THE

QUARTERLY

EDITED BY

GORDON LISH

THE QUARTERLY

1 / SPRING 1987

VINTAGE BOOKS

A DIVISION OF RANDOM HOUSE

NEW YORK

THE QUARTERLY IS EDITED BY GORDON LISH
AND IS PUBLISHED FOUR TIMES A YEAR BY VINTAGE BOOKS.
THE QUARTERLY WELCOMES THE OPPORTUNITY TO READ WORK
OF EVERY CHARACTER, AND IS ESPECIALLY CONCERNED
TO KEEP ITSELF AN OPEN FORUM. MANUSCRIPTS
SHOULD BE ACCOMPANIED BY THE USUAL RETURN MATERIALS
AND SHOULD BE ADDRESSED TO THE EDITOR,
THE QUARTERLY, 201 EAST 50TH STREET,
NEW YORK, NEW YORK 10022. *THE QUARTERLY*
WILL MAKE THE UTMOST EFFORT TO OFFER ITS RESPONSE TO
MANUSCRIPTS NO LATER THAN ONE WEEK SUBSEQUENT TO RECEIPT.
OPINIONS EXPRESSED HEREIN ARE NOT NECESSARILY THOSE
OF THE EDITOR OR OF THE PUBLISHER.
BUSINESS MATTERS SHOULD BE ADDRESSED TO THE ATTENTION
OF THE PUBLISHER, *THE QUARTERLY,* VINTAGE BOOKS,
201 EAST 50TH STREET, NEW YORK, NEW YORK 10022.

ISBN: 0-394-74697-X

DESIGN BY ANDREW ROBERTS

MANUFACTURED IN THE UNITED STATES OF AMERICA

THE QUARTERLY

1 / SPRING 1987

A NACE PAGE　　2

AMY HEMPEL / *The Harvest*　　3

TOM SPANBAUER / *Sea Animals*　　7

MATTHEW LEVINE /
　Noises of Astonishing Satisfaction　　19

CHRIS SPAIN / *Playing Iwo Jima*　　24

PAMELA SCHIRMEISTER / *Squirrels*　　30

YANNICK MURPHY / *The Slit*　　37

J.S. MARCUS /
　It's Freezing Here in Milwaukee　　44

DARRELL SPENCER / *Pots of Impatiens*　　52

KAYE GIBBONS / *The Proof*　　60

PETER CHRISTOPHER / *The Careerist*　　73

JANET KAUFFMAN / *Anton's Album*　　83

TOM RAYFIEL / *Another Night in Tunisia*　　89

JANE SMILEY / *The Age of Grief*　　104

ANOTHER NACE PAGE　　190

PAULETTE JILES　　191

LINDA GREGG　　234

ROBERT GIBB　　237

JOHN ALLMAN　　246

WILLIAM FREEDMAN　　248

THE QUARTERLY

JACK GILBERT   253

ANSIE BAIRD   259

DIANE DESANDERS   262

HARVEY SHAPIRO   263

ONE MORE NACE PAGE   268

NANCY LEMANN *to* Q   269

PAGAN KENNEDY *to* Q   276

HAROLD BRODKEY *to* Q   280

JAMES LAUGHLIN *to* Q   291

AMY HEMPEL *to* Q   295

PATTY MARX *to* Q   298

ROBERT JONES *to* Q   304

E.J. CULLEN *to* Q   307

DAN DUFFY *to* Q   309

THE LAST NACE PAGE   312

THE
QUARTERLY

a mother's Love

The Harvest

The year I began to say *vahz* instead of *vase,* a man I barely knew nearly accidentally killed me.

The man was not hurt when the other car hit ours. The man I had known for one week held me in the street in a way that meant I couldn't see my legs. I remember knowing that I shouldn't look, and knowing that I *would* look if it wasn't that I couldn't.

My blood was on the front of this man's clothes.

He said, "You'll be okay, but this sweater is ruined."

I screamed from the fear of pain. But I did not feel any pain. In the hospital, after injections, I knew there was pain in the room—I just didn't know whose pain it was.

What happened to one of my legs required four hundred stitches, which, when I told it, became five hundred stitches, because nothing is ever quite as bad as it *could* be.

The five days they didn't know if they could save my leg or not I stretched to ten.

The lawyer was the one who used the word. But I won't get around to that until a couple of paragraphs.

We were having the looks discussion—how important *are* they. Crucial is what I had said.

I think looks are crucial.

But this guy was a lawyer. He sat in an aqua vinyl chair drawn up to my bed. What he meant by looks was how much my loss of them was worth in a court of law.

I could tell that the lawyer liked to say *court of law.* He told me he had taken the bar three times before he had passed. He said that his friends had given him handsomely embossed business cards, but where these lovely cards were supposed to say *Attorney-at-Law,* his cards said *Attorney-at-Last.*

He had already covered loss of earnings, that I could not now become an airline stewardess. That I had never considered becoming one was immaterial, he said, legally.

"There's another thing," he said. "We have to talk here about marriageability."

The tendency was to say marriage-a-*what?* although I knew what he meant the first time I heard it.

I was eighteen years old. I said, "First, don't we talk about *date*ability?"

The man of a week was already gone, the accident driving him back to his wife.

"Do you think looks are important?" I asked the man before he left.

"Not at first," he said.

In my neighborhood there is a fellow who was a chemistry teacher until an explosion took his face and left what was left behind. The rest of him is neatly dressed in dark suits and shined shoes. He carries a briefcase to the college campus. What a comfort—his family, people said—until his wife took the kids and moved out.

In the solarium, a woman showed me a snapshot. She said, "This is what my son used to look like."

I spent my evenings in Dialysis. They didn't mind when a lounger was free. They had wide-screen color TV, better than they had in Rehab. Wednesday nights we watched a show where women in expensive clothes appeared on lavish sets and promised to ruin one another.

On one side of me was a man who spoke only in phone numbers. You would ask him how he felt, he would say, "924–3130." Or he would say, "757–1366." We guessed what these numbers might be, but nobody spent the dime.

There was sometimes, on the other side of me, a twelve-year-old boy. His lashes were thick and dark from blood-pressure medication. He was next on the transplant list, as soon as —the word they used was *harvest*—as soon as a kidney was harvested.

The boy's mother prayed for drunk drivers.

I prayed for men who were not discriminating.

Aren't we all, I thought, somebody's harvest?

The hour would end, and a floor nurse would wheel me back to my room. She would say, "Why watch that trash? Why not just ask me how my day went?"

I spent fifteen minutes before going to bed squeezing rubber grips. The anticoagulant was making my fingers stiffen. The doctor said he'd give it to me till I couldn't button my blouse—a figure of speech to someone in a cotton gown.

The lawyer said, "Charitable works."

He opened his shirt and showed me where an acupuncture person had dabbed at his chest with cola syrup, sunk four needles, and told him that the real cure was charitable works.

I said, "Cure for what?"

The lawyer said, "Immaterial."

As soon as I knew that I would be all right, I was sure that I was dead and didn't know it. I moved through the days like a severed head that finishes a sentence. I waited for the moment that would snap me out of my seeming life.

The accident happened at sunset, so that is when I felt this way the most. The man I had met the week before was driving me to dinner when it happened. The place was at the beach, a beach on a bay that you can look across and see the city lights, a place where you can see everything without having to listen to any of it.

A long time later I went to that beach myself. *I* drove the car. It was the first good beach day; I wore shorts.

5

At the edge of the sand I unwound the elastic bandage and waded into the surf. A boy in a wetsuit looked at my leg. He asked me if a shark had done it; there were sightings of great whites along that part of the coast.

I said that, yes, a shark had done it.

"And you're going back in?" the boy asked.

I said, "And I'm going back in." **Q**

Sea Animals

I asked her to show me what was wrong with him. It was still winter when I asked, sometime within the first ten days of his one hundred days, after he got home from the hospital, before the time when she thought she had smothered him, before the time when the pigs got out, before he died in the spring, after the chores were done, and after school and before supper. I asked her to show me in the late afternoon what was wrong with him, when it was not day and not night, when the shadows were long and running in together and when the chickens flew up to roost, to sit, and to listen to the world.

On the porch, before I went in, before I asked her, I could smell her bathing him. I took off my coat, my cap, my mittens, pried off my overshoes on the top step, and all the while, in there, in the kitchen, I could smell her: the Ivory soap, the steaming water in the porcelain pan, the baby oil, and the clean diapers. All of those were her smell, and his.

These were my chores: to water and feed the hens, to gather the eggs, to water and feed the baby chicks under the brood lamp, and to slop the kitchen garbage to the pigs.

They were Barbara's chores, too, but most of the time I liked to surprise Barbara when she came home from the third grade at the St. Joseph's School and tell her that everything was done and that we were free to do things, to play if Russell wasn't crying; free, for instance, to make cocoa and sit in the kitchen, and free for Barbara to try to show me how to write in longhand the way she could do, and sometimes Mom would come and have some cocoa, too, if Russell was sleeping and wasn't crying.

Another part of my chores was making sure that the doors

were locked and that the windows were shut up tight in the coop for the hens, and especially for the chicks. Dad said that if an owl or a hawk or some kind of varmint got in there we'd lose all of the chicks for sure, because the ones who weren't killed right off would suffocate in a heap trying to get away. I want you to know that Dad gave this chore to me especially, not to Barbara, and I was always careful to lock the doors, and I always checked the windows, even though they were too high for me to reach, and sometimes at night I would wake up and think I had forgotten to lock the doors and to check the windows.

Before Russell was born, the new word that everybody said was *brood lamp.* After he was born, they were *incubator, disease,* and *cripple.* That's what I heard the doctor tell Mom, that she had a cripple, and because of his disease, he had to be in an incubator. I heard those words all the time and thought about them all the time, even when I did my chores. I asked Barbara to write them out for me in longhand. I thought about them even more after Russell came home, after they let him out of the incubator and he came home. But he looked just like a baby to me. After all that talk, after all those words so many times, my brother looked like a baby to me.

When I asked her, she did something that she hadn't done in a long time. She picked me up. She leaned her body so that her hip held me. Her arm was around me, the flesh of her arm against my arm, the smell from her armpit under the red housedress. She showed me Russell's head and said, "You see how his head is so much larger than the rest of him is?" And then she showed me his foot. It went over to the side, and she moved it up so that it was straight, and then she let it go, and the foot went crooked again. "That's his foot," she said, and then she sat me on the table. She took Russell's hands in hers. "They will not open," she said. "I have to open them for him and put powder in there for him."

She pried open his right hand and told me to put my finger in there. I didn't want to do it because his palm looked like a terrible blossom to me, or like an egg that the rooster had got to.

She said, "Come on, you wanted to know."

So I put my finger in there and my brother grasped my finger.

Before Russell came home, I don't remember much. There are some photos of me and Barbara, and sometimes of Mom, standing and squinting into the sun that I think I remember living in. But it's hard to say which came first, the photo of me and the experience of living it from it, or the living of it reminded by the photo.

I do remember six things: I remember when our dog Toby died. He came over to me and stood next to me for a while and then did the same thing with Barbara, and then he went into the barn and died on the hay.

I remember Mom saying that animals do that, that they say goodbye before they die.

I remember a lightning storm that blew one of the poplars in front of the house over. The sky was black and it was day and we prayed the rosary loud and lit a candle and Dad wasn't home.

I remember Mom taking the paring knife out of where the silverware was in the kitchen and going outside and sitting on the patch of lawn she had planted and digging dandelions out of the grass with the paring knife.

I remember the Door of the Dead. It was a game that Barbara and I played, and the way you played it was you would go into a room, into the room which Barbara and I had together, and we'd close the door and then you'd say that the closed door was the Door of the Dead, and then we'd get scared, or I should say that I would get scared, and then after saying "The Door of the Dead, the Door of the Dead" over and over again, we'd make scary sounds and then Barbara would open the door, and it was always the same thing, I always was the one who ended up yelling, no matter how many times I told myself I wouldn't yell this time.

I remember that everybody said *brood lamp*.

Before Russell came home, that's it: six memories. But after Russell came home and before he died, those one hundred days, are not just a memory, not just some things I am recalling, and it has always been that way for me.

The house was warm all winter, that winter, and there was steam on the windows that I was not allowed to swipe through, which was ice in the morning and blue, and orange when the sun was up. Dad carried in wood and stacked it high by the stove and on the porch. Sometimes I helped.

Russell cried all the time and never slept, although I know that's not the truth. There were times that he was not crying, times when I stood by his crib and he wasn't crying and he was sleeping. I wasn't allowed near him because he had a lot of mucus and I had a lot of childhood diseases in me like measles and mumps that he could catch and make him more sick, but I still snuck in a lot and looked at his head and his foot, but mostly I looked at his hands, to see if they had opened up yet. Sometimes Russell was awake and not crying and he just lay there quiet, his eyes rolled back up a little, as if he was looking at his head, too, as if he was wondering what to do with all the mucus I could hear up there, wondering when the egg would hatch, as if it was a problem and he was planning a solution, a way to make it go away, and he was trying so hard that it made his hands fists.

I woke up once.

It was spring I think by then, the river was high, and Russell was crying and I was surprised that he was crying just the same way that I had been surprised by his crying when he first got home in the winter, and then I wondered if my brother had always been crying and if I just didn't hear him anymore or if he had stopped for a while, for days, for weeks, and then started up again. My brother's cries were like the sound the pipes made when you turned on the water in the bathtub, that sound, and then the sound like the pipes were singing high, off tune. Sometimes the pipes didn't make that sound, but mostly they did, and sometimes I didn't hear them when they did, and only remembered that they had made that sound when it was over.

That afternoon she ran out of the bedroom and walked around the house, inside, near the walls. I was making incubators with my Tinkertoys on the floor of the front room, Barbara wasn't back from school, and Dad wasn't home. I could hear my mother crying and walking around and around. I thought she might run out into the field and that Dad would have to go bring her back again and he wasn't even home like the last time. I didn't know what to do when she cried but cry, and I didn't know at all what to do if she ran out into the field. And then she said, "Tommy, you have to be a grownup now. I'll make us some coffee and we'll put the cloth tablecloth on the table and we'll have a cigarette. I've got something I've got to tell you, but you must be a grownup for it to work, and then you must never tell anybody ever. Do you promise?"

"Yes," I promised.

She took out the tablecloth as she spoke to me, and floated it down onto the table. I had seen her do that with Russell, float his blanket up in the air like that, like a fan, and then let it settle on him, and then flip it up again and then let it settle again. Russell liked that. I think I could see him almost smile whenever she floated the blanket down on him like that, floated it onto him, so soft, like a big bird flying.

I was watching her when she took out the tablecloth, and I wanted to be lying on the table and let it come down on top of me; that clean wave of air, her smell, the slow graceful descent.

She put four tablespoons of coffee into the percolator and plugged it in. She went to the bathroom and pulled the bobby pins from her hair and fluffed it out, and put lipstick onto her lips, and blotted her lips with a square of toilet paper, and let the square float from her hand into the air onto the floor by her high heels with no toes in them. She had put on her high heels and her nylons with the seams in them and her brown dress with the orchid all the way down the front. I wet my hair and parted it, and put the clip-on tie on my white shirt on the collar, and polished my shoes the way I would do if I was going to church. She poured us coffee in the cups that matched the saucers and she smoked. I smoked, too, French-inhaling, my hair slick, me in my tie with her, with her having coffee in the afternoon.

But it's not the truth.

I didn't smoke.

There was her lipstick on her Lucky Strike, and there was her lipstick on her cup.

"Just now, when I was sleeping with Russell," she said, "I woke up and I was laying on top of him. I thought I had smothered him. I thought he was dead. Tommy, you know what that means, don't you? Dead?"

"Yes," I lied. I didn't know.

I knew the Door of the Dead. I knew that my dog Toby said goodbye first.

"I thought I had killed him," she said. "And this is the part where you have to be a grownup and never tell, Tommy. Thomas? I was glad," my mother said.

It was spring when the pigs got out. Sometime within the last ten days of his one hundred days, and this day, the day that started out with the pigs getting out, is the most important of all of the one hundred of those days.

Mom had bought a window fan for the window in her bedroom for Russell with her S&H Green Stamps. The June grass was already going dry and the river was back down. Dad had built a pen out of wire fencing and old doors in the corral behind the barn, with part of the pen in the river so that the pigs could lay around in the water and the mud.

Those pigs were in that water all the time. Dad called them the bathing beauties. The brood sow he called Esther. Esther Williams, he called the brood sow.

That day when they all got out was a Saturday, because school was still on and Barbara was home and wasn't sick, and it wasn't Sunday, because we didn't have our Sunday clothes on and didn't go to church. Dad was usually home on Sundays, because there wasn't supposed to be any servile work on Sundays and he wasn't there that day, and so that was the day when Barbara and I walked out the back door of the barn and there were the pigs, out of their pen, squealing around the corral.

"Pigs are out! Pigs are out!" Barbara yelled, and then I yelled it, too.

Mom flipped her fingers the way she always did when she was nervous when she heard anything about the pigs, and went into the bedroom and looked at Russell, who was sleeping. Barbara and I looked in after her. The room was dark and the fan was on. My mother turned to us and put her finger to her lips and motioned for us to get out of there, so we went into the kitchen. We weren't in there long before suddenly a streak of red shot past us. It was Mom.

"Last one to the corral gate is a cow's tail!" my mother yelled, already down the steps of the back porch, opening the screen door, stretching out the screen-door spring and going into the bright large flat dusty world; we followed her, first past the little green square of lawn with no dandelions in it, then past the rose hanging on to the back fence, then past the gas pump, then past the Buick, then onto the graveled yard that stretched out acres between us and the corral gate, Mom ahead, the skirt of her red housedress flying up above her knees, Barbara right behind her, my sister's hair blowing like her mother's, her legs like her mother's—those females.

I stopped running.

I stopped running and stood and watched them running.

Mom cleared the three poles of the fence like a bird flying, like something wild leaping, and Barbara never hesitated. My sister dived under the bottom pole and rolled and stood up next to her mother. They smiled at each other. I stood there and watched, and my mother and my sister smiled at each other. A flock of sparrows flew over the ridgepole of the barn then, between me and the sun, and I was there watching things. The barn, the house, the pole fence, the gate, the pigs out, Mom and Barbara, everything different, everything different and bright, nothing the same, and I felt as if I had never even been anything before.

"Come on! Come on, cow's tail!" my sister yelled at me, waving her arm. "We have to get these pigs in before they get to the river!"

"Sooo-eeee! Soooo-eeee!" Mom yelled.

"Sooo-eeee! Soooo-eeee!" Barbara yelled, and so did I.

We circled the pigs. Mom got between them and the river, Barbara got in the middle and me on the other side, and we herded them slowly back into the pen, our arms out to make us wider.

"Sooo-eeee!" we all yelled.

One of the doors of the pen was down, the closest one to

the barn, so we had a corner to herd them into. We were doing pretty well until Barbara pointed to the door lying on the ground, to the door that was part of the pigpen, which the pigs had knocked over, which was lying there like a door into the ground, underneath the dry cow manure. My sister pointed to that door and said, just only so I could hear, "The Door of the Dead."

I was almost standing on it.

I was almost standing on the Door of the Dead.

I jumped right out of there and yelled with all my might, which spooked the pigs, and they ran back out into the corral, through the place where I was supposed to be standing, and went straight to the river, Esther Williams in the lead, and the rest of them after her, the rest of the bathing beauties running after Esther Williams.

When that fat sow dived off the riverbank, the same way I think a ballerina would dive, poised in the air, and then, when she hit the water, gliding like a seal, gliding as I thought Esther Williams would glide, through the current toward the small island of brambles and scrub elms some feet off from the bank, when that pig just went like that, I stopped and looked again, looked as I had looked before, stopped and looked at what the world looked like. It was a world that was suddenly full of things, mysterious things, things that weren't me.

I could see my mother and my sister doing everything they could do to keep those pigs out of the drink. They were screaming and waving their arms and putting their bodies in front of the pigs, but it was no use. Mom was able to grab one pig by a hind leg and drag it away, but the pig kicked and squealed and Mom didn't have enough energy to pull it any farther, so there they stood, Mom and the pig in the middle of the corral, a standoff, the pig kicking and my mother jerking with every kick. Finally she just had to let go. The pig ran and dived, just like the others, and swam, just like the others, to the island, to where Esther Williams was with the rest of the bathing beauties.

It got quiet then.

Mom just sat down right there in the manure.

They were gone.

All the pigs got wild, got crazy on us, and swam away, dived the way they weren't supposed to, got out of there, swam like other animals, like sea animals, not like pigs, swimming, dumb farm animals diving, swimming, escaping, showing off.

It was then that I saw the owl in the tree on the other side of the river, just above the bank, just a little ways past the island where the pigs were, in shallow water you could wade through right to the tree where the owl was. If you moved your eyes a little, the owl would disappear like magic, but then, if you knew how to look, it would appear again, out of the leaves and out of the twigs, there were its eyes,

"Sons of bitches!" Mom yelled.

She picked herself up off the ground and picked up a hard horse turd and threw it at Esther Williams. And then she picked up a rock. She spun in circles, around and around, winding up for the pitch, twirling, a dust devil, her arms in the air, her skirt riding up, a dance, and hurled the rock with a sound from her inside and deep, a grunt, and the rock sailed through the air and went through the window of the chicken coop, the side where the baby chicks were. There was a little sound, a slight shattering in the sunny afternoon, and that was all.

"Sons of bitches!" my mother cried, her fists, like Russell's, aimed at the sky. "Damned sows, damned sows sons of bitches!"

I didn't tell Dad about the broken window in the coop, because Russell died the next day. No, actually, it was Monday that Russell died, because the next day, the day after the pigs got out, was Sunday, and on that day Dad got the pigs back in with the horse, had to lasso each pig and bring it across one at a time, even though it was a Sunday, but it was an emergency and not that servile.

I was picking up my Lincoln Logs off the floor of the front room, or Tinkertoys; Barbara hadn't been home long, and I had done the chores. I had leaned a board in front of the broken window and was going to tell Dad about it at supper. We were going to make cocoa, because Russell wasn't crying. Mom was sitting in her special chair, she and Russell's special chair, holding him the way she always did, rocking, when she said, "Go get your father—Russell's dead."

This part is not as clear as the other parts.

What happened next are these things: Monsignor Cody was there, and so were Aunt Marguerite and Uncle Pat, and more people. I was supposed to stay in my room and so was Barbara. In the kitchen, on the table, was the cloth tablecloth and the percolator and the cups with matching saucers, a chocolate cake and red Jell-O with fruit cocktail in it and bananas. They put Russell in his bassinet in the bedroom. I wasn't supposed to go in there, but I went in there when nobody was in there, even though there were people everywhere, some of them crying. The fan was off and there were candles all around him and everything was white: the blankets, the bassinet, his nightie.

It smelled like him in there, like her.

He was just lying in there the same way I had seen him so many times, his eyes closed, the covers pulled around him. I touched him a little on the shoulder, through his nightie, and he was no different. But then I pulled the cover back and saw his hands. They were open, palms up, sunny-side.

On the day of the funeral it rained. Barbara says it was sunny, but I remember that there were umbrellas and that we all stood under umbrellas, and that I was wearing my overshoes. I stood to the right of the Monsignor and the altar boys. I got to smell the incense. My grandmother was behind me. Barbara stood by me on the side, and then Aunt Marie, Aunt Zita, Aunt Alma, Aunt Marguerite, and then Mom here on the other. Dad had bought her a new coat. It was navy-blue, with big buttons. Behind Dad stood my other grandma and Great-aunt Monica.

When they lowered the casket, I thought about the Door of the Dead in the corral on the ground that day the pigs got out and that Russell was still alive, but this is what is most important about what happened that day and the thing that I remember most of anything, in those days, those one hundred days. It's that Dad started crying so hard that they had to wipe the rain off the folding chair so he could sit down. As soon as I saw him sit down like that, I was on my way to him, and I was halfway there, just past Aunt Alma and almost to Aunt Marguerite, before Grandma, the one behind me, got ahold of my arm and pulled me back, past the flowers, past the Door of the Dead, and put me back in my place; in my place in front of her, back in my place, seven females from my father.

There was a reception at St. Joseph's Hall.

Barbara showed me her classroom, although we weren't supposed to go upstairs. I heard Aunt Zita say that it was a blessing, because there was so much wrong with him. Afterward, we went home. Mom drove, and when we got home I changed my clothes and did my chores. The board was down from the window of the coop and all the chicks were dead. It looked to me that those who weren't killed right off by the owl had smothered in the corner, in a heap, trying to get away. **Q**

Noises of Astonishing Satisfaction

We lived in a condemned building above a former Japanese revolutionary and his wife. I suspected him of having designs on the building. In this country the Jap had turned architect. Not only was he an architect, but he had turned sculptor too. He made colossal leaves out of metal and left them in public places, outside of mental institutions, places where they would not be noticed. It wasn't so much a building we lived in as four walls, a floor, and a roof all leaned together like a house of cards. Wind blew in through gaps in the window frames and we stopped up the gaps with old underwear. My wife played piano around and I did whatever. Twice a month I was food buyer for the food co-op two doors down and my pay was in food. That's how we ate.

This Jap had been kicked out of Japan, I don't know what for. There was something deliberate in the way he did things. He had an unmoving face and he never looked right at you, always to the side, at your temple or the side of your neck.

The Jap and I owned vans and there was one parking spot in front of the building. When he slipped out, I slipped in, and vice versa. When my wife played piano, he banged on metal and cranked his radio. He smoked cigars and I pushed the smoke back down the holes in the floor with some water. When it rained and the rain ran down the walls, he slammed on our door and came in with a bucket of tools. He hammered at the rain-soaked wall and left a butterfly sort of thing hanging there. He turned to me and barked, "Empty bucket."

After he left I saw what it was hanging there. He had attached a V of wood to the wall. He had angled two sheets of newspaper against the wall so they overlapped in the middle and formed the wings of a butterfly. From the lower tips of the wings he had tacked strips of plastic. These fed gathered water into the bucket.

My wife and I would look at the thing for long stretches. We would fall quiet. Rain after rain it stuck to the wall with the discipline of a thing well placed. I ran my fingers over it. The Jap had driven the nails in to a perfect depth. The surface of the wood was smooth. To the last I did not take it down.

Mice lived with us. While we slept they pattered on our chests, on the blankets, and they shrieked and fought across the floors. My wife said, "Are there mice in the bed, if there are mice in the bed I'm not staying another minute." And I said, "Nonsense, big as we are, why should there be mice in the bed?"

I woke up early and swept the pellets from the sheets. I cleaned the place immaculate to force the mice down, but this Jap, he was cleaner, and the mice lived with us.

I had to fake it when the traps went off. I had invented my own traps. "Book falling," I'd say, and I would pick up the big illustrated dictionary with the little body stuck under it. Or, "Bad wiring," I'd say, when smoke came from the baseboard where I had exposed some wiring and left a crumb of cheese. For a time, I thought I was winning.

My wife could pull anything out of a piano. She played from the hips from what I could see, but she said that was not all. She tried to tell me how there was as much in the pulling away as there was in the going in, maybe more, though the feelings were different. My wife had a belief in the spirit that I could not fathom. I imagined that it maybe gave you something to sleep with.

To get at sleep, I replayed my greatest victories, my worst defeats. I went all the way with them. I heard little patterings and I knew the mice were running and then I felt a pattering on my shoulder. It was my wife, her fingers playing in sleep. I tried to calm myself so I could feel what it was that she was playing, but my pulse was rough and unsteady and somehow I filled all of the quiet rests with my frenzied beating.

I do not dislike Japs. Why should I have anything against Japs? This Jap ex-revolutionary, though, had himself right under me and he was building up. He was building something with that deliberateness. He was getting closer. Every so often I heard something slam against his ceiling, my floor.

At night, beams of light came into our place through the holes in the floor. When my wife was good and asleep I put my eye to a hole and I watched the Jap cover his wife. All I could see was the smooth of his shoulder and the open look on her face at the ceiling, at me. That was all I saw of her. But from what I saw, I saw she was smooth. The two of them were smooth. From then on even the smallest pimple killed me. I bought my wife bath soaps. I soaked her twice a week and rubbed her down with lavender talc. She said she loved it.

One night, after we had finished, I smiled down on her and said, "Make some noises." She opened her eyes and said, "What noises?" "Noises," I said, "noises of gratitude, noises out of your control, noises it would kill people to hear." It was just a thought I had. Nothing issued from her and, eventually, my wife said, "Make them yourself, I'm going to sleep."

It was the day dried leaves scuffed the pavement that we had it out. The Jap left me a note. He had bought the building.

I stormed downstairs. There was nothing I had in mind other than putting my body in front of him. I rang his bell. The mice were quiet. His open-faced wife answered the door. She had on a big white T-shirt as a dress that barely caught her where her smooth legs started out from her hips. The Jap was there over her shoulder. He had a tool in his hand. There was one of those big leaves behind him. It was curled over like a dead, fallen leaf. Even curled, the thing was so big you could climb to the ceiling on it.

"Yes?" she said, then she cast down her eyes. I took my advantage. I let my eyes rest on the smooths of her arms, on the smoothness under that white shirt. She caught me with a smile. The control of that smile was mutilating.

I looked at the Jap. I looked him right in the eye and he met me in the eye and his face didn't move. Something started to drain out of me.

Somehow I was on the stairs and I was going up, but halfway up the stairs I sat down. I could have fallen asleep right then and there.

The Jap started his banging.

My wife was upstairs at the piano. She was putting everything into that instrument, slowly, pressing and pulling. It was the quiet between the notes that tore into me. The quiet left me to wonder what it was I thought I was doing there with my forehead pressed against the metal edge of a step.

When I was a boy in bed I tried to shut my body off. I propped my legs straight up against the wall, my shoulders to the mattress, arms out to the sides, and I gathered my blood to my head. First I shut off my feet, then legs, hands, arms, and stomach, until I reached my chest. The heart was hardest because it had a life of its own that I had to choke down until it was beat out. I had to fight that heart hard, because it kept on wrenching free. I fought the heart so hard that my legs came back on. After a while I would give in and curl up on my side and focus on the wedge of light that came out of my closet.

Once, a mouse came out of the closet and stood in the wedge of light on its hind legs. I could make out every whisker. The mouse was carrying a shred of something. I wondered why it stood there, so obvious, in the light. I wondered why it had come out precisely then, to see me. **Q**

Playing Iwo Jima

What I am doing now is I am butt-welded to a John Deere 4020, unzipping the earth west of Muleshoe, lifting her dusty dress. I am probably alone out here, only who knows? I will put it together for you the way I put it together for myself. There is heat waving off my tractor's fenders, dust devils jumping the farm to market road, and Sarah waiting in the turn row with a bag full of Ogallala water. Sarah waiting in the turn row is the only part of this that is for sure a lie. There is no question I am plowing the beaches of Iwo Jima, turning up bones from Frog Wars fifteen years ago.

The rules were that there weren't any rules, but if you got frog on you you were dead. I had no arm, Harold called me woman, so mostly I was dead. When they picked armies, Jap and Marine, I was last—last to go, even after Sarah. The Japs defended the milk barn, Iwo Jima, and the Marines waded ashore through the cotton. You combated with a pocket full of black cats, a pocket full of frogs, and a punk between your teeth. The punk's glow gave you away, but when you torched that fuse it was like pulling a pin. Stick a finger-thick black cat in old frog's mouth, make him look cigar-smoking, torch that fuse, and hurl the frog grenade across the West Texas sky. Last-ditch assaults were pure carnage, frog bombs dropping everywhere. When you got a direct hit, you would say, "Take that, fuckhead, I frogged your ass!" And if they got you, you would say, "Oh fuck, I been frogged!"

When I did my firefly-smeared-on-cement imitation, when I sparklered across the Delta's high black tent, I said, "Oh fuck, I been frogged." I was in my baby Piper with thirty-foot mufflers and exhaust shields. I was hawking, not making a noise, except my prop soft-chewing the Mekong muck. I was looking for somebody's ass to frog when they frogged my own. It was all swirling smoke. I grabbed my sky blanket and went looking for a door. I thought, This is what they call difficulty leaving the aircraft, and I tried to remember what they said about that. I couldn't see to see until the phosphorus lit. Then I saw myself reflected on the air like it was a mirror, a mirror of me and a mirror of Harold the night of the Frog War to End All Frog Wars.

Flashbulb-caught is how Harold looked the night of the Frog War to End All Frog Wars, which was also the night he frogged his own ass. It was the day after the Fourth of July. We had gunpowder enough to blow away half the farm, and the wind was blowing warm through the tree strip. The run had been made to the tail-water pit, what we called the ammo dump, where the frogs were, and we had grenades for days. Sarah was chosen a Jap and me a Marine, so I resigned myself to battle. It was dark already and the moon was shining off the tin tractor shed and the round water of the horse tank. Iwo Jima was just a black lump. We could hear Japs talking bold, trying to make themselves brave because they did not know where we were coming from. Harold drew the plan in the dirt. The Marines with shoes would attack out of the orchard, what we called the mine field, where the goatheads were. Harold and I, the only barefoots, we would commando out of the cotton when the mine-field attack had their attention.

I was flying over what I called the mine field in the Delta when they got my attention. I had that Delta laid out in my head just like our farm. There was the cotton patch, which was mostly friendly; the tractor shed and the horse tank, which about you never knew; and the mine field and Iwo Jima, which were always trouble. So when they direct-hit me, it wasn't that

I wasn't expecting, but I wasn't expecting the phosphorus to do like it did. The phosphorus, what I called my party candles, was what I laid down on the so-called to-be-frogged asses. Where my candles landed, soon followed large amounts of destruction. What the phosphorus did was ash my retinas. It left me sideways to the world. What it does is, it doesn't let me see what is out in front.

When you are tractor-driving, it is what is out in front that counts. You decide what gets it and what doesn't, and what you leave behind can't be undone. My dad raised his boys to plow Kansas-straight straight lines. When I came back, all I could do was draw snakes on his fields. He put a roll bar on the tractor so if I back-flipped it I wouldn't kill myself, and started with his mirrors. The first year I plowed under half his cotton, but he didn't quit it on me, and he finally got it so I could practically see what I was doing. Anymore, I'm just dangerous to fence post and irrigation pipe.

Waiting in the cotton for the mine-field attack to happen, I didn't feel dangerous to anything. I was a deserter in my heart. All I wanted was Sarah in the tree strip. Dead Marines and Japs both were supposed to bleed together in the tree strip until the war was over. Whenever Sarah got it first, I would frog myself to be with her. It undid Harold. He called Sarah a Jima-whore, and me a Marine-woman disgrace. When the first range rounds whomped in, raising dust, Harold and I crawled forward through the furrows, butt low, hunkered down on our faces. We gave the mine-field attack time to convince those Japs. Then we came out of the cotton, skirting the Case tractor broken down so long it was growing roots. We were in a charge so strong that even I thought we wouldn't be stopped. We had nearly made the wide-open when we went sprawling, howling to the ground. In a stroke of genius, in a tactic we had never known, the Japs had goathead-mined it. They threw frog down on us.

It is afternoon now and the sun has an angle on me so that when I am heading west my horizon is mostly orange. At the end of the field is a bar ditch. It is where my dad was lying when his brother came yelling through the dead cotton to tell him there had been a Pearl Harbor. My dad was resting his sights on a rabbit. He says it was the last unhuman thing he ever pointed a gun at. He says that jack got saved by a war. In the turn row, I lift my cultivator, and I am swallowed in a red-dirt storm. Plowed earth and blown-up earth smell the same to me. It is a tornado-shelter smell, a wet-cement smell, the frog breath in a Texas loblolly. The dust settles in my elbows as I head back toward where the dark is coming from.

When I was the boy called woman by Harold, I would thread two miles of that red dust and dark through my toes to watch Sarah pull a dress over her head. The dark between our place and their place was country dark. I walked the tree strip, listening to wind walk on trees, running when bull bats spooked up from the dirt. Sarah waited until she knew I was there, standing on the wheel rim against the outside wall. She opened the curtain so that mosquito screen was all that was between us. Then she pulled her dress over her head, and did her desert-place dance.

The day I left I asked Sarah to drive the farm with me. I wanted to take one last look, just in case. It was late summer, the growing was over, the well motors were quiet. We could hardly see the farm for the waist-high cotton and head-and-a-half field corn. I asked Sarah if she wanted to skip frogs on the tail-water pit for old times. She didn't say but walked on the dam and down to the water. I told her she looked so mighty in her white dress that it was what I would remember to come back to. She hung the white dress on the barbed wire of the fence. We lay down in the dirt, and I let her pour dirt over my head. She said we had to throw a penny in the water and say this-is-fors. We couldn't find one. All we could find was a lockjaw-rusty nail. Sarah dropped it in the tail water and said, "This is for you getting back here, and for everything staying the way it is."

The way it was was that Harold and I were completely routed from the field. We found ourselves belly in the cotton, listening to our retreating hearts on the dirt. Harold said we had been Dresdened. Dresdened, Dunkirked, and Water-looed. In the humiliation of impending defeat, he decided to win the war with firepower. I followed him to the tractor shed, where he reached into the dead air space between the walls. His hand came out with a gunpowder-monster. He said he had engineered it himself, said it was the secret weapon, the one that would turn the tide, the atom frog-bomb. I asked if a bomb like that wouldn't be against the rules. Harold looked at me and said, "War is fair and all love."

When I came home from war, and Harold took me home to meet his wife, he had to lead me by the hand with the one hand he still has. When he turned in the drive and stopped short, I asked, "What?" He said she was standing there. I asked how she looked, and he said, "Same as always." I asked what she was wearing, and he said, "A white dress." I waited for something to happen. I asked Harold what was happening. He said, "Let's get out." I listened to him get out. Then I tried to remember what the rules were for difficulty leaving the aircraft, or anything. I waited until I wondered if I was alone. Then I felt her hand on my arm, and I said to myself, "You been frogged like you'll never know."

Harold said we were going to Hiroshima their asses. He said we had to search for a frog with a big enough mouth. We stalked the sides of the tail-water pit, slipping in mud as we groped with our hands. We took the biggest frog we found and pried open his mouth. He looked like he had been telephone-poled. Then Harold made his charge, rose up out of the cotton like the hordes himself, his black outline hanging on the end of a spark. When he pulled up to light the fuse, Harold looked bigger than life. He looked as bronze and as famous as that statue of the Marines lifting the flag. He was leaning back in a heave when the atom frog-bomb went off. He was flashbulb-caught, and then he disappeared in a shower of frog and finger mist.

The sun has gone where it goes to. The engine casing pops as it cools. I take off my boots and hang my pants on the barbed wire of the fence. Out in the middle of the tail-water pit, I can't get any hint of light, and I feel like I am swimming beneath the rim of a bomb crater. I dive down into it. With my fingers I sift through layers of bones on the bottom. What I am looking for, what I can't find here, is a tenpenny nail. When I come up for air, someone has killed the water well. It is the quiet of quiet after battle. All I can hear is breathing from the mud. I stand naked in the water. I try to wash myself with the soft caliche. I try to clean it from me. But what I have on me won't come off, what I think I have on me is frog for always. Q

Squirrels

Out on the end of a point sits a fine old house facing the sea. Evenings, you can see a thin blue curl of smoke issuing from its chimney, and inside, I sit by the fire, listening for the noises overhead. A scraping, or maybe a whirring, but in any case, something like the irregular sound of objects being dragged across a floor. At first, I hoped that it had to do with my ears. I would be the first to admit that I am not a man of appalling self-knowledge, but I have large ears, and I know this. They are veritable echo chambers. But this was no wonderful ventriloquist prowling around my attic. Nor was it a mischievous wind wreaking havoc with my chimney, despite what the wife would say. My wife, when she was alive, and when she still lived in the house, wanted to pull the chimney down before it fell around us. The plaster cannot hold forever, she said. But before she would get any further about how loose the bricks had become, and how she could fit her little finger between the mantel and the chimneypiece itself, before she got as far as the sigh which always prefaced these remarks, I would wall myself up in the soundest of sleeps. Still, even in the depths, I could not insulate myself from the wife howling about my chimney. And so, I would stir in my chair to ward off her despair and then return to my sleep, dreamless. She did not speak the last word concerning the imminent demise of my chimney, and now she is gone. I live in the house with fourteen rooms and no other people. The chimney has, beyond dispute, asserted its superiority in the argument with her.

At present, however, it is neither my chimney nor its fortunes that most concern me. Racked though I am by my late wife's suspicions, they are unfounded and do not support a theory of the noises from above. In fact, no theory can be constructed to explain these noises, and there need be none. I do not like to say so, but there are sounds overhead because there are squirrels in the attic. It has to be, because ever since the noises started, I have had trouble keeping the house heated. I suppose that the squirrels crept in along the drain-pipe and through a chink in the shingling, or even down the stalwart chimney. However they have gotten in, their comings and goings must have worn a space larger than was there before, so that, now, an imperceptible draft sucks the heat under the attic door from my part of the house. For this rea-son, the fact of the squirrels cannot be whitewashed into a theoretical matter. It is a question of economy—these are en-ergy-saving times—a practical question. It requires only cun-ning, a proper assessment of the situation, and a knowledge of squirrels.

My first impulse was to burn the house down and collect the insurance. I know, everyone entertains this idea at one time or another. But then I could move to Spain, alone, which has always been on my mind, or at least for as long as I can remember. Moreover, this plan, which includes buying a large château, has plausibility to recommend it. The trees back of the house, mostly oaks and hawthorns, have long been rotting from within. Wizened and hollow, they want little provocation and a well-struck match to disappear in a blaze of flame and to take the house with them. This Chekhovian vision appeals to me. But even as I see the frames of wood blistering and snapping to consume themselves at last in one long, low-pitched whistle, my vision comes to grief. Suppose that long after the last ashes had smoldered, long after I had purchased the airline ticket (first class, because of the insurance money), long after all the necessary arrangements had been made, I did not like Spain. It would be my fate not to like Spain. When I think about not liking Spain, I begin to doubt that I would like it anywhere at all but where I am, for which reason even the more modest plot of putting the house up for sale has to be shelved. I cannot leave the house, because then where would I be?

Better not to answer that and to reconceive the possibilities. Professional exterminators are out of the question. I appreciate that they still make house calls, but once you bring them in, there is no getting rid of them. They arrive with their paraphernalia and poke around, checking the moldings, running inventories, leaving Styrofoam coffee cups on the tables. The house gets smaller once they are here. You can feel it shrinking around you. When they have successfully diagnosed the problem, they spray something or other wherever it is they spray it, and then the rugs and the drapes hold the stench for days. To their credit, they usually rout whatever you have hired them to rout in the first place. But no sooner does one menace disappear than another and still more pestilential vermin materializes. Like weeds grown in dragon's blood—the more you chop them down, the harder they grow. Dragon's blood, this is what the exterminators have in their spray guns and, in this way, keep their business up, even as they pretend to settle their bills in permanent ink.

I worry about calling down an interminable plague upon my house, and besides, I am not at all sure that exterminating work can be applied to the case of squirrels. Thinking of the exterminators has caused me a good deal of remorse, because I have always been fond of small animals, so long as they are not rats. That would be why the squirrels came to inhabit my attic to begin with. I think that animals have a second sense about such things; they know if you harbor an obscure sympathy for them. I did, after all, when I was sure that the noises *were* squirrels, try to make friends so that I could induce them away without having to kill them off. If they could have been domesticated, they might have become a blessing—you know, something to have around the house for the hard moments,

like childhood snapshots. Squirrels will eat just about anything, and the peace offerings left at the base of the rainspout
have disappeared. But the squirrels, judging from the noises,
have remained. My gesture was thwarted, and what else would
it be? You didn't think that squirrels, with squirrelish minds,
would distinguish between a bribe and an invitation to stay on.
Did you?

I am wistful when I think about the failed attempt to do-
mesticate the squirrels, much as I am wistful about the time
before Spain was spoiled by my intention to move there. Wan-
dering around the upstairs rooms to get my bearings is no help
for it, either. Instead, later I went downstairs and tried to get
a fire going in the hearth, but it would not catch. Still, sitting
by my chimney, I thought far into the night and still farther,
nursing the fire and studying my nostalgias. There is not too
much to be said or done about them, so that after a time I
drifted into my proverbial sleep. No longer does the wife's
voice haunt my slumbers, but neither are my sleeps dreamless.
In this particular sleep, urged, no doubt, by my proximity to
the chimney, which, after all, runs right through the attic to
where I was sitting, I was visited by the sight of the attic itself.
Everything that belonged to everyone had been put up there.
Whatever was left by my parents when they died, including a
metal hat rack and old newspapers that had been kept in the
attics of their houses. My entire collection of comics, or maybe
they were the children's collections of comics, and dog-eared
travel guides with phone numbers written on the inside covers.
Filing boxes filled with cards, and empty boxes in which had
arrived gifts, long ago thrown out, from a maiden aunt who
lived in Poughkeepsie. Catalogues of lawn furniture that
would never look right on the lawn, and a great, baroque
mirror that has been in the family for years, my grandfather's,
or maybe his grandfather's grandfather's. I am sure that other
people's property was stored up there, too, people I have

forgotten, if indeed I ever knew them at all. It was a common-place dream, but the details of what I saw puzzle me. I have not been in the attic for years and really have no waking idea whatever of its contents. In the meantime, the attic continued to contain everything, and I could see it all very clearly. It could not be expected that things would be quiet up there.

When I awoke, it was not yet morning, but this short sleep had renovated my spirits. Enough, at least, that I could begin to conceive a good once-over for the attic, a thorough clean-ing. The prospect daunted me, but I was inspired by thoughts of a vengeful yard sale, a redistribution of the extraneous possessions that crowd my attic. Here, I might turn current loss to gain or, in any case, make up for the heating bills, which had become astronomical. It was the time of beginning. But on the way upstairs I wondered if it was right to dispose of other people's pasts with such short shrift, if the deed didn't require some permission it was not mine to give. If only I could have devised a cleaning-out that was not a throwing-out. But there was no place other than the attic to put all of these things, and besides, it is misgivings such as this one that landed me in the present predicament.

I believe I would have gone through with the sale, except that when I got to the attic door it was locked. I do not recall there ever having been a key that unlocked it or, in fact, there having been a lock on the door at all. It is pointless to look for a key that may not be lost, but all the same I went down to the cellar to where I keep a glass jar full of odd hardware. You can never tell when a stray screw, or whatever else is in that jar, might be useful. I did not find a key in the jar. But I did select a handful of nails, and a hammer and leftover shingling that were lying in a heap on the floor. Then I went outside to get the ladder from its place at the edge of the house. Balancing my climb, with the nails in my mouth, a hammer slung in pocket and shingles in arm, I could see that it really was too late in the season for a spring cleaning, anyway. The sky was already ribbed with the thin rows of cloud that mean May has come and gone, even though it had been unseasonably cold, especially with the draft from the attic. I was not distracted by the sky from my purpose. When I had finished, the dormer window that had let what light there is into the attic was boarded shut. Presently I went inside and sealed up the attic door, nail by nail, so that, key or no key, it no longer mattered. Now nothing remained but the chimney. There was no way of closing it off at the top—the ladder wouldn't reach that high —but downstairs, where I had taken to dreaming lately, I pulled the flue shut and dragged a chest onto the hearth. No more fires would burn here, but then, no more would I be troubled by drafts. Eventually the noises overhead would cease. Squirrels will not survive long in a sealed-off attic, or if they do, you would never know.

This shutting-down business was grim, but it was finished, and I will still defend what I have done. For a long time I had been fighting it off. Even after it was over, there was some resistance, and I thought it might do me good to go for a drive. Whenever I am caught like this, I go for a drive, mostly across the causeway to Greenport and back. From the causeway you can see along the Sound, sometimes all the way to Connecticut. Actually, Connecticut is too far away to be visible. What you see is just a dark line of haze that hangs on the horizon, especially when the weather is clearest. There are always a lot of gulls around the causeway, too. In their frenzied attacks and retreats, shrieking, they remind me of rats with wings. But there are also, occasionally, beautiful birds that outsoar the gulls and cut untraceable arcs above them. I do not know what they are called, but they help to mitigate my disgust with the gulls. By the time I reach Greenport, a matter of about twenty minutes, I usually have also reached a perspective that allows me a little more freedom in my dealings with myself. Then I have a beer at the Tribe on. It used to be the Tiburone, which is the word for *shark* in some language, but a storm last spring, maybe in late March, ripped down the sign. When the owner put it up again, the *u* had been lost and the name was mangled. He picked up the pieces as best he could and made a new sign that says TRIBE ON. The change no longer disturbs me, although it took some getting used to. Now, Tribe on seems preferable. It doesn't mean anything in any language. It is only the name of the bar where I like to stop for a beer.

This time, though, when I got to the Tribe on, it was closed. I just swung the car around without stopping and headed back over the causeway to where my house rests, on the end of the point, near the ferry station. I have visited a lot of famous houses, and I have read a lot about houses, too. Crossing the causeway was time enough to catalogue them, famous houses—of Seven Gables, of Usher, that Jack Built, of Mirth, houses by the sea. This is best of all, the way mine is founded right on the sea, poised at the water's edge, but it must be, after so many years, poised perfectly. I like the image of the house standing, long empty and overgrown with beach vegetation, with one shutter flapping when the wind is full. Better still, I like the image of the solitary chimney, chiseled against a bright November sky, supported only by the remnants of the brick foundation. Driving home, I revolved these pictures in my head for a minute, thought about how different the house always looks after a drive over the causeway, a house that looms, monster-like, a house that is a giant, a child, whatever I say it to be. I tried to imagine what the house would be like on this day. Then I looked out across the Sound and, mostly, ahead to where it is I live. **Q**

The Slit

Her mother was fat and she was fat and when her mother threw herself down into the grave, on top of her daughter's box, what I thought was that she was doing the Fat Man Dance with her daughter. Then I remembered that not every family did the Fat Man Dance.

It was the same with pogo. It was not until I went to school and got sick and lay on the floor in the bathroom, and the girls came up around me, and what they told me was that they could see my belly button.

I had never heard of belly button. It had always been pogo.

I thought, What is belly button? I thought, What kind of a name is that for my pogo? I wanted to go home and I wanted to ask someone at home who started it that we had pogos, and why was it that all the other people had belly buttons.

I thought, I bet the daughter's glad she's dead, because what her mother was doing, throwing herself into the grave on top of the box like that, looked funny. It looked funny because her mother was fat, and it looked so much like the mother was doing the Fat Man Dance because her arms were spread out, too, as if she were waiting for her daughter to spread out her arms also, and then they could hold hands and smack bellies together and dance in circles on the box, just the way we always did in the summer when we did the Fat Man Dance. Because we always did the Fat Man Dance in the summer when we ran around with no clothes on and danced a lot because it was summer.

Then I realized that there were no flowers in the place. I looked around, at the other headstones, and there were no flowers. I thought to myself that this must be the wrong place to bury the daughter, that her mother had made a mistake,

37

because if the mother wanted to do the Fat Man Dance with the daughter, she would have also probably brought flowers to put on the daughter's headstone. I thought to myself that my mother would not have buried me here. I do not know where my mother might have buried me, but maybe she would have done it out back, in our backyard. Maybe my mother would have buried me under our pool, in our backyard, and then in the summer she could swim over me, her belly facing down.

The daughter's father told us a story.

He told us that when the daughter was little she went home from school, at lunch, and after she ate lunch she started playing with her dolls, and she forgot about the time, and she didn't know what to do—if she should go back to school and have her teacher get mad at her, or if she should just stay at home and keep playing with her dolls—so what she did was she wrote a note, and she went back to school, and what the note said was *Dear Teacher, please excuse Jody for being late—she had to feed her dolls.*

I heard someone call it a VJ. But we had always been calling it a free-free. Maybe this was because my sister and I used to always look at the back of cereal boxes where there was a toy inside the box, and what the back of the box said was FREE-FREE. *Inside This Box Is a Toy,* and I think my sister and I would think to ourselves it was a free-free inside the box.

The last thing I did with Jody, I think, was play Foot.

We were on a bunk bed, on the top bunk bed, and we were just talking—and then we started kicking at each other, and then we started playing Foot.

I never understood Foot. It was something you did just to see how long you could push your foot up against the other person's foot, or see who could push the other person off first off the bunk bed. It was something like that. Maybe it wasn't really the last thing that I did with Jody, maybe it was just the last time that I touched her.

There was a drop of blood on the ground. When I think about it, I still don't know why I didn't think there was something wrong. It looked like something our dog would leave behind on the floor when she was in heat, and we could know where the dog was going across the house that way, and my mother would say, "Oh, the dog is in heat," when she saw the blood, and it was all right because we knew it, so no one was supposed to get upset about it or worry. I don't even think we even cleaned the drop of blood up from the dog. I think we just left the drop of blood on the floor in the house.

There were also people standing in their doorways. But everyone does that. But later I should have thought to myself that it wasn't summer and that people only stand in their doorways for no reason like that if it is summer.

When I got upstairs, there was no answer at her door. Then I saw that the neighbor's door was open and I heard Jody's mother inside the neighbor's place.

Her mother wasn't saying anything that I could understand. She just sounded like she was laughing. Jody and I were supposed to go out that night and I wanted to know if Jody was going to come out. But her mother was laughing and it was hard to understand what was going on. Then I saw her mother and I saw that she was crying, not laughing, and then she came over to me and gave me a hug. But to me it felt more like a hang. She just let all of her body hang down on my back and I thought my legs were going to give. She was crying into my hair and I thought about how I had just washed my hair because Jody and I were going to go out that night.

"Where is Jody?" I said.

Her mother could not say. But the neighbor said, and then I left.

Going down the stairs, I touched my hair—and it was wet where her mother had cried against it, but the even more amazing thing was the blood I saw in the street when I looked down. I saw that there were more drops of blood than I had thought there were before, and they were all over, spread out, as if our dog, in heat, had run in circles on the ground.

I saw the people still standing in their doorways. I thought that maybe they thought that if they stayed out there long enough that it would happen again, or that Jody would come back and open the door to her place.

Then I thought her mother pushed her.

Sometimes I have dreams where someone is trying to show me a picture of the way Jody looked on the ground, or sometimes she comes back and I think to myself that I can't wait to wake up and tell everybody that Jody is back. Sometimes I tell Jody that she should have stayed around. Sometimes she shows me a bed with the sheet pulled back and the window open. Sometimes she makes hairbrushes and bottles and things move in the room by just looking at them in my dreams.

Maybe the last time I touched Jody was in the bathroom when I was passing her a napkin under the stall door—and when she took the napkin from my hand, she touched my hand at the same time.

Her father pulled out a rose from inside his jacket. I did not understand how her father could have kept it there so long and how it still was in good shape and the petals weren't bent.

My father gave us the names of mushrooms. My sisters were Fairyrings and Moonlights, and I was an Inkycap.

My mother gave us butterfly kisses on our cheeks.

When her mother threw herself onto her daughter's box,

I thought that maybe she did not throw herself onto the box right, that maybe she threw herself only half onto the box, and where her face was on the box was where Jody's free-free was instead, and what Jody's mother was doing was giving Jody's free-free one of those butterfly kisses that my mother used to give to us.

Her window was the kind that is low to the floor, and when you stood next to it, it hit you in the place in your legs that made you feel as though it would be so easy to fall out of it.

We used to rub butter onto our pogos.

Really, we rubbed it all over.

It felt good.

We would hold the stick of butter in its wrapper just the way you would if you were buttering a pan for a cake, and we would move the stick of butter around and in circles.

You could tell that her father wanted to throw the rose on top of the box, but that he could not because her mother was still on top of the box. Then he got down next to the box, and he pulled on her mother's arm.

Once, we got pencils and put them in our free-frees so that they hung down, and we said that we were cows. Other times we played Superman, and put towels between our cheeks in our bottoms and ran down a hill and yelled, "Superman!" and hoped that the towels would lift up into the air, like a cape would do, if we were wearing capes and running down a hill.

Before they put her into the box, they told us they dressed her in her St. Claire's confirmation dress. She had already grown out of that dress and I didn't know how they could have fit her into it. I pictured a slit in the back of her dress that they made so that the dress would look like it fit Jody from the front.

Then I thought, maybe, for some reason, they don't put them in faceup, but they put them in facedown, and that if the top of the box was taken away we would see the slit in the back of her dress.

I thought, If the top of the box was taken away, then Jody's mother's face would be in the slit on the back of Jody's dress if they had put Jody in facedown.

I saw her father pull on her mother's arm a little more. Her mother put her arms around the box like she was hugging the box and she would not move. The rose he was holding started to bend where his hand was around it.

Lately, I have been dreaming that she is standing over me in my bed. When I wake up, I do not let myself open my eyes. I think, Maybe now that the dress is very, very small for her, she is a doll wearing a dress. Then sometimes I think that when I wake up that I can smell her, or that I can smell dirt, but then the wind comes through my window and I can't smell the smell.

Now I hear them saying Ur*an*us instead of *U*ranus, the way it always used to be said.

My father wrote our mushroom names on a wall in our house, but we don't live in that house anymore.

When her father was getting her mother to get off the box, and when her mother was standing up, after he had pulled her up, her father slipped and his leg hit the box and it made him fall down onto the box, and what he was doing was sitting on top of the box, with the rose still in his hand, and what it looked like he was doing was that he was asking her mother to marry him all over again, as if her father was sitting on a log in the woods and that she was just standing there, listening to him, and we, all the mourners, were the trees.

I guess if my mother could, if people allowed it, she would bury me under her bed, so that when she was sleeping she could sleep belly down.

Then he put the rose on top of the box, and we all walked away and heard them shoveling the dirt on top of the box.

I thought about the rose being on top of Jody's belly and about the dirt being on top of Jody's belly and I thought about Jody doing the Fat Man Dance even after her mother walked away. **Q**

It's Freezing Here in Milwaukee

Sometimes I'm in excruciating pain—so excruciating that I can barely walk across the room. I have to have my feet propped up on pillows to keep the pain away. It's very simple, really: the arches—the metatarsal arches of both my feet—are falling, and when I try to walk in any direction, or stand up, the bones of my toes start to throb and my eyes start to water. It's unbearable. My surgeon, the man who is supposed to operate on my falling arches, is in Italy, and I am waiting at my parents' house for him to get back. Every day, I read the weather report in the newspaper: "Rome—84°F," or "Rome—91°F." My surgeon is in Rome, and my parents live in Milwaukee.

I don't have to stay in bed all the time. I could go down to the family room and sit on the La-Z-Boy, or into the basement and sprawl out on our old sofa. Sometimes, in the afternoons, I go into my parents' bedroom and lie down on their king-size bed. The bedspread, which is frayed and colorless, smells like the kitchen. It's like lying down on a tablecloth.

The surgeon is supposed to be the best in the country for this kind of surgery, so I gave up my apartment, took a leave of absence from my job, and came home to see him at his suburban clinic. After my second visit, the nurse gave me some cork-and-leather inserts for my shoes so I could get out of the house and do things.

The cork-and-leather inserts are too big and slip underneath the soles of my feet, and they remind me of portable oxygen tanks. When I was in high school, I had a summer job at a factory on the south side of Milwaukee. The factory made portable oxygen tanks for people with severe respiratory illnesses so they could leave their houses without passing out.

The company liked using real people instead of models for their brochures, and I remember one of the vice-presidents coming around every July to pick people out. He would take them to the parking lot, fit them with an oxygen tank, then get a photographer to take pictures of them getting in and out of the company car. Somewhere, in some part of the house, there is a brochure with a picture of me and a caption reading: *It really works!*

I've spent the last three years of my life working for the metropolitan staff of a newspaper in New York. Outside, everything seemed to be falling apart, but inside, in the newsroom, it only got better and better: new carpeting, new display terminals, record-setting circulation. I was a copy aide for two years, which meant that I clipped other people's articles and answered the telephones. In September of last year, the deputy editor called me in and said, "Danny, we're going to make you election coverage coordinator." Later that day, I officially became "election coverage coordinator," which meant that in early October I was supposed to call the telephone company and order the extra telephones.

This past winter, I was promoted to editorial aide and sent to the Westchester bureau. My job there was pretty similar: answering phones and clipping articles. But about twice a month they would let me write a brief for the "Westchester in Brief" column. Right before my arches collapsed, they sent me on my first story. It was about a python escaping from a vet's office in Tarrytown and getting itself caught in the engine of a nearby station wagon.

A few weeks after I was sent to the Westchester bureau, Sally-Ann arrived. She had been a reporter for a Dallas paper and had just been hired by the metro editor. Sally-Ann lied about everything: her age, her salary, where she went to college. And she used me as a personal slave. "Daniel," she'd scream, "I need that clip ASAP!" The bureau chief editor, who is twenty-five (a year younger than I am), had been working on an investigative story for ten months; something about cocaine smugglers and a Larchmont pizza parlor. When he discovered a link with a pizza parlor in Amarillo, Sally-Ann said, "Let me work on this story. Get the paper to send me to Texas. I know Amarillo. I covered the Panhandle."

Sally-Ann had to stay in Westchester and was only allowed to cover the municipal courts. One afternoon at the courthouse, she saw Tony Seligman. (Tony Seligman writes for the national desk and has a Pulitzer Prize.) Sally-Ann came back to the bureau and started asking questions. Why was Tony Seligman in Westchester? What was he doing at the courthouse? Why didn't anybody tell her that Tony Seligman was doing a story at the courthouse? Sally-Ann was getting frantic, so she called up the national desk. "Hello, Tony?" she said. "This is Sally-Ann Hughes. Remember me? I work up at the Westchester bureau. I heard you were doing a story up here at the courthouse, and I thought, if you need any help, that perhaps we should meet to talk about it. I know the courthouse, it's a pretty closed place without contacts." Tony Seligman didn't want to have lunch with Sally-Ann and wasn't interested in meeting her contacts. He was getting married in three days and had gone to the courthouse to pick up a marriage license.

On my last day of work, Sally-Ann came up to where I was sitting and handed me a list of forty names. She wanted me to find out the people's phone numbers, and then call and invite them to her birthday party. "Of course," she said, "I would have invited you, but you'll be back in Iowa by then, won't you?" Most of the people had to be reminded of Sally-Ann's last name before they remembered who she was. Tony Seligman and his new wife were on the list, but I couldn't get up enough nerve to call them.

When I went downtown to ask if I could take a year off, the

metro editor said, "Of course. We can't afford to lose you. The year you were election coverage coordinator, everything went as smooth as silk." A few times since I've been home, my father has bought a national edition of the paper and left it on the dining room table as a surprise. I spend the afternoon going through it as if I've never been inside a newsroom, and never lived in New York.

When I first moved there—to New York—I tried to get all points of view. I tried and succeeded in befriending the couple who lived across the hall. She had a genetics degree from M.I.T., a law degree from Harvard, and a medical degree from Yale. Her husband used to joke that the only thing left was divinity school. The first time I saw her, she was walking down the stairs as I was walking up. She was pregnant and wearing high heels, and I remember expecting her to fall, or at least stumble. After the pains in my feet got worse, and I could think of nothing but my own suffering, she gave me a list of five specialists: four in New York, and Dr. Platt in Milwaukee.

Their names were Carol and Ron Bellamy, and for the majority of the time that I lived across the hall, they introduced me to their friends. One of the friends, a man from India with advanced degrees in mathematics and philosophy, would throw dinner parties in his small apartment and explain things using mathematical metaphors. He'd begin: "There isn't a society, there isn't an individual consciousness, that doesn't start out believing it is getting closer and closer to one, and further and further from zero. We move, step by step, away from the latter and toward the former. But with each step, our courage diminishes and our steps become smaller. You see, we eventually realize—the sane ones—that there is an infinite quantity of numbers between zero and one. We realize that we've never been at zero, and we will never reach one: Our past remains a fiction and our future an impossibility." Then someone would ask him if he'd ever been compared to Bertrand Russell, and he'd say, "Of course, dear girl."

The summer before I was sent to Westchester, I slept with a woman who lived in the mathematician-philosopher's building—one of those giant fortresses on Second Avenue. It was August, and I was supposed to be on vacation. I couldn't afford to leave New York, and I went to a party with a copy aide from the foreign desk. It was hot and crowded, and I didn't know anybody except the copy aide. I remember a man there of about thirty, slightly overweight, who was refusing to take his suit coat off. He was surrounded by people who seemed to know him. They were chanting "Take it off! Take it off!" Someone had put bottles of wine underneath the air-conditioner to keep them cold. I took one of the open bottles and sat on the floor next to the window. I could see the copy aide looking around the room for me, then I could see him go into the hallway. Standing above me, leaning on the air-conditioner, was a woman in a green T-shirt and a long skirt. She moved closer, and the air-conditioner blew the hem of her skirt against my face. She was looking down at me, keeping her hair up in a bun with one hand and holding a bottle of beer with the other. She seemed to be swaying back and forth, and I thought she might be drunk. Coming toward me, she let her hair fall down around her shoulders. She put the beer next to the wine, and ran her fingers across my forehead. "Hot?" she said. She had my head between her hands. "We'll have to make it go faster," she said, tilting her head toward the air-conditioner. "We'll have to make it go as fast as it can!"

During the cab ride to her apartment, the driver stopped to buy cigarettes. She rolled down the window and started screaming. Then she opened up the door and grabbed my hand, pulling me into the street. She kept saying she was a stockbroker and that she'd had a bad day at the market. "Really, really bad," she kept saying. "Really bad." As we walked the rest of the way, I decided to ask her if she'd lost her job, if she'd been fired. "Really, really bad day," she said.

Her apartment was on the twenty-third floor, and it wasn't until I looked out the window that I realized the man from India lived a few floors above her. She turned on the air-conditioner and stood in front of it, holding her hair above her head again.

It looked as if she was either moving in or moving out. There were paintings stacked on the floor, and a very large television set next to its box. She must have sensed I was looking around, because she walked away from the air-conditioner and kicked a pile of paintings. She kissed me on the mouth, and we stood in the hot darkness, taking each other's clothes off, waiting for the room to get cold.

In the middle of the night, I walked around the apartment. There was a basket of unopened mail addressed to Judith Simms—her last name was Simms. In the bathroom, there was a bottle of French shampoo made from walnut leaves and an unused bar of soap. I was hungry, and I went into the kitchen. She had two gallons of olive oil, an empty refrigerator, and empty cupboards.

The next morning I woke up and she was sitting on the couch, wearing her green T-shirt. She wasn't wearing any underwear, and when I got out of bed, she put her hands in her lap. "I don't know what's the matter with me," she said. "I feel real sick. Do you?" I thought about staying and taking a shower with the walnut-leaves shampoo, but she seemed to want me to leave. "I have to get to work," I said, lying.

It was about seven-thirty. I stood in front of the elevator with two men and two women, all in suits. After five minutes, I decided to walk down. The stairs were wide and well lit. I remember speeding down the stairs, flight after flight, talking to myself. I was sure I was the only person not waiting for the elevator. But I'd overestimated my endurance, or under-

estimated how long twenty-three flights of stairs are. It got to
the point where I was so dizzy and hot that I had to sit down.
There was something awful about the situation: spending my
vacation, surrounded by stairs, running away from some girl
I never wanted to see again. I leaned back against the concrete
to catch my breath.

When I first moved to New York, I couldn't wait for anything; I could feel myself crackling inside. But it all changed.
It must have changed because I fled New York the first chance
that came along.

Here in Milwaukee everything is beginning to freeze. Yesterday my father took our cars in to have the snow tires put on;
neighbors' yards are starting to look like tundra. I stare outside, and I can't help thinking about my surgeon. In Italy,
they're having the hottest November in history. It's over 100
degrees. People are passing out in the streets. I try to imagine
what my surgeon is doing. Has he abandoned Rome and gone
to the beach? Has he sacrificed his vacation to treat the heat-
stroke victims? Or perhaps, like the Romans they showed
on the evening news, he has given up and lain down in a
fountain.

While I wait for him, I often lie in bed with my feet on the
headboard. I follow the ceiling as it slopes down to the windows, then look out to the backyard. When I was a child, we
had a pear tree and an apple tree growing next to each other.
In late summer, the ground would be covered with pale green
things; you could never tell whether they were apples or pears.
From far away—from my bedroom, for instance—they all
looked round and indisputably like apples. From closer up—
the back porch or the driveway—they would become yellow
and irregular, like hourglasses. Not until you got on your
hands and knees, or picked them up—not until after that—
could you possibly know for sure.

My parents cut down that apple tree so they could install central air conditioning, and the pear tree has stopped bearing fruit. Its leaves are all gray and brittle.

In a way, nothing turns out to be what you think it is. Sometimes the yard looks empty—it doesn't even look familiar. But if I rushed outside, I could feel those pear leaves, like wet sticks between my toes, and know exactly where I was. And I could look up to my bedroom window, just able to make out a corner of the room, the place I'm looking at right now. Q

Pots of Impatiens

The sun made by the window sits on me. I have just returned from running and put together a bowl of cottage cheese and corn flakes. I picture myself out there. I am down to two miles a day, and there is something froggy about my style.

My ribs ache, and my breasts itch. Approaching muffin-hood is what mother used to say. I am eight months into it. My baby, they tell me, is sliding toward home.

The landlady brings pots of impatiens and hangs them in the trees. I don't water them, and they die. She persists. She is a pleasant woman. When she comes we sit in chairs strung with plastic the color of turquoise and we talk. She sneaks looks at the impatiens. The dead ones hang like flying saucers with dreadlocked hairdos.

People bring food. I used to meet them at the door, thank them. But the food was mostly freezer-burned. Now they knock, and I sit. They can see me here in the big window. They leave their food on the steps.

Here's the deal: If my time comes between 8 and 10 A.M., I phone Alice, and I *try* her first if it's between four and five in the afternoon. No answer, then I call Alex. Alex is Alice's father-in-law. His son Alexander is married to Alice. I phone him any other time, day or night. Alexander has call-waiting, call-forwarding, and a phone in his Riviera.

After I make contact, I'm to get to the couch and begin my forehead-to-toe relaxation exercises. Alice can be here in ten to twenty minutes, depending on how she hits the lights. Alex in thirty, and Alexander in five to forty-five. Sometimes he's in the neighborhood.

Alex. Alexander. Alice.

This is confusing. Let me explain.

You need to know that Alice and Alexander are habitual aborters.

The key here is that I am giving them my baby.

Everything is legal. Alexander is a lawyer, and other lawyers have been called in. We've signed papers. All that. Picture the god of adoption smiling on us.

Then picture this: Earlier me and Alex and Alexander are going over who I call and when. This is something we do often. They come over. They quiz me. I have 3 × 5s by the phone. *Who* is in black. The times are in red, and the phone numbers in blue. Like this: Alice, 8–10, 4–5, 542–9087.

Alex brings coffee and brews it. I drink juice. Today I looked around. There they sat, Alex and Alexander, two men who looked like they had just surrendered, leaning back in chairs that won't give. Their hands behind their heads. Their elbows sticking straight out. They had on rubber-soled shoes. Alex's were black, and Alexander's brown. I wanted to say something in German, but couldn't. So I wrote on a card: *Learn German.* After they left, I swallowed those words. They are for baby.

Alex, who is the uncle of a friend of a friend, arranged everything. The first thing Alexander said to me was: We get pregnant, then we abort. Spontaneously. He said it like I wouldn't believe him. Alice herself just sort of drifted around, acted like it's the human way of things.

I told them what I tell everyone: I watch too much television. I'm confessing, and I want to know what we can talk about. Like this: *The Paper Chase* and Kingsfield. If I tell you that Alex looks like Kingsfield, can you see him? Big man, not just fat, but tall. Like God in a bad dream. With a bow tie and vested suits. Put the black, rubber-soled shoes on Kingsfield and you've got Alex. Alexander himself is shorter, and the jowls haven't settled yet.

I won't watch Carson unless Joan Rivers is guesting. That woman is a hoot. Carson's a goat who's lost his whistle. And the people he has on. Who wants to see Shelley Winters or hear Steve and Edie?

I get cable and two movie channels. My show is *WKRP in Cincinnati.* If I say Bailey, do you picture her? *She of the jugs hung so well* is the way Freddy put it. Freddy is my baby's father. He looks like Johnny Fever. The Doc-*tour.* That's how Fever says it. Over the air, he says, "Fellow babies, this is the Doc-*tour.* We are all in critical condition." Fever and Freddy keep a three-day stubble going. Fever has eyes like sparklers. Hair's going. Freddy's isn't. In fact, Freddy is working on a California pompadour.

Freddy is no dummy. IQ off the charts. I'm telling baby about him. Writing notes and eating them, like with the German. It'll all come back to her, and she'll do unspeakable things and not know why. She'll astonish fools. Some of what I write is mean. Like: *Suck your thumb, hard.* Alexander has the money, and he needs to pay for this kid. Pay and pay. $12,000 in dental bills.

Baby's a girl. I did the tests. My age is no blessing, and there are no guarantees, but baby is cleared for landing.

Freddy has gone to Vegas to work as a troller. One of those guys who walk up and down Fremont, trying to get you inside the souvenir shops. Some do some magic. I saw one bouncing around a ball of Silly Putty. Anything to get you talking. What state you from? That kind of line. Then they give you a coupon for a roll of dimes or a free drink. There are a few slot machines inside, maybe a row, but the real business is anything with Vegas on it. Pencils, mugs, I.D. bracelets, combs, towels. T-shirts in Day-Glow colors. Me and Freddy would drive up there some weekends.

Freddy'll get people in. He has talent. He has looks. He has a smile like Presley.

When I picture Freddy I picture him slipping out the front door. I see the back of his Dodger jacket. Blue satin like a flag in the breeze. I hear organ music. I've drawn up a picture of that in living color, and eaten it. In small pieces. For baby. She'll be ready.

Mother always told me, "Just because the bus driver doesn't smile at you doesn't mean you can't keep on smiling and saying hello." Be an actor, she said, not a *re-*actor. It was something she had read.

My baby'll be an actor.

Freddy thinks I took away his instincts, and if he thinks that, then I did. I'm too old for him. I'm old enough to be pissed off at Nixon. I threw jelly beans at the Beatles.

I'm too old to have a baby. I pee a lot.

Soon as she comes, I'm cutting my hair, and I'll hit Vegas. To Freddy, I'll say, *Friends only.* He'll smile like Presley.

For now, I take care of my girl. Alexander tells me she is lowering herself or she may be already in position. He reads the books. He shows me pictures and tells me stories. Eight months means she has eyes to see with and ears to hear.

Alexander and Alice think I'm ill-bred myself, but I am far from that. Here's what I do and don't do. No alcohol, no drugs, no aspirin. And no red meat. You watch enough television and you'll learn to do without meat. I eat tuna. Brain food.

I don't smoke. I grind wheat and bake bread, my grandmother's recipe. As they say: Color me adult. I rinse the fat from cottage cheese. It only takes a minute. All you do is put it in a sieve and run sink water over it. My baby will hate fat. I cut a picture from *Life.* Fattest woman on earth. She looked like fill dirt. I ate that, the picture, quickly. I ate the cover of *Time.* It had on it the Woman of the Eighties. Tall and thin, and looking like a boxer. Muscles like stones. A woman who could throw a jab and take a punch.

When I clean the kitty litter, I wear a surgeon's mask. You

don't, and you could end up with a kid with heart trouble. Chemicals do worse things than kill. There are things you don't want to know. Pictures you don't want to see.

I call kitten Whips. She was a gift from the friend of the friend who told Alex about me. I called her Ruth. Then it became KIT-ten. Soon it was Kitten-with-a-whip, because I saw that movie on the set. Ann-Margret looking mean enough to hump Russians. There's a woman for baby.

I want Freddy to tell baby the real story of Pocahontas. She needs to hear it. Picture this: He calls, and I coax him into it. Can you see baby's face? See her ears turn like radar? Freddy's version has Captain Smith in it.

I don't expect him to phone.

This is a note I wrote baby: *Your real daddy is a redheaded bandit who drinks like a fish.* Freddy's hair is black as plastic can be.

Alexander calls every day. We don't use names. No hello. He just starts in. The lawyer in him, I guess. It's like we're in the same house and he's just drifted back in from taking a leak. Alex is like that, too.

So, Alexander is full of worries. A month ago, it was my running. He calls. "Did I see you on Birch?" he says.

I say, "Running?"

"Yes."

"Could have."

He says, "Is that right?"

I say, "Doctor's orders."

His doctor. We are playing Alexander's game; he's upset but doesn't want to push it. Surely he is dealing with a loony. A daughter of the moon was what my mother called me. Alexander's on eggshells. Who knows, any day I could say, *Papers or no papers, I'm keeping kiddo. Take me to court. I'll turn up on* 60 Minutes, *and you'll refuse to be interviewed.*

I won't, but daughter of the moon that I am, I could, and

then laugh and say, *Only joking.* I'd laugh like Bette Davis in *Burnt Offerings.* God, her laugh. And when she broke her neck, you could feel your own snap and paralysis creeping north and south, moving like water when you overfill a plant and it seeps onto the coffee table.

Alexander and I should talk more. Maybe I should screw him. Can you see that? I invite him over. I tell his secretary to tell him it's important. He arrives, all business in his brown rubber-soled shoes. Here is one worried lawyer, a lawyer trying to remember his lawyer's number. I pour him a drink. I counter his Scotch with my Perrier. I smile at him, and the curl returns to my hair. I coo and coo. He realizes that he is about to be laid. His mind says, *You're okay. She's offering; you're taking. Don't upset her. Only doing what the crazy woman wants to do.* This is a man who I'm sure has never cheated on Alice. I begin slowly, so slowly he thinks we might be under water. I coo. And then I fuck his eyes out.

Or maybe I should do Alex.

It's too late.

And Alice and I have never talked, not even about iron. I want to tell her how sleepy I am. She feeds me things and then stands by like a waitress. *Coffee?* she asked when they had me over. I outlined its dangers and then rub-a-dub-dubbed my belly. I asked if there was lard in the rolls. Salt in the potatoes, I wondered. I let her know these things are under suspicion.

I wasn't supposed to get to know them. But I came by. Alex was there. "We were just talking about you," he said. I touched my ears. Alex's chin said, *You should not be here. We had an agreement.* Everyone sort of retreated and acted like *they'd* come to see me.

They want this baby. I walked around, sat on their bed, lifted the lid to the clothes hamper. "Eat?" they said.

Over a Pepsi Free I said, "Whose fault?"

So that's when Alexander told me they were habitual

aborters, and I told them about TV. I can't explain this, but as I sat there I pictured a half-finished cup of coffee on a café counter.

Afterward, on the bus home, I wrote baby her first note. It said: *Your father is not your father. He did not make you.* And because these things happen this way, my baby turned inside me. It could have gone unnoticed. I've learned that she was tiny enough to do a somersault.

A lady from up the street, who has wax hair and who defines her Indian cheekbones with an orange blusher, comes to the door with food. She can see me here in the sun. Like the others, she leaves her dish behind.

I am painting my nails the colors of M & Ms.

I picture myself in a German concentration camp. Outside the gate there is a guard and a Doberman. The guard kisses the dog, and his helmet falls off because he has to bend over. They both laugh, the guard and the dog. So the guard closes his eyes and bends to kiss the Doberman again, and the dog holds up a shovel, one of those snub-nosed kind. The guard kisses it. He opens his eyes and laughs. The Doberman laughs. They are laughing so hard they are on their backs.

Now I want to tell you something true. I am in junior high when the local television station comes to my class. They talk to me. I see myself on the set that night. There is me and a microphone and someone is saying, "What do you want to be when you grow up?" I must say something stupid, because I can still see my mom pointing to my dad and saying, "You're like him; you're a sitter. You'll be a sitter all your life. Nothing changes."

When it gets dark here I sit in this window and it seems that always one of those moons they call a strawberry moon is sitting on me. And I hear a voice. It is my mother nagging my father to take out the trash. I look at the pots of impatiens, and I say to nights that have turned a mute silver, *Take me to your leader.*

And now I sit, in the sun, my legs spread like a celebrated cellist's. I can't explain my goofball love for the sun, but I am passing it on. Baby and me are catching rays. Someone is on the radio singing in a Betty Boop voice of perpetual woe: "Girls just want to have fun." "Listen," I say to my girl.

She kicks. My ribs hurt.

KIT-ten has become the long-haired tortoiseshell she promised to be. At night she rises up in front of the TV and runs her claws down the screen. I think she wants out, so I know it is time to get her fixed.

When this is over, I'll advertise and find KIT-ten a good home. I won't go to Vegas till I've done that.

I close my eyes and look toward the sun. KIT-ten rubs my ankle. Out? Food? On the inside of my eyelids I make the shape of my girl's face. It is a primitive and red picture. I'm no artist. But it's her face. And I know that my baby will arrive like incoming fire. Q

The Proof

I did not kill my daddy. He drank his own self to death the year after the county moved me out. I heard how they found him shut up in the house dead. Next thing I know, he's in the ground and the house is rented out to a family of four. Now I live in a clean brick house and mostly am left to myself. When I start to carry an odor, I take a bath and folks tell me how sweet I look.

There is aplenty to eat here, and if we run out of something we just go to the store and get some more. I had me a egg sandwich for breakfast, mayonnaise on both sides. And I may fix me another one for lunch. I keep my elbows off the table and wipe my mouth like a lady. Nobody barks, farts, or feeds the dogs under the table here. When everybody is done eating, my new mama puts the dishes in a thing, shuts the door, cuts it on, and wala they are clean.

Now at my new mama's I lay up in the bed and watch the rain fall outside. Not one thing is pressing on me to get done here. I have a bag of candy to eat on. One piece at a time. Make it last. All I have left to do today is eat supper and wash myself. Look around my room. It is so nice. When I accumulate enough money I plan to get some colored glass things that you dangle from the window glass. I lay here and feature how that would look. I already got pink checkerboard curtains with dingleballs around the edges. My new mama sewed them for me. Everything matches. It is all so neat and clean. When I finish laying here with these malted-milk balls, I will smooth the covers down and generally clean up after myself. Maybe then I will play with the other people. But I might just lay here until the chicken frying smells ready to eat. I always love to eat a good supper, brush my teeth, and go to bed early. If I am not sleepy I will always find something to do.

Lately I lay up in my bed and read old books. I told the library teacher I wanted to read everything of some count, so she made me a list. That was two years ago and I'm up to the Brontë sisters now. I do not read comic books or the newspaper. I find out what news I need off the television. I can hardly tolerate the stories we read for school. Cindy or Lou with the dog or cat. Always setting out on some adventure. They might meet a bandit or they might hop a freight, but the policeman or the engineer always brings them home and they are still good children. I myself prefer the old stories. When I started my project I enjoyed the laughing Middle Ages lady that wore red boots. She was on a trip with a group of folks swapping stories, carrying on, slapping each other on the back.

What I am reading now is a little fancy for me but it is on the list. Just men and women sneaking around in a big dark house with one all into the other's business. The library teacher said the author and her sisters wrote books because in their day they could not go out and get jobs. I bet they were just well off and did not need to work.

I could lay here and read all night. I am not able to fall asleep without reading. You have that time when your brain has nothing constructive to do, so it rambles. I fool my brain out of that by making it read until it shuts off. I just think it is best to do something right up until you fall asleep. If I absolutely have to think, then I think about how good I have it now. I believe I have made out pretty good considering the rest of my family is either dead or crazy.

Every Tuesday a man comes and gets me out of Social Studies and we talk about it all. Last week he spread out pictures of flat bats for me to comment on. I mostly saw flat bats. Then I saw big holes a body could fall right into. Big black deep holes through the table and the floor. And he took off his glasses and screwed his face up to mine and tells me I'm scared. I used to be but I am not now is what I told him. I might get a little nervous but I am never scared.

Oh, but I do remember when I was scared. Everything was so wrong, like somebody had knocked something loose and my family was shaking itself to death. Some wild ride broke, and the one in charge strolled off and let us spin and shake and fly off the rail. And they both died tired of the wild crazy spinning. Now you tell me if that is not a fine style to die in. She sick and he drunk with the moving. They finally gave in to the motion and let the wind take them from here to there.

My mama could not help getting sick, but nobody made her marry him. You see, when she was my age she had romantic fever, I think it is called, and since then she has not had a good heart. She would come home from the hospital sometimes. If I was her I would stay there. All laid up in the air conditioning with folks patting your head and bringing you fruit baskets. But oh no. She comes in the house and he lets into her right away. Carrying on. Set up in his E-Z lounger like he is King for a Day. You bring me this or that, he might say.

She comes in the door and he asks about supper right off. What does she have planned, he wants to know. Wouldn't he like to know what I myself have planned? She would look at him square in the face, but not at his eyes or mouth but at his whole face and the ugliness getting out through the front. On he goes about how come weeds are growed up in the yard. More like a big mean baby than a grown man. I believe somebody recently operated on needs to stay in bed without some husband on their back all the time. But she does not go to the bedroom but turns and goes into the kitchen. What can I do but go and reach the tall things for her?

Mama puts the food on the table and he wants to know what I am staring at. At you humped over your plate like one of us is about to snatch it from you. You old hog. But I do not say it.

Why don't you eat, he wants to know.

I don't have a appetite, I say back.

Well, you better eat. Your mama looks like this might be her last supper.

He is so sure he's funny that he laughs at his own self.

All the time I look at him and at her and try to figure out why he hates her so bad. When he is not looking I give him the evil eye. And my mama looks like she could crawl under the table and cry.

We leave his nasty self at the table and go to the bedroom. She is sore all up through her chest and bruised up the neck. It makes me want to turn my head. We peel her dress off over the head and slip on something loose to sleep in. I help her get herself laid out, and then I slide in beside her. She just turns her head into the pillow.

I will stay here with you. Just for a little nap I will stay here with you.

His yelling makes my mama jump, and if she was asleep she is awake now.

By the time the dog races come on television he's stretched out on the bathroom floor and can't get up. I know I need to go in there and poke him. Same thing every Saturday. I go tell him to get up, that folks got to come in here and do their business. He can go lay in the truck.

He just grunts and grabs at my ankle and misses. Get on up, I say again to him. You have to be firm when he is like this. It makes me want to heave, my own self, seeing him pull himself up on the sink. He zigzags out through the living room and I guess he makes it out the door. I don't hear him fall down the steps.

So where did she come from? Standing in the door looking at all this. Please get back in the bed, I say to my mama.

63

I said I had rather go to the reform school or get on the chain gang than be sent to my mama's mama's house. I did not know her good and it made me nervous to be around her. But somebody had to take me. She came and picked me up in her long car that was like my mama's funeral car, only hers was cream. I said to myself, If we have to live together, the least you can do is act like you know I am in this car with you. I figured she might warm up to me, but all she asked was, When does school start again?

Lord, it just ended and I sure am looking forward to staying on your farm, I said for the icebreaker.

I asked you when school starts again. I do not need the commentary, she said back to me hot.

So September. I said my answer quick and on time like the army way. I saluted in my head.

I decided I would make the best of the situation, because you can generally adjust to somebody with money to burn. She might be a witch but she has the dough is what I kept telling myself.

By July all the money in the world did not matter to me, and that is really something when you consider how greedy I am.

My bedroom was my mama's room she had when she was little. It had a canopy and a fireplace for show. My mama's mama said she gave me that room because I deserved it. It took me awhile to figure out that the room was not a present or a prize for being sweet. I started to think she knew what all I would see dancing around in that fireplace and how I would need the lights on all night.

She would catch me snooping around the house sometimes and say, I'll break your little hand if you touch that vase! She would say that not joking but serious, to make me think of how a broke hand might feel.

I was there for a week when she said she had finally found something to do with me. She has found a summer job for me, I thought. I hoped it was delivering newspapers. She could drive and I would pitch them out the car window. Early one morning we did get in the car, but we did not deliver newspapers. She drove me instead to the field and said to come back home for lunch. Ask a nigger what to do is what she said before she drove off.

Five or six people were already chopping and they were way far down the row and not noticing me. I just looked. Then the biggest lady yelled, You better get on a row!

And I'll be damned if I do it, I said to myself.

You better get on a row! she yelled to me again. The boss lady left you here to work, not to stand. Now get you a hoe. When I gets to the ends of my row, I'll catch you up with the rest of us.

That was the first thing I had heard reasonable, so I started work.

I lived on a farm with my mama and daddy but they hired colored people to do my part of the slave labor. Lord, how did they stand it so hot, I wondered.

The biggest lady, named Mavis, helped me catch up to them, and then she said she was curious. She told me it must be a mighty bad debt you is out here working off. They is no sense in a white chile out here in this heat. I can hardly stands it my own hot self. Then one day when I had gotten to know her pretty good she asked me why my mama's mama sent me out to the fields and why I was not in Vacation Bible School, or at least somewhere out of the sun. I told her exactly what I was told. My mama's mama said I was under her feet, and besides that she could not bear to look in my face day in and day out. Also, she said I might learn a thing or two there. Which I did. I bet she never counted on me learning everything old Mavis had to teach me. The hotter the summer got, the more Mavis loved to talk. And I loved to listen. One day she said flat out, You look just like your mama. Lord, chile, you got that same black hair all down your back.

Did you know my mama?

Yes, chile! I was raised up beside her on this farm. I knowed her good as I know my own self. I never knowed anybody sweet like your mama. Smart as a whip too!

She was?

Lord, yes! she said.

Did her mama make her work out here?

Lord, no! She won't cut out for hot work. She made the other ones work like dogs, but not your mama. You don't plan to tell the boss lady I been talking like this, do you?

Oh no, I said, so maybe she would tell me more.

She told me enough that summer to let me know I was not the only one who thought my mama's mama was off the rocker. She said the boss lady had always acted peculiar, but ever since my mama died she had acted touched.

I did not need to ask touched with what, because I already knew. But still it is hard to believe in your head what you feel in your heart about somebody. I figured one day I would do some encyclopedia research and find if there is a name for what ailed my mama's mama. But that would be like trying to look up a word you don't know how to spell. What would I look under? Meanness? Angry? Just crazy? Then I figured out it was a little bit of everything. And anyway, my family never was the kind that could fit into a handy category.

By July I was like a boy. When I started out both my hands were a red blister, but by July I was toughened up good. If I just looked at my arms and legs up to where my shorts and shirt started, I said I could pass for colored now. I was so dark from the sun I was just this side of colored. Under it all I was pinky white.

At the end of each day the colored workers went to their shack and I walked to my mama's mama's. On workdays she

left a plate of something on the stove for me. That might not
sound social to you but it was perfect for me. We ate right
many miniature chickens or turkeys. I do not know the difference. But they were baked and not crunchy the way I most
enjoy chicken. When we both ate at the same Sunday table, we
both picked at our little individual chickens or turkeys and did
not talk. And still it was okay by me.

After supper each night it was not raining I walked up the
colored path and spied on Mavis and her family. It looked like
slavery times with them all hanging out on the porch picking
at each other. They fought strong as they played and laughed.
I looked regularly but they never saw me, or at least they did
not mention for me to stay away from their house. I wondered
right much about the way they got along.

My mama's mama did not pay them doodly-squat. I saw
the amount she had wrote on their envelope every Friday. She
did not pay me a cent except room and board. I kept figuring
up how much I was worth by the hour.

While I was eavesdropping at the colored house I started
a list of all that a family should have. Of course there is the
mama and the daddy, but if one has to be missing, then it is
okay if the one left can count for two. But not just anybody can
count for his or her self.

While I watched Mavis and her family I thought I would
bust open if I did not get one of them for my own self soon.
Back then I had not figured out how to go about getting one,
but I was sure one could be got. I only wanted one white and
with a little more money. At least we can have running water
is what I thought. You would think that when you get older you
get slow and weak, but that was not true in my mama's mama's
case. Meanness made her quick like a jungle animal.

I started to think she wanted me around as a substitute for
my daddy. And each day I was not exactly him but just enough
of his eyes or nose to tease her, oh, she boiled violent inside.

It must have been hard on her to keep in mind that I was a girl Ellen and not a man she hated and wanted alive by her so she could work her power on him. And she had that kind of power that will suck out all your good sense and leave you limp like a old zombie. That is what I felt like on some days. An old monster zombie who was a girl awhile back. But I got my fire back in me now.

She wanted me so hard to be like him. She reminded me all the time of how me and him favored and acted alike. I never told her how Mavis said I looked just like my mama. Sometimes she talked so strong to me that I had to check in the mirror to see if I had changed into him without my knowing or feeling it. Maybe her wishing so hard had made it so, I thought. I decided I would jump off the bridge if I was different from my old self.

It gives me nerves to worry like that. My mama's mama would shake a little like this too. I hide my hands under my desk if it happens at school. Her hands shook right much when she told me about my daddy dying. She said, Your bastard of a daddy is dead, and then she slapped my face. That might not make sense, but that is what she did.

I had not planned to cry over him when he died. I had practiced it all so many times that all I wondered was if he had died one of the ways I had planned. All varieties of accidents and unfortunate mishaps.

Go ahead and cry for your damn daddy, she got in my face and said to me. Go ahead and cry. Just make sure you cry more than you did for your mama.

Why did she say that to me, I wondered, and reached up to catch a tear I felt had just rolled over my eye ledge.

You can bet we did not go to his funeral. I know they had one, because my daddy's brother Rudolph brought me the flag they laid on his coffin. He got the flag because he was in

the war. They put my mama in a box too and him in a box—
oh, shut the lid down hard and nail it with the strongest nails.
Do all you can to keep it shut and him in it always.

Go ahead and look, said the magician.

I do not want to look.

It is all illusion. Look in the box and see what is there.

I do not want to see.

Go ahead, said the magician. There is nothing to be afraid
of. Everything has vanished. See!

Where did it go, I need to know.

Oh, I suppose they put him in the hole and everybody
walked away talking just like before and they wished they were
already home.

Rudolph came straight from the graveyard to my mama's
mama's. She sent me to my room and told me to stay there
until he left. I knew that what I was not supposed to hear was
most likely juicy, so I listened in.

What are you bringing that trash here for? she met him at
the back door and asked.

He said in a hangdog way he thought Ellen should
have it.

I watched her get stiff, and then she spit on the flag he had
folded up in a neat triangle and handed to her like an expensive present. Rudolph kept saying he thought he was doing the
right thing. Then she called him a worm and a farm boy too
big for his britches, and if you don't think I can ruin you like
I ruined him, then just hide and watch me! Rudolph turned
and ran out the door. He left the flag, though.

That night I woke up from my sleep because I heard something outside, and I looked out my window and saw her standing by a wood fire she had made herself, poking what was left
of some stripes farther into the flames.

I do not know why I thought she would be happy when my
daddy died. She was the kind of woman you cannot even die

to suit. She would swear you did it to spite her. We all did things against her, she said. She even fired her colored help because, she swore, they were an infernal conspiracy and were stealing out from her nose. And when they were gone it was just her and me. Me to look after her, not the other way around like you might expect. That did not surprise me, because I had just about given up on what you expect. I just lived to see what would happen next.

At least taking care of her took me out of the fields. When she got bad sick with the flu all she wanted to do was talk. That was about all she was able to do. I called her doctor, who checked her over and told me to feed her particular foods, which I sent Mavis's husband to the store after. She told the doctor to leave and never come back and on his way out the door he could unload all the silverware and jewelry he'd stole. He just chuckled like she was joking with him. Ha.

Then she said, I don't need a doctor with Ellen here to nurse me.

Which I did the best way I could.

She wanted to talk mainly about my daddy, and most of what she said did not make any sense. It was like listening to three different conversations at once. She could ask questions and answer for all three folks. And one day she got up on her elbows and said clear to me like she had come out of a long fever, Ellen, you helped him, didn't you?

Why did she say that to me, I thought, Lord, did I do the wrong thing? But he said she would just sleep, and if that didn't convince me then the knife by his hand would. And it is easy to see·him now in the fog of his not knowing she would be dead soon. It is like when you are sick and you know all the things you ever ate or just wanted to eat are churning in you now and you will be sick to relieve yourself, but the relief is a dream you let yourself believe because you know the churning is all there is to you. And through all the churning and spinning I saw her face. A big clown smile looking down at me while she said to me, You best take better care of me than you did of your mama.

My daddy gave me a guarantee the pills would not hurt her bad.

She got herself out of bed during the night. I must have slept hard not to hear her. In the morning I went to the kitchen and saw her sitting at one end of the table and him at the other end going through her pocketbook. Some of her heart pills were rolling off the table and the bottle was in her lap.

Give me the bottle and let me put the pills back in it. They cost money, I said to my mama.

She took almost the whole damn bottle, he looked at her and told me.

Lord vomit them up, Mama. I'll stick my finger down your throat and you can vomit them up. She looked at me and would not vomit. She would not move.

Well, I'll just go to the store and use the telephone.

But my daddy said he would kill us both with the knife if I tried to leave the house. All the time I knew he was evil, but I did not have the proof.

Hell, all she needs is some sleep is what he kept telling me. Take her to the bedroom and see if she don't sleep it off.

And now I will rest with my mama. The day is early and we need more rest.

She is so easy to tend to. She is just stiff and hard to move around. I get her in the bed and tell her to listen to the door closing. He is leaving the house. She starts to whimper and I say it is no reason to cry.

And a storm is coming up. And I will lay here with my mama until I see her chest rise up and sink down regular. Deep and regular and far away from the man outside. I can smell the storm and see the air thick with the rain coming.

I always want to lay here. And she moves her arm up and I push my head down by her side. And I will crawl in and make room for myself. My heart can be the one that beats.

Hers has stopped.

Damn him to the bottom of hell, damn him. Oh, how I have my rage and desire for the lightning to strike a vengeance on him. But I do not control the clouds or the thunder.

The way the Lord moves is his business. **Q**

The Careerist

Ever think what do chicken-sexers think all day?

Well, this chicken-sexer thinks mostly him and me and Sweet Miss Stringbean.

Make him Billy Boillit, sometime mill rat, most time drunk, my best friend. Make me Sarno, chicken-sexer. Make Sweet Miss Stringbean Billy's sweetheart.

So there is Billy and me and Sweet Miss Stringbean and working as a chicken-sexer all . . . make that as a chicken-sexer all night. I work the night shift. Working the night shift, once you know what you're doing, once you tune out the peeping, allows plenty of time for thinking. Mostly me thinking how Billy, my forever best friend, does what he wants whether he wants to or not.

And me almost happy when bow-hunting, although I never get anything bow-hunting, or watching TV over at Sweet Miss Stringbean's, although I never get anything over there, either.

And Sweet Miss Stringbean almost happy when her kids, who likely will make her a grandmother before she is thirty, are also almost happy.

In other words, like everybody else we know, none of us are happy. If we are, none of us know it. And *that*, chicken-sexer or not, is plenty to think about.

But there is always the Legion and who goes there.

This chicken-sexer goes to the Legion before going home to . . . make that to supper and sleep.

The Legion's the same as most legions—the same dark, the same smells, the same smoke, the same TV shows on the same TV that is always on the same kind of shelf sticking out over the same kind of stick.

What makes the Legion different is Desperado and Billy.

Desperado, who works behind the stick, is what everybody here at the Legion calls him. The unclean rag he wears to cover his mouth and everything right up to his eyes is why.

Billy, who everybody here calls Billy, slumps on the stick doing shots and beers and watching Desperado's unclean rag suck in, blow out, suck in, blow out.

Billy watches and weeps.

"Billy," says I, "what's up with you?"

"Me and Sweet Miss Stringbean," Billy says. "I say marry me to Sweet Miss Stringbean and she says to me only when I quit drinking and getting marihoochied up and getting otherwise crazier than I get."

"Oh no," says I.

"Oh yes," Billy says. "So I says marry me to Sweet Miss Stringbean, or else."

"Aw, Billy," says I, not knowing what else to say to Billy.

"I say marry me," Billy says, "or else I'll get drunk and marihoochied up and otherwise crazier than I've ever gotten, whether I want to or not."

"Aw, Billy," says I, because what else can anyone say to Billy?

You know where and when I do most of my thinking? It is when I'm wearing egg-white booties, egg-white jumpsuit, egg-white shower cap in a just-hosed-down room full of peeping.

Other than the peeping, which you tune out after a while, there is no noise except the noise of what you could hear if you could hear us chicken-sexers thinking and looking for that tiny bump that means a boy chicken. Looking for that tiny bump is, I like to say, eggciting work.

That's the kind of yoke—make that joke—that us chicken-sexers say when us chicken-sexers say anything. Most chicken-sexers don't say anything while sexing, at least not the good chicken-sexers. The good chicken-sexers, like Emile and unlike me, sex about nine hundred chicks an hour. Every joke amounts to almost twenty chicks and forty cents less.

This chicken-sexer would rather have forty cents less—make that a whole lot less—than think what this chicken-sexer is thinking.

Everybody here at the Legion knows everybody else from going to the same grade school, to the same junior high school, to the same high school.

And as long as everybody here has known Desperado, we have never heard him say much. Now he says even less. Now Desperado works the stick without saying anything.

After work and before going you-know-where, I watch that unclean rag suck in, blow out, day in, day out. I watch that unclean rag suck in, blow out of the place where Desperado's nose used to be, until Billy, drunk and marihoochied up at the Legion's New Year's Eve party two New Year's Eves ago, bit it off.

This chicken-sexer usually goes over to Sweet Miss Stringbean's before going to work. Me and Sweet Miss Stringbean and Sweet Miss Stringbean's two kids sit on the couch watching *Wheel of Fortune* and other family-type game shows.

The couch and TV are just about all the furniture Sweet Miss Stringbean owns. So we sit on the couch with the two kids, with Dana and Cara crawling all over each other and all over us.

Cara, the kid who is the youngest kid, wriggles around and yells out the right answers before the people on the shows can yell them out and way before I could ever do it. It takes me too long to think. So it's me mostly trying to think and wrestling around with the kids and with Sweet Miss Stringbean yelling for us to stop.

In other words, going over to Sweet Miss Stringbean's before going to work is like bow-hunting, with me never getting anything and being almost always happy anyway.

Desperado is what everybody here at the Legion calls Desperado.

Billy is what everybody here calls Billy.

Sweet Miss Stringbean is what Billy and me call Sweet Miss Stringbean.

Billy started calling Sweet Miss Stringbean Sweet Miss Stringbean first, saying she was so skinny and her legs were so long and she was so young and fresh as to remind him of a young, fresh stringbean.

Sweet Miss Stringbean's sweetest feature, Billy says, is how those long stringbean legs of hers lead all the way up to her snap.

The best thing about bow-hunting is time in the woods. Time in the woods, going around with a bow in my hand, makes me feel, well . . . make that almost happy.

I think getting something, getting anything, must be like getting to be something you're not.

Except when she yells, Sweet Miss Stringbean is sweet.

Sweet Miss Stringbean is sweet for a brick-eater.

Brick-eater is what Billy and me call women with no teeth. Sweet Miss Stringbean has teeth, just not her upper teeth, the big ones in front.

Billy, my forever best friend, punched out Sweet Miss Stringbean's teeth on Sweet Miss Stringbean's fifteenth birthday. What Billy's birthday present to Sweet Miss Stringbean was was to wait until me and the kids weren't looking at it when he punched her teeth out.

Except for what Billy says and for what everybody here at the Legion wonders out loud, there is no way I would know.

"What do you mean?" says I.

"What do you think I mean?" Billy says.

"Aw, Billy, I'm not sure," says I.

"Are you Sarno the chicken-sexer?" Billy says.

"Sure," says I.

"Then think, you chicken-sexer you," Billy says. "Think what that bump that means a boy chick feels like, only think of that bump as big as the end of your little finger right there in all that snap."

"Aw, Billy," says I, thinking of all that peeping.

I'm in my skivvies making ready for sleep when I hear knocking on the door.

"Sarno, it's me! Come quick!"

It's Sweet Miss Stringbean, sobbing and sucking in her top lip where her teeth are missing.

"It's Billy," Sweet Miss Stringbean sobs. "Billy's gotten drunk and marihoochied up and otherwise crazier than he's ever gotten."

"Oh no," says I.

"Oh yes," Sweet Miss Stringbean sobs. "And he's got Cara. Billy's got Cara and says he's not giving her back except in pieces until I say I do."

"Call the staties," says I, putting on what's handy.

What's handy are the day's—make that the night's—egg-white booties, egg-white jumpsuit, egg-white shower cap.

"Get your bow!" Sweet Miss Stringbean sobs. "There's no telling what Billy will do!" she sobs.

"Call the staties!" says I, getting my bow and a handful of broadheads and going out into first light.

"Hey, Emile," says I during last night's shift.

Emile looks up, but keeps on sexing.

"Emile," says I, "want to hear a poem?"

Emile keeps on sexing.

"Here goes," says I. "Had a little chicken, she wouldn't lay an egg, I poured hot water up and down her leg. Little chicken cried, little chicken begged, little chicken laid a hard-boiled egg."

That fucking Emile just keeps on sexing.

I live crawling distance from the Legion.

Outside the Legion, there in the first light, is Billy's old ride.

Inside the Legion, there is the same dark, the same smells, the same smoke, the same TV shows on the same TV, and behind the stick, smelling it all and watching it all, is Desperado.

Slumped at the stick doing shots and beers, watching Desperado suck in, blow out, suck in, blow out, is Billy.

"Aw, Billy," says I. "What's up with you?"

"Me and Sweet Miss Stringbean and Sweet Miss Stringbean's Cara," Billy says.

"Where's Cara?" says I.

"Cara's at my place asleep," Billy says. "Cara was watching TV and wriggling around and yelling out the right answers before the people on the shows could do it and now she's asleep."

"Oh no," says I.

"Oh yes," Billy says. "And now she's asleep."

"Aw, Billy," says I. "In how many pieces?"

"In one piece," Billy says.

"Hey, Emile," says I during last night's shift.

That fucking Emile looks up, but keeps on sexing.

"Ever hear the one about the two chickens sitting together in the chicken coop?" says I.

That fucking Emile never stops sexing.

"Well, there's two chickens sitting together in the chicken coop," says I. "The first chicken says, 'Bawk, bawk, bawk,' and lays a fifty-cent egg."

That fucker.

"The second chicken says, 'Bawk, bawk, bawk, bawk,' and lays a fifty-five-cent egg," says I. "So the first chicken says to the second chicken, 'So? For a nickel more, for a lousy five cents more, I should break my ass?'"

Hey, let's not even talk about that Emile, okay?

Not knowing what else to say to Billy, I don't say anything to Billy, just look at him and at Desperado and around the big bigness of the Legion.

But Billy, he looks at my egg-whites and bow.

"Sarno, you chicken-sexer you," Billy says. "Are you my best friend?"

"Sure," says I. "I'm your forever best friend, Billy."

"Then load your bow and do me," Billy says.

"Aw, Billy," says I. "You're my forever best friend."

"Then do him," Desperado says.

"What?" says I, not sure I'm hearing Desperado say anything.

"Do him," Desperado says, his unclean rag sucking in, staying in, blowing out, blowing all the way out.

"Do me," Billy says. "Whether you want to or not."

"Aw, Billy," says I, loading my bow and weeping.

I tug back the bowstring and broadhead and take aim. I hold back while the shakes set in, then hold back some more, then let the broadhead fly.

"Hey, Sarno," Emile says to me during last night's shift.

I look up from sexing. I look up, thinking that I am hearing something other than peeping.

"Sarno?" Emile says, "why does the chicken cross the road?"

"What?" says I, not sure I am hearing that fucker say anything.

"Why does the chicken cross the road?" Emile says.

"I'm not sure," says I.

"The chicken crosses the road because the chicken can," that Emile says.

The broadhead thunks deep into the stick and way wide of Billy.

"Aw, Sarno, you chicken-sexer you," Billy says. "No wonder you never get anything. Try again."

"Aw, Billy," says I, weeping and loading my bow again. I tug back the bowstring and broadhead and take aim. I hold back while the shakes and the ringing sets in. There's ringing and more ringing and me holding the bowstring and the broadhead back until I can't hold anything back anymore.

"Hold it until I get the phone," says I, tramping over in my egg-white booties, my egg-white jumpsuit, my egg-white shower cap to the pay phone.

"The Legion," says I, getting the pay phone.

"Sarno?" Sweet Miss Stringbean sobs.

"Sweet Miss Stringbean," weeps I.

"Where's Cara?" Sweet Miss Stringbean sobs.

"Cara's at Billy's asleep," says I.

"In how many pieces?" Sweet Miss Stringbean sobs.

"In one piece," says I.

Sweet Miss Stringbean sobs and I just listen to her sob. Oh, God, she's such a Sweet Miss Stringbean, thinks I.

"Tell Billy I'll say I do when Billy quits getting drunk and marihoochied up and getting otherwise crazier than he gets," Sweet Miss Stringbean sobs. "Tell Billy now, Sarno."

"Hold on," says I.

"Billy," says I, tramping back to the stick in my you-know-whats. "Sweet Miss Stringbean says she'll say I do when you quit getting drunk and marihoochied up and otherwise crazier than you do."

"Aw, Sarno," Billy says.

"Aw, Billy," says I.

"Aw, nothing," Billy says. "Do me."

"Do him," Desperado says.

"Don't think," Billy says. "Do me."

So I do Billy. Just as quick as that, I thack a broadhead into Billy.

Billy, looking surprised, looks at the broadhead feathering his blue jeans.

"Billy!" says I, weeping and amazed.

Billy fingers the blood that's darkening his jeans, then holds the fingers up. Billy looks like he just made the discovery of his life. Billy gives me, then Desperado, that look—then looks once more at the broadhead—and then passes right the fuck out.

Ever think what do cow-manicurists think all day?

Well, this cow-manicurist thinks mostly him and me and Sweet Miss Stringbean.

Make him Billy "The Gimp" Boillit, full-time mill rat, most time sober, my best friend. Make me Sarno, cow-manicurist. Make Sweet Miss Stringbean Sweet Mrs. Stringbean Boillit.

So there's Billy and me and Sweet Mrs. Stringbean Boillit and working as a cow-manicurist all—make that all day. Working all day, manicuring cow hooves with wood chisels and mallet, allows me to go over to Billy's after work.

Billy's is the same as Sweet Miss Stringbean's was before she became Sweet Mrs. Stringbean Boillit, or I guess I should say it's almost all the same except for the new big couch I bought all of us when they exchanged the I-dos. It's almost all the same, with us sitting on the new big couch, watching the same TV with the same two kids, Dana and Cara, crawling all over each other and all over us.

In other words, it's almost all the same except for Billy and Sweet Mrs. Stringbean Boillit and me almost happy. And me —once I tune out the mooing—as almost happy as I have ever been, and that is plenty to think about, whether you want to or not. Q

Anton's Album

1—All right. In the grape arbor, and in the shadows, you can see me. He put me in there, just to look out. This is September, and he had forgot to prune in the spring. Look at the tangle.

2—The Embassy, the rear door; and those are two bluebirds, one caught in flight, landing on the gravel the way they often do, tilting their wings and flashing that bluey blue. He's caught the corner of Geoffrey's car, accidentally, the gray blur over there.

3—That's not me, not on your life. That's Angelique. When he called the Embassy and ordered up an angel, she's the one who showed.

4—Me again, I think this was the birthday dinner for Geoffrey. Anton called this shot: Consideration. He asked me to bring in the butter dish, and I only said, just as he would, "Give me a chance to consider."
My hair was longer then, what a shame.

5—When Geoffrey moved out, Anton blamed the neighborhood. People with money were buying the houses, and there were two seasons: sandblasting season and winter. Anton hated it. "Literacy does this to a neighborhood," he said. "The bums move out."
He took a picture when the couple across the street came outside in coveralls to paint their wrought-iron fence.

6—These two, I'm not sure I can remember their names. Anton ignored introductions; he had the idea that people would make themselves known. These two stopped in about once a year and brought tins of smoked salmon; and Anton took a day off and we got some Bibb lettuce and cheese from Gaccione, two blocks down. Gaccione'd say, "Tony baby. Tony, you deserve the best!" Always the same lip-smacking.

After a while, the wine bottles arranged themselves on the table like bowling pins. These two guys, one was called Bob White, I believe that was it, a bird's name, told long stories involving motor troubles, leaking boats on the Yukon River, and Anton would sit there tearing a lettuce leaf down the middle and shaking his head side to side; "Oh no, don't tell me."

I like the way they stood here, though, one behind the other, the same shoulders, like a two-headed man.

7—It's hard to believe, but this is Anton's mother. She came by train before Christmas that year, and when I kissed her cheek she said, "I take it this is the child." From then on, she was like anybody else.

When I did her hair, Ice White, Anton took a picture and she touched one hand behind her head and tipped up her chin, like a star.

8—Another picture of Anton's mother and me. Anton never made excuses—he wasn't a photographer. If somebody turned and the face washed out, that suited him. He said what he wanted was evidence.

"You two were here," he said about this one. "Here's the evidence."

9—Angelique again, in her blue dress, all the sequins. I'll tell you what I know about her. Her mother was Serbo-Croatian and her father a Marriott-Hilton. She told this story as a way of accounting for how easily she could "dance in rooms—or not!" Then she howled, with her very smart laugh.

Anton was taken, I won't say smitten. He was taken. We had special foods, artichokes, fresh shrimp, red lettuce, asparagus with lemon grass and butter. Geoffrey did his work in the living room, reports on his lap, some secret, some not, he was just there, comfortable, out of the way, while Angelique put on music. I didn't mind. Why should I? I learned how to lounge, how to sprawl on a chair with upholstered arms, how to listen to anything, you name it.

Anton said, "What a sad life," talking about her; but he never would say it about himself.

10—And Geoffrey, in the Arboretum. He came along as a favor, although he claimed no admiration for trees and no liking for gravel paths, which suggested corduroy to him, a texture he found unnatural. I gave him a walking stick—it was sassafras, and I peeled the bark off—and he sunk his teeth into that, as I suggested, for a taste, before walking through the beech wood. By the time Anton took this picture, Geoffrey admitted there might be a pleasure or two somewhere in the wild; and so he waved the walking stick, and he smiled. That's how simple he was.

11—True Value Hardware, that's right. This was my birthday, and my present was: I could take a picture anywhere I chose. Anton said, "Anywhere. You choose."

I said, "The place on the calendar."

And, very quick, Anton said, "And I say which calendar!"

If I had said one word—Crete, Lapland, anywhere—I'd have been there, to this day. It could have happened. Anton was not much for premeditation. His idea was, you could only think something through after the fact.

Since it was his present to me, I accepted. I'd forgot we had more than one calendar.

After the cake, instead of boarding a plane and flying to England to take a picture, or flying to the Arctic Circle, we took Geoffrey's gray Olds over to Nebraska Avenue. The boxwood at the entrance to the store is sliced off the edge, just like the calendar picture, and the sun on the glass doors is about as bright.

12—I suppose this is Anton's favorite photo of the Embassy, an incomprehensible picture, the heads of everybody lost off the top. But Anton said it was all right, he liked the colors. At the swimming party, the men posed in the pool, and here they are, the big shots, naked chest after chest after chest. They're columns of pink, peach pink, and the water is plain blue.

13—Geoffrey sent a picture of his room in Paris, the rue Victor-Cousin.

"Rue," Anton said. "Ruin." He gave me the photograph to throw in the wastebasket.

It was a dark room, if I remember correctly, with the camera aimed out the window toward the rooftops across the street, with some of the windows over there shuttered and some open.

Anton decided to take this picture, out the front window of our place, with the frame of the window the frame of the picture, and the roof of the house across the street cutting a low triangle, green-shingled, and the white sky above it, all around, very bright, your large city sky, no color, probably ozone.

You can see, though, he never sent the picture to Geoffrey. He kept it here.

14—All right, look. Here he is. Nothing I can say will show you Anton better than this, enthroned, on the back porch in the ratty gold chair. That's not his Amish hat, that's mine, to match my hair, and Geoffrey took this picture.

These are all out of order.

This was the summer, and we were celebrating Independence Day, waiting for the fireworks, doing nothing the way we did it best.

Anton set up the tripod, the timer, and tried to take a picture of the three of us, arranged, he said, so that nobody outshone anybody else, but it didn't work. After a couple of foul-ups, Anton picked my hat off my head and said to Geoffrey, "There's one shot left. Take me."

He sat back in the chair, the wide-brimmed hat on his head. In the shade, he grinned with his eyes, but you can see the uneven tips of his front teeth, which hardly anybody ever saw.

It's a good picture. That's how he looked that afternoon. This was a lucky shot, and I'm lucky to have it, because usually Anton wasn't very good at looking good.

15—Here is the old woman who moved into Geoffrey's car in the alley for three nights. She didn't speak English. Anton finally gave up pointing at the door.

16—There aren't any other pictures, those last months. Anton stopped taking pictures. I was ready for it when he told me to leave, that I should be on my own. I kissed his fingers.

I said, "What's far away?"

"Calcutta," he said. "Anchorage. How about a ticket to Anchorage?" His mouth stayed open.

"One-way to Anchorage, that's fine."

"It's not a pretty place," he said.

I let my mouth sag, too, and didn't say anything. I just looked back at him until he said, the way I always say it, "All right."

At the airport, I asked if I could take a picture, and Anton rolled down the car window and looked out. He didn't look pretty, not that day. I took this picture, though, and I'm glad he let me take it. I took his album, too, out of the living room rubble.

I wouldn't take anything else. I owe him too much. His idea was, it was the same with humans beings as with God: after you saw the ruin, that's all there was. The rest did not matter. The idea pleased him, when it did not make him ugly. And it pleases me, too. Q

Another Night in Tunisia

Ennui, having once again planted its sweaty buttocks on my face, drove me to Great Lengths, the local hippified gin mill run by a purple-haired diva named Stella Artois. Stella, who was handy with a chain saw, had done most of the decorating herself, but because of my degree in literature asked if I would glue shut some six hundred editions of Shakespeare bought wholesale from a failing grade school. This I agreed to do in return for unlimited credit at the bar; a coffin actually, propped on sawhorses. The rest of the place was similarly done up, hi-tech *objets trouvés et volés* vying with wall-sized drip/splash paintings that looked like late Pollock, just after his accident.

Without disturbing her torso she managed to toss coaster, glass, and bottle of Bourbon Supreme—three shovelfuls of dirt—onto the bar, and mop her forehead. I poured just a splash.

"How come you always give me *Coriolanus?*"

"I don't always give you *Coriolanus.*"

The building across the street blew up and for a while we watched that. Stella even waddled to the window, where she attracted almost as much attention as the fire trucks. Knots of little boys gawked at her operatic breasts. Naturally, in such a parched provincial town she was a sight.

Will came in for what was left of his lunch hour.

"Gas leak, they think. Still looking for an old lady."

By now the dust had cleared enough to reveal pipes sprouting through brick rubble, fragments of walls, and a crowd of aimless spectators.

"Please, Stella," he called. "I only got fifteen minutes."

She huffed back behind the bar and made him a sloe-gin fizz.

"How can you drink that stuff?" I asked, mesmerized by the shining head of lather.

"It's good for you."

"Good for you? Who says so?"

He puzzled a moment, then brightened. "Doctors."

Stella abhorred a vacuum, so the cloud of pulverized mortar ushered in by the lunch rush didn't noticeably alter her menu's grit content. Under their nibbling murmur, Will described the latest office game at the Ministry, Hotspot. During the day each player chose an area of world tension. Then, after work, they all tumbled to the Club Crucible and watched TV news. Every time a contestant's hotspot was mentioned, he drank a shot of whiskey. Whoever, at the end of the hour, had collected the most empty glasses won, and was paid for by the others. The theory being, I suppose, that he with such clear foresight needed all the free liquor he could get.

"It was Afghanistan last night. Tonight I'm playing a hunch: Moscow. There's a rumor Brezhnev kicked off."

"What about Tehran, isn't that still big?"

"That's back-page stuff now," he said scornfully. "You ought to get out more. When's the last time you bought a newspaper?"

"Why, this is the world, nor am I out of it. Besides, I'm still on *Coriolanus.*"

"Yeah? I never read that one." He looked down. "*The Merry Wives of Windsor.*"

"Lucky dog."

"Matter of temperament, really." He drained his glass and licked the mustache off his upper lip. "Tell Stella I'll see her tomorrow."

When things quieted down, she settled her three hundred

plus pounds onto an adjacent barstool and joined me in admiring our tableau in the mirror. Two Sybarites, One Massive, One Wan.

"Do me a favor, Juan," she muttered. "See if that kiwi omelette by the jukebox has a saber scar over his left eye."

Now, like any other customer, I had heard about Stella's brother, Rainer Maria Artois; thrown out of the army for dueling, crack shot with both javelin and any make of foreign sportscar, a psychopathic big-game hunter who had once placed in an Olympic rowing event. The prospect of determining whether the commonplace Trotsky look-alike who subdivided his pile of green eggs while reading *Soldier of Fortune* magazine was in fact this long-lost black sheep loomed like a cloud bank over what was left of my sunny afternoon. There was, however, the matter of my unpaid bar bill, a subject she deftly emphasized by snatching away the bourbon moments before my own fingers trembled into pouring position.

"*Mort à crédit?*" I asked.

"It'll be here when you get back."

I punched up Nev Torsion and The Encumbrances doing "A Blast from the Past," their three-minute forty-second microchip rendering of *Swann's Way*. He sat very straight in an unremarkable caned chair, the top of his thinning scalp rising no higher than the water glass. That and four feet makes a quadruped, I thought cheerily, kick-starting the next table's arthritic wicker rocker.

"An abstract-pointillist friend of mine"—he stiffened at the accompanying all-inclusive gesture—"who literally lies on a bed of nails, then tips himself over the canvas like a sprinkling can. What do you think?"

The glossy fortress made no response. On its back cover, a heavily made-up girl straddled a grenade launcher.

"I know your type, Grub Street first, then aesthetics. Personally, I think hanging's too good for them. I mean, sure, art comes from your entrails or bowels or whatever. But there has to be more of a distinction between . . ."*

Gaius Calculus Cinna was born in Bithynia and flourished briefly during the eventful reign of Caligula in the first century A.D. Fragments of what is assumed to be his lost *Roman in the Gloamin'* were recently discovered in the Maison Carrée in Nîmes and appear here for the first time, freely translated into American patois. The highly allusive nature of the work has led me to substitute Western for Classical references in hopes of making it more accessible to the lay reader.

Little is known of the author, who had previously survived only in brief quotations by later writers illustrating what they felt to be his poor grammar and style. He accompanied Caligula on the Emperor's farcical German expedition, presumably to immortalize the events in a (no longer extant) epic poem. After this, he disappears completely from the historical record.

. . . stumbled out, sidestepping the rubble, the crowd, the frail, ever hopeful ambulance.†

"On your right," continuing in my tour guide's voice, pretending only to steady him from behind as he leaned over the rail, "our civilization's most hackneyed metaphor: the moon reflected in a canal. Eternity and the staunchless wound of time."

"The staunchless wound," he repeated admiringly, and bent far enough over the edge so that, by lifting his flimsy tunic, I should have been able to do a little staunching of my own and secure satisfaction for us both had not Gravity chosen

* Here there is a gap.
† Concluding, apparently, this "adventure."

that moment to reappear and, seeing what threatened the treasure he also coveted, insisted we . . .

> Orange in patches like a bell pepper,
> the sky's gone to seed. Otherwise this roof
> has little going for it. Such a sag
> I have to crawl its concavity to watch
> the college boys patronize the bars.

> Earlier the dancer in 5A held
> a photo session through which I had trundled
> with my garbage bag. But now the tripod,
> lamps, her stylized wide Italian eyes,
> are gone. It's dusk in the provinces. Soon

"Okay, okay," I interrupted, throwing down a quarter. "Ashbery jam, I get the idea. Haven't you got anything else?"

"The poetry you seek is in my state, not my statements."

"You Christians," I complained, "what's your problem? Can't you see that in our eyes your cult is the punk rock of religions? Derivative ritual. Presumptuous, infantile theology . . ."

"I am not," he replied indignantly, "the religious fanatic you describe, but a conceptual artist of no mean degree."

"Ah."

I circled the traffic sign admiringly.

A contortionist I could just barely picture nailing his own feet to either edge of the red Yield triangle without help. But some obliging soul must have lashed each hand to the notched tent pegs, whose little fringes of splinter suggested their being hammered deep into the ground. Apart from the video camera and some coins tossed on a blanket it was your standard Petrine crucifixion.

Truck headlights shot over him like a quick feel as a VW microbus eased off the road. Before it had stopped moving, the back doors opened to shit six neo-greasist headbreakers, their tucked-in T-shirts bulging over belt buckles like breakfast sausage stitched up in white muslin. Naturally—the conceptual artist's muddled iconography demanded it—they literally gave us the cold shoulder, picking up and hurling sharp bits of gravel until I lay on my stomach and begged them to stop. One, whose octagonal wire-rimmed spectacles served only to magnify his porcine eyes, pulled me upright by the neck, while the others puzzled which limb of the unfortunate artist to "free" first.

"You are interfering with a carefully planned aesthetic endeavor," I heard him say menacingly.

To struggle was pointless. I . . .

The Hyperborean Apollo, angry after snapping yet another guitar string, for the millionth consecutive time accidentally kicked over the night's bucket of accumulated urine as he rose for breakfast. Sun spilled down the street, gilding nocturnal stragglers into horror-film-sized chocolate-covered ants.

"My next project," the artist was saying, sucking gingerly at his stigmata, "is to live inside a Xerox machine for a week. When people feed me papers, I'll either make them a quick sketch if it's a drawing or type out duplicates to documents."

"Tough way to make a dime." I yawned, holding my head as a performing seal balances a particolored beach ball on its dank, whiskery nose.

The road in front of Gravity's was cordoned off for a procession.

"If it's Cybele, I'm leaving," someone behind me said. "With those amps they use, the priests ought to cut off their ears, not their cocks."

"Rock n' roll," his companion replied philosophically.*

A lady with binoculars spotted them on the next hill.

"No musicians, no dancers," she reported disappointedly. "Just a bunch of costumes and a funny-looking priest with a beard."

"Druids? They got a lot of Gaul, coming this far south."

"Yom Kippur," a vendor in advance of the march called. "Day of Atonement. Get your red-hots."

The crowd groaned.

Led by a rabbi, twenty or thirty men in business suits of pastel blue or light red, as if milk had been poured in all the dyes, solemnly passed.

"Must be the Reformed Temple," the conceptual artist opined. "Atonement, huh? They look pretty comfy to me in their guilt-edged security."

My gaze was higher, where the drapes of Gravity's apartment had blown open, revealing him and Simon pawing each other on the water bed. I unhesitatingly jumped the barrier, bulled through the pitiful procession, and kicked in the door, to find Gravity now alone, inchwormed up against the headboard with fingers laced comfortably behind his hair.

"How come I'm only attracted to my friends' lovers?" he asked. "I mean, is it repressed homosexuality, you think?"†

I told him no, I did not think so.

"Sometimes it gets me down," he confessed.

Simon returned from the other room, where he had taken the opportunity to scent himself, and snuggled against my companion beneath the orchid-colored sheets. I noted him rubbing the side of his golden head vigorously against the skin

---

* The cult of Cybele worshipped a small black stone, probably a meteorite. Its priests practiced self-emasculation. Processions were known for their "clashing of cymbals . . . drums, and peculiar ululating cries," cf., the "Attis" of Catullus.

† It is unclear, in this context, what the word signifies.

between Gravity's breast and armpit, an animal preparing its bed for the night. How painful the familiar caress, seen instead of felt!

"Still raining?"

"No." I examined the shoulder of my trench coat for confirmation. "This just seemed to fit the part."

"Don't you see?" the boy complained. "He followed me here."

"Shhh." Gravity placed perpendicular to his soft scarlet lips one finger. "Be cool."

"It is difficult to lose friend and lover in one blow," I said dryly.

The artist sauntered in behind me, examining the apartment. He removed a bullwhip from the wall and brandished it experimentally.

"Maybe we better leave these guys to their own devices, huh?"

"Be honest, Gravity. Do you ache one tenth as much as I for this boy?"

Ever glib, he replied: "I wish you'd see it as a fraternal effusion rather than in terms of seduction and/or betrayal."

The artist replaced the bullwhip, having discovered a Claes Oldenburg electric dildo.

"Hemorrhoids, anyone?"

". . . or how about as a tribute to your own exquisite taste?"

"I thought these guys were taking us out to brunch."

"Interesting slip." Gravity yawned. "Forgetting it's a bisextile year. The twenty-fifth's tomorrow. Now will you please leave us?"*

Thus rejected, scorned, after a night weeping under the star-pocked sky and drinking through *Good Morning America,* I

---

* Roman equivalent of leap year. Every four years the twenty-fourth of February lasted two days.

felt an enormous craving for chopped liver. Two stores in this
menopausal backwater call themselves delicatessens. One has
nothing but reconstituted "loaf" products you can imagine
being extruded from the asshole of some stainless-steel Mo-
loch while frantically mooing cows are prodded down its skid-
way throat entire. At the other, I did a deep knee bend before
the slanted glass case. Tender, my eyes avoided the ultraviolet
bug trap to light first on headcheese, a nauseating mosaic of
hosed-out viscera suspended in slime-shiny gelatin; then on a
craggy, scorched hunk of pastrami, its slicing edge iridescent
in the sun like a diamond facet . . . and comparably priced, I
reminded myself.

"Where's the chopped liver?"

"We're out," the owner-proprietor said. "Had to send
back the whole order. Tongue had freezer burns."

"The what?"

"Yeah, should be Thursday. Can I get you something
else?"

I refused to be conned by his balding eagerness (faded
Grand Opening banner still taped to the window, along with
all sorts of complex 99¢ breakfast specials) and rejected some
proffered ham inlaid with plastic pineapple ring and cherry
bulls-eye.

"Yup, a good chopped liver's hard to find," he para-
phrased Flannery O'Connor. "You know why, don't you?"

"Freezer burns," I said. "The tongue."

"No, I mean all over." He walked around the register and
came insanely close. "Because it's got to have the sweat of a
concentration-camp survivor."

We nodded in sync, for different reasons. I felt for the
door, without looking down.

"Thursday."

"I seen it," he called after me, apron burring in the breeze.
"Factories. Hundreds of old geezers kneading the stuff,

stripped to the waist. You can see where they were marked, glistening. Glistening in the heat!"

So instead I bought from the ancient Greeks a small pizza and was trying to keep it level in the stiff winter wind when a streetwalker—black skin, hair in a thousand tiny immobile braids like obsidian linguine, white denim, purple silk, coral beads—shot across my chivalrous bow into Joe's Aqueduct. The wind delayed the bar's glass door from closing just long enough to pang my sozzled heart. But what no doubt highly paid working girl lets herself get picked up by an unshaven, unsteady, all-night bum reeking of Scotch and half-congealed pizza? Then again, perhaps my forlorn state could be worked to advantage, a hug at the tart strings.

"Yes, Joyce was a great writer. And you know many of those myths are still valid today."

A bearded student, trying to make time.* Flashing in her eyes already was the bored VACANCY sign of the Piss-Off Motel.

"If the lady was interested in modern fiction, I'm sure your virility would be one of the first she'd consider, son," I said. "Now, why don't you make like the Roanoke Colony?"

The boy muttered off. She eyed me sideways.

"Whatever you've got there is just about soaked through."

I dropped the box on the bar and examined a hand nearly tanned to leather.

"Makes you leery on nuclear power, trying to contain one of these pizzas."

She looked up coolly. "I didn't notice. What kind is it?"

"Half salami, half hummingbird tongue. Glib but gut-satisfying."

"And now you're after a slice of life." She wrote a price in the sky. Astronomical.

"Don't need any books glued shut, do you? Classics A Specialty."

* "Beardless" in the original; so times change.

Joe walked over, one of those upper-body types who can get away with wearing just an undershirt with exaggerated cutouts around the arms.

"You seem like a nice guy," she said. "But in my line, charity isn't deductible."

"Delores and me," Joe explained, "we got to make ends meet."

The student, who'd been steeling himself with a boiler-maker, came back.

"You want to step outside?"

"We are outside." I sighed, sidling out, when Joe called: "Hey, ain't you a friend of Gravity's?"

"In that I'm earthbound, yeah. What . . ."

"So what do you do?" my landlord asked.

"I make a nice round dent in the wall with my head," I answered.

Both sauced at 10 a.m., we swayed like seaweed in the hall outside his curio-stuffed office. Showing great presence of mind, I congratulated him on his recent appointment to the bench. He made a sound that wasn't a word and put my check in his breast pocket. We'd still be out there if his phone hadn't started playing the theme from Pac Man. Upstairs, I made a great show of virtue by not eating the Andean crust surrounding the greased-over lump of pizza. The roaches were impressed . . . and grateful.

On TV, Phil Noxious, eponymous host of the "issue-oriented" talk show to which millions of housewives ironed their cortexes each morning—smoothing out wrinkles until they attained a blissful state of marble-brained moronity—discussed whether or not a transsexual should be allowed to join the Vestal Virgins. The educational station was rerunning its 600-part dramatization of Thucydides. I watched Pericles mount the Parthenon steps and address the assembled population of Athens.

"Well, folks, it's great to be back at the Pallas."

The pizza's trickle of olive oil down my chin conjured Proustian backflashes of time with Simon—sunlight in our old apartment, an aimless next-door guitar pursuing half-recognizable pop tunes, the rainfall of his shower, the still and smell of a summer Sunday morning.

On the weatherman's advice, we once tried frying an egg on the hood of my car and instead watched the white's amoeba-like fingers dribble into the engine block. The yolk, more stately, tore on itself. I stood in the middle of the road with spatula and plates of toast, stupid with heat.

"Ungrateful child," I now cried. "After I worked my bone to the fingers indulging your every whim."

The door opened with a familiar purr . . .*

". . . like wet tea bags," I murmured, touching each . . . ."

The New Grand Central, wrapped in foil,
ignores a frieze of taxicabs.
Across the street a busker jabs
his rubber snake that won't uncoil.

Torn denim lined with Ultrasuede
has come and gone as this year's look.
Now Warhol, in a picture book,
extolls the use of razor blade.

The Yankees drop their manager
by parachute on Wrigley Field.

* The medieval copyist to whom we are indebted for what survives of this work here apparently omits a prurient scene. The interpolation is from another source.

"Which World Series was that?" Gravity interrupted.

"It's urban lieder," he explained. "I call it 'Autumn in New York.'"

"What did Auden call it? In the lawsuit, I mean."

Our party walked through the quiet town. Contrite, Simon once tried guiding my hand to the site of so many previous ecstasies. But I pulled away, telling myself who's good for the goose is good for the pander. In time and circumstances more fitting, his repentance could be more effectually reaped.

"Motion motion motion, then rest," the artist sighed. "Does this place serve drinks before twelve?"

Gravity was irked.

"This is a private dwelling I'm taking you to. It overlooks the Colosseum."

"You said brunch, not Grapefruit League action," I pointed out.

"Delores was a quarter finalist in the Pillsbury Bake-Off. And I was instrumental in helping Joe score half a pound of Macedonian blow last month."

"You're making a lot of bourgeois friends in early middle age, aren't you?"

"Take me out to the ball game," the artist hummed.

"These Nubians," Joe said, reclining in a plastic chaise next to a hamper full of chipped ice and beer. "They're fast as hell, but don't have much power."

As if to illustrate the point, a dark lanky figure raced into left field, easily outdistancing two charioteers before coming up against an ax-wielding centurion. Moments later, his head appeared on one of the flagpoles surrounding the stadium, where pennants and vultures flapped.

"DELORES ."

"I'm *basting*, Hun."*

* An affectionate nickname, comparable to our "Beast."

"Last week's game almost didn't happen. There was talk about a *players'* strike, can you believe it? I told 'em, put the damn Christian on the field and see what happens. Care for a toot, anyone?"

Our skulls made bongo sounds in the casual rush to hunch forward. Talk turned, as consciousness-razed chat always does, in on itself. Joe told us how he'd driven a rented car across the Peloponnesus and sat three days in a tourist-trap Acropolis café waiting for Gravity's connection; then of the deliberately disorienting chase through tangled dockside capillaries where the apparition had suddenly turned, thrown down the stuff, grabbed Joe's money, and vanished. ("I don't mean he ran away, either. I mean 'Hey, Joe, how come you're talking to that *wall* all of a sudden?'") Stranger, though, was Joe looking up to wonder where he was; noting the lap of hidden water, the natives' hostile stares ("like I was a *Cretan* or something!"), the street's narrow canopy of sky.

"Man, was I spooked. Getting too old for that."

"Narcotic paranoia," Gravity scoffed.

"Where'd you end up, Joe?"

"Oh, he left me just ten feet from the hotel, only on the other side. Big circle."

The home team roared as the crowd trotted out. Meanwhile, the sun had gone de Chirico, dissecting the field into its constituent blades of grass, transforming each building into a façade.

"What?"

"Nothing." I sniffled mistily. "All this beer."

Dribbling my medicine-ball bladder to the kitchen, I found Delores assembling a huge plate of ribs, home fries, hush puppies, melon balls, onion dip, and M & M's.

"Down there on your left," she said.

Some children's art affixed to the refrigerator door by magnets delayed me.

"That's Johnny's, our youngest."

I admired the bright, mica-like sheets of color, how the edge of a crayon mesa crumbled and flaked above the sordid gray drawing paper. Children at play, brown stick figures on a green fringe of grass under a disk of desperately reinforced yellow. This glimpsed transition between the glyphic and the representational interested me profoundly in the moment my legs allowed before hotfooting me down the hall to piss.

"How long you going to be in there?" I called, panicking and pushing at the door, whose flimsy lock gave way on the tableau of the conceptual artist taking full advantage of my faithless little brother.* Simon's eyes widened at the intrusion.† I smashed the neck off an unguent jar and advanced slowly.

"This is just a little aesthetical investigation," the conceptual artist tried explaining, looking nervously to either side. "You know, like a painter sketching all the time. Doodling."

> I stare
> Blankly into space as if space were time
> And I at the end of my rope saying
> Here, Mr. Rochefoucauld, is the *Daily News.* Catch.

The full-length mirror he had been pushing with his foot tipped over. I caught my surprised face swooping like a shooting star and shattering, extinguishing its source.

Ennui, having once again . . .‡ Q

* A common term of sexual endearment, cf., the *Satyricon* of Petronius Arbiter.
† Again, it is difficult to say how this is supposed to be taken.
‡ From here on, the text becomes increasingly corrupt.

JANE SMILEY

The Age of Grief

Dana was the only woman in our freshman dental class, one of two that year, in the whole dental school. The next year things changed, and a fifth of them were women, so maybe Professor Perl, who taught freshman biochemistry, didn't persist in his habit of turning to the only woman in the class and saying, "Miss McManus, did you understand that?" assuming that if Dana got it, so had everyone else (male). In fact, Dana majored in biochemistry, and so her predictable nod of understanding was a betrayal to us all, and our class got the reputation among the faculty of being especially poor in biochemistry, a statistical anomaly, guys flunking out who would have passed any other year. Of course, Perl never blamed himself.

Dentists' offices are very neat, and dentists are always washing their hands, and so their hands are cool and white and right under the nose, to be smelled. People would be offended if dentists weren't as clean as possible, but they hold it against us. On television they always make us out to be prissy and compulsive. If a murder has been committed and a dentist is in the show, he will certainly have done it, and he will probably have lived with his mother well into his thirties, to boot. Actors who play dentists blink a lot.

Dentists on television never have the people coming in like the man who came to me today. His teeth were hurting him over the weekend, and so he went out to his toolbox and found a pliers and began to pull them all out, with only some whiskey to kill the pain. Pulling teeth takes a lot of strength and a certain finesse, one of which the man had and the other of which he lacked. What drove him into my office today, after fifteen years away from the dentist, was twenty-four broken teeth, some in fragments below the gumline, some merely smashed around the crown. Teeth are important. Eskimo cultures used to abandon their old folks in the snow when their teeth went, no matter how good their health was otherwise. People in our culture have a lot of privileges. One of them is having no teeth.

Dana was terrifically enthusiastic about dental school, or maybe the word is *defiant*. When she came into the lecture hall every day she would pause and look around the room, at all the guys, daring them to dismiss her, daring them, in fact, to have any thoughts about her at all. To me, dental school seemed more like a very large meal that I had to eat all by myself. The dishes were arrayed before me, and so I took my spoon and went at it as deliberately as possible, chewing up biochemistry and physiology, then fixed prosthodontics and operative dentistry, then periodontics and anesthesia and pain control.

I was happy during lab, when we were let loose on the patients. They would file in and sit down in the rows of chairs; then they would lie back, and we would stretch these wire-and-rubber frameworks over their mouths. They were called "rubber dams." You lodged the wires in the patient's mouth and then pulled the affected tooth through a tight hole in the rubber sheet. Our professors said that they made the tooth easier to see and get at. Really, I think, they were meant to keep the students from dropping something, a tooth or even an instrument, down that open throat. They also kept the patients quiet. That little barrier let them know that they didn't have to talk. Patients feel as if they ought to make conversation. Anyway, that huge hall would hush, and you would simply concentrate on that white tooth against that dark rubber, and the time would fly. That was the last time that I felt I could really meditate over my work. For a dentist, the social nature of the situation is the hardest thing.

I did well in dental school, but it seemed to me that I deserved more drama in my life, especially after I quit the building crew I had worked on every summer since I was sixteen. I quit the crew because I was making $4 an hour and one day I nearly crushed my left hand trying to lift a bunch of loose two-by-fours. It hurt, but before I even felt the pain (your neurons, if you're tall, take awhile) I remembered the exact cost of my first year of dental school, which was $8,792.38. A lot of hours at $4 an hour.

I took on Dana. I felt about her the way she felt about dental school. I dared her to dismiss me, and I was determined to scare the pants off her. I took the front basket off my bike, and then I would make her sit on the handlebars at midnight while we coasted down the longest, steepest street in town. We did it over and over, eight nights in a row once. I figured the more likely outcome, death, was cheaper in the end than just wrecking my hands. Besides, it was like falling in love with Dana. I couldn't stop doing it and I was afraid she could.

After that, we'd go back to her place and make love until the adrenaline in our systems had broken down. Sometimes that was a long time. But we were up at six, fresh and sexy, Dana pumped up for the daily challenge of crushing the dental school between her two fists like a beer can, and me for the daily challenge of Dana. Now we have three daughters. We strap them in the car and jerk the belts to test them. One of us walks the older ones to school every day, although the distance is two blocks. The oldest, Lizzie, would be floored by the knowledge that Dana and I haven't always crept fearfully from potential accident to potential accident the way we do now.

If Dana were reminded these days that she hadn't graduated first in our class but third, she would pretend indifference, but she was furious then. What did it matter that Phil Levine, who was first, hadn't been out of his apartment after dark in three years and his wife seemed to have taken a vow of silence, which she broke only when she told him she was going to live with another guy? Or that Marty Crockett, number two, was a certified genius and headed for NASA as the first dentist in space? The result of her fury was an enormous loan, for office, house, equipment, everything the best, the most tasteful, the most up-to-date, for our joint office and our new joint practice. We had been intending to join two separate and established practices, etc. etc., the conservative path to prosperity. Another result of her fury was that the loan officer and his secretary were our first patients, then his wife, her five children, one of her cousins. The secretary has proved, in fact, an inexhaustible fount of new patients, since she is related to everyone in three counties and she calls them all regularly on the bank's Wats line. I root-canaled three of her teeth last year alone.

Anyway, we dropped without pause from the drama of Dana's four-point grade average into the drama of a $2500 mortgage payment in a town where we knew no one and that already had four dental clinics. Dana put our picture in the paper, "Dr. David Hurst and Dr. Dana Hurst, opening their new clinic on Front Street." I was handsome, she was pretty, people weren't accustomed to going to good-looking dentists, she said. They would like it. Our office was next to the fanciest restaurant in town, far from "Orthodontia Row," as Dana called it. It wasn't easy, and some of those huge mortgage checks were real victories of accounting procedure. As soon as it got easy, just a little easy, Dana got pregnant with Lizzie.

Dana likes being pregnant, even though, or because, each of our fetuses has negotiated a successful but harrowing path through early bleeding, threatened miscarriage, threatened breech presentation, and long labor. She likes knowing, perhaps, that when Dr. Dana Hurst comes through the obstetrician's door with the news that she is pregnant, the man had better get out his best machines and give his assistants a little extra training, because it isn't going to be easy, and wasn't meant to be.

Then there was the drama of motherhood—babies in the office, nursing between appointments, babysitter interviews that went on for hours while Dana probed into the deepest corners of the candidate's psyche, breasts that gushed in front of the dourest, least maternal patients. Assistants with twins. Those were the only kind she would hire for a while, just, I thought, to raise even higher the possibility that we wouldn't make it through the morning, through the week, through our marriage. I used to meditate over my patients in the dental school, but it wasn't enough. I wanted to be a dentist and have drama, too.

Now the children are all in school, or at least off the breast, we are prosperous and established on a semi-part-time schedule, and all Dana has to do is dentistry. Little machines. Itsy-bitsy pieces of cotton. Fragments of gold you can't pick up with your fingers. I think she thought it would get bigger, like Cinerama, and instead it gets smaller and smaller.

If she were writing this, she would say that I was an exotically reckless graduate student, not dental at all, and that she pegged me for that the first day of classes, when I came in late, with my bike helmet under my arm, and sat down right in front of the teacher, stuck my feet into the aisle, and burped in the silence of his pause, loud enough for three rows to hear. But it was the only seat, I was too rattled to suppress my digestive grind, and I always stuck my feet into the aisle because my legs didn't fit under the desk. It was she who wanted me, she would say, to give her life a little variety and color. When I tell her that all I've ever longed for is the opportunity to meditate over my work, she doesn't believe me.

Dana would say that she loves routine. That is how she got through a biochemistry major and through dental school, after all, with an ironclad routine that included hours of studying, but also nourishing meals, lots of sex, and irresponsible activities with me. Her vision of routine is a lot broader than most people's is. You might say that she has a genius for knowing what has to be included. She has a joke lately, though. At night, standing in the bathroom brushing her teeth, she will say, "There it goes!" or she might get up on Saturday morning and exclaim, "Zap! another one vanished!" What she is referring to is the passage of the days and weeks. A year is nothing anymore. Last fall it happened that we got Lizzie the wrong snow boots, fat rather than thin, and not acceptable to Lizzie's very decided tastes. Without even a pause, Dana countered Lizzie's complaints with the promise that she could have some new ones next year, in no time at all, she seemed to be saying.

It used not to be like this. Time used to stretch and bunch up. Minutes would inflate like balloons, and the two months of our beginning acquaintance seem in retrospect as long as all the time from then until now. A day was like a cloth sack. You could always fit something else in, it would just bulge a little more. Routine is the culprit, isn't it? Something is the culprit. The other thing about routine is that it frees you for a more independent mental life, one that is partly detached from the business at hand. Even when I was pulling out all of that guy's teeth today, I wasn't paying much attention. His drama was interesting as an anecdote, but it was his. To me it was just twenty-four teeth in a row, in a row of hundreds of teeth stretching back years. I have a friend named Henry, who is an oral surgeon at the University Hospital. He is still excited when he finds someone's wisdom tooth up under the eyeball, where they sometimes migrate. He can talk about his patients for hours. They come from all over the state, with facial disfigurations of all types, no two alike, Henry says. But does his enthusiasm have its source in him or in them? In ten years, is he going to move to New York City, because he's tired of car wrecks and wondering about gunshot wounds? Should Dana have gone into oral surgery? I don't know any women who do that.

I sound as if we never forget that we are dentists, as if when someone smiles we automatically class their teeth as "gray range" or "yellow range." Of course we are also parents. These are my three daughters, Lizzie, Stephanie, and Leah. They are seven, five, and two. The most important thing in the world to Lizzie and Stephanie is the social world of the grammar school playground. The most important thing to Leah is me. Apart from the fact that Lizzie and Stephanie are my daughters, I am very fond of them.

Lizzie is naturally graceful and cool, with a high, domed forehead and a good deal of disdain for things that don't suit her taste, for instance, turtleneck shirts and pajamas with feet in them. She prefers blouses and nightgowns. Propriety is important to her and wars with her extremely ready sense of humor. She knows I exploit her sense of humor to get my way, and I would like to get out of the habit of tricking her into doing things she doesn't want to do, but it is hard. The tricks always work.

Stephanie is our boy. She is tall, and strong, and not interested in rearranging the family's feelings. She would rather be out. Sometimes she seems to not recognize us in public. She feels about kindergarten the way people used to feel about going away to college: at last she is out of the house, out of her parents' control, on her own in the great world. I think she has an irrational faith that she won't always be two years younger than Lizzie.

There is a lot of chitchat in the media about how things have changed since the fifties and sixties, but I think that is because nothing has really changed at all, except the details. Lizzie and Stephanie live in a neighborhood of older houses, as I did, and walk home from the same sort of brick schoolhouse. When they get home, they watch Superman cartoons and eat Hershey bars, as I did. They swing on their swing set and play with Barbie and talk about "murdering" the boys.

They have a lot of confidence, and even power, when it comes to the boys. To hear them tell it, the boys walk the playground in fear. Dana says, "Don't talk about the boys so much. When you grow up, you're going to resent them for it." It is tempting, from their school tales, to think of the boys as hapless dopes—always in the lowest reading group, never earning behavior stars for the week, picking their noses, exposing the elastic of their underpants. It is tempting to avoid mentioning that I was a boy once myself.

It's not as if they ever ask. The unknown age they wish to know all about is their own—what were their peculiarities as babies, and toddlers, in the misty pasts of five years ago, three years ago, last year, even. When Dana pulls out a jacket for Leah that was originally Lizzie's, Lizzie greets it with amazed delight—how can it possibly still exist, when the three-year-old who wore it has vanished without a trace?

For Leah, the misty past is still the present, and no amount of future dredging will bring to the surface her daily events of right now—her friend Tessa, at preschool, whose claim on Leah is that she wears a tiny ponytail smack on the top of her head, for example. Were we to move this year, that might furnish her with a memory of this house—a ghostly sense of lines and the fall of light that would present itself to her in some future half-waking state. I wish that Leah's state of mind weren't so unavailable to us all, including herself, because she is driving us crazy.

Dana was glad to get Leah for her third, because Leah was big and cuddly and slept through on the tenth day. There is no subsequent achievement that parent wants of child with more ardor than the accomplishment of eight hours at a stretch, during the night. Leah slept ten, and then, at three months, fourteen rock-solid nightly hours, and woke up smiling. She didn't even crawl until ten months, and could be counted on to stay happily in one place when infants who had been neonates with her were already biting electrical cords and falling down the stairs. At one, when she said her first word, it was "song," a request that Dana sing to her. Since the others were already by this time covering their ears and saying, "Oh, God!" whenever Dana launched into a tune, Dana thought that her last chance for that musical mother's fantasy was a dream come true. Everyone, especially me, liked the way Leah gave spontaneous hugs and said, "I love you," at the drop of a hat. She seemed to have an instinctive understanding of your deepest parental wishes, and a need to fulfill them. Patients who had seen her at the office would stop us and say, "That Leah is such a wonderful baby. You don't know how lucky you are." My brother would get on the phone from Cincinnati and shout in her baby ear, "Leah! Cheer up!"

Dana was overjoyed but suspicious. She would say, "No one grows up to be this nice. How are we going to wreck it?" But she would say it in a smug tone, as if experience alone assured that we wouldn't. Dana felt especially close to Leah, physically close and blindly trusting. They nursed, they sang, they read books, they got lost in the aisles of the grocery store companionably choosing this and that. "The others are like you," she often said, "but she is like me, lazy." That's what she said, but she meant "everything anyone could want." Leah was everything she could want and she, as far as she knew, was everything that Leah could want.

Not long ago, Dana got up first and went into Leah's room to get her out of her crib, and Leah said distinctly, "I want Daddy." Dana came back to the bedroom, chuckling, and I got Leah up. The next morning it happened again, but the days went on as before, with Dana sitting in the mornings and me taking the early appointments, then Dana dropping Leah at preschool, where she said, "Bye-bye, Mom, I love you."

At three I leave the office and go home to meet the school-girls. At five we pick up Leah, at six Dana comes home to dinner. Twelve hours of dentistry at about $100 an hour. We work alternate Saturday mornings, another $500 a week. Simple multiplication will reveal our gross income for part-time work. This is what we went to dental school for, isn't it? Since they got the dental plan over at the university, people ask me if business is better. I say, "You can't beat them off with a stick," meaning new patients. The idea of Dana and myself on the front stoop of our office building beating hordes of new patients off with sticks makes me laugh every time.

Anyway, other things were going on. They always are. A patient called me at nine-thirty in the evening and said that her entire lower face was swollen and throbbing, an abscess resulting from a long overdue root canal. You remove the dead tissue and stir up the bacteria that have colonized the region and they spread. That's what an abscess is. I met her at the office and gave her six shots of novocaine, which basically numbed her from the neck up. Meanwhile, at home, Leah awakened and began crying out. Dana went in to comfort her, and Leah began crying, "I want my daddy! I want my daddy!" as if Dana were a stranger. Dana was a little taken aback, but picked Leah up, to hug and soothe her, and this made Leah so hysterical that Dana had to put her back in bed and tiptoe out, as if in shame.

By the time I had taken Mrs. Ver Steeg home and put the car in the garage, all was quiet. I was tired. I drank three beers and went to bed, and was thus unconscious for the second bout of the night, and the third. In each instance, Leah woke up crying for me, Dana went to comfort her, and was sent packing. The longer she stayed and the more things she tried, the wilder Leah got. The first bout lasted from midnight to twelve-thirty and the second from two-forty-five until three-forty. Leah began calling for me to get her out of bed at six.

I woke up at last, wondering what Dana was doing, motionless beside me, and Dana said, "I won't go to her. You have to go to her." That was the beginning.

She lay on the living room carpet, rolled in her blanket, watching Woody Woodpecker cartoons from the forties. I drank coffee. She was happy. Between cartoons, she would get up and walk over to me and begin to talk. Some of the words were understandable, the names Lizzie and Stephanie, the words *oatmeal* and *lollipop.* But more intelligible was the tone. She was trying to please and entertain me. She looked into my face for smiles. She gestured with her hands, shrugged, glanced away from me and back.

When Stephanie and Lizzie came down at seven, attracted by the opening theme from *Challenge of the Superfriends,* she retreated to the couch. When Dana got up and staggered down the stairs in her robe, looking only for a place to deposit her exhaustion, Leah shouted, "No! Go away! Don't sit here! My couch!" She would take her oatmeal only from me. Only I was allowed to dress her. If Dana or Lizzie or Stephanie happened to glance at her, she would scowl at them and begin to cry. Dana, forgetting herself, happened to kiss her on the forehead, and she exclaimed, "Yuck! Ouch!" and wiped the kiss off. When I went to the bathroom and closed the door, she climbed the stairs behind me, saying "I go get my daddy back." We were embarrassed. By eight-forty-five, when I was ready to leave for the office, we had run out of little jokes.

It was not simply that she didn't want Dana near her, for she would allow that most of the time, it was also that she had exacting requirements for me and was indignant if I deviated from them in the slightest. If she expected to climb the stairs and find me in my bedroom, and I made the mistake of meeting her in the hallway, she would burst into tears and shout, "Go back in room! Go back in room!" I would have to go back in the bedroom and pretend to be ignoring her, and wait for her to come find me and announce herself.

I don't think this ever happened to my father, who had a plumbing supply business and wore a white dress shirt to work every day. He referred to my brother and sisters and me as "the kids," in a slightly disparaging, amused tone of voice that assumed alliance with the great world of adult men, the only audience he ever really addressed himself to. I don't know anyone who calls his children "the kids." It would be like calling his spouse "the wife," not done these days. We call them "our children," "our daughters," very respectful. Would Leah thrive more certainly on a little neglect? Should we intentionally overlook her romantic obsession, as our parents might have done naturally?

At any rate, at dinner that night, there seemed no alternative to my serving her food, cutting her meat, sitting as close to her as possible. When I got up and went into the living room without taking her down from her high chair (Dana and Stephanie were still eating, Lizzie wanted me to adjust the television set), she allowed the others to leave the table without asking either of them to get her down. Dana said, "I can get you down, honey. Let me untie your strap here." Leah said, "No! No! Daddy do it."

I stayed in the living room.

Dana said, "I'll untie you and you can get yourself down. You're big enough for that."

"No! No!" said Leah. "Tie strap! Tie strap!" Dana tied it again. I stayed in the living room. Leah sat in front of her little bowl for ten minutes. Dana sent first Stephanie, then Lizzie as emissaries, first to ask if they could get her down, then if she, Dana, could get her down. Leah was adamant, with the two-year-old advantage that no one knew for sure if she knew what she was talking about, or what any of them were offering. This advantage enables her to be much more stubborn than the average speaker, whose eyes, at least, must register understanding.

After a minute or so, she began calling, "Daddy! Daddy!"

in a tone of voice that suggested I was far away but willing. Dana and I looked at each other. She looked hurt and resentful, then she shrugged. I got up and took Leah down from her chair. She did not greet me with the elation I expected, but after we went into the living room, she puttered around me, chattering mostly nonsense and looking to me for approval every so often. I said, "Let's go along with her for a while. It shouldn't be too hard."

Dana lifted one eyebrow and went back to her book.

It was nearly impossible. At first I thought the worst thing was the grief at parting: "Oh, Daddy! Daddy! Daddy!" hardly intelligible through the howls of betrayal. I was only going to the lumberyard or the Quiktrip, ten minutes, fifteen at the outside. Taking a child turns the errand into a forced march. "She'll be good with you," Dana would say, and she would, and the household would be relieved of screaming, but at the price of constant engagement with equipment. A snap, two threadings, and two buckles into the car seat. The reverse for getting out of the car seat. Opening an extra door for the stroller. Unfolding the stroller, locking it into stroller-rictus, wheeling it around the car, a threading and a buckle into the stroller. Up curbs, through doors, down narrow aisles, all to find a package of wood screws or a six-pack of beer. Or I could carry her, thirty-four pounds. Doing an errand by myself came to seem a lot like flying—glorious, quick, and impossible.

But grief wasn't restricted to my leaving the house. Leaving the room was enough to arouse panic, and the worst thing about it was that at first I was so unaware, and there was the labor of being trained to alert her that I was going outside, or upstairs. Then there came the negotiations. One of the first things she learned to do was to tell me not to do what I had originally intended to do. After all, she had her own activities. "She loves you," said Dana. "It won't last."

There were three more elements, too. I notice that there

is a certain pleasure for a meditative person like myself in laying down one thread and picking up another, as if everything isn't happening at once. One of these elements was that Dana's choir group was practicing four days a week so that they might join the chorus of the opera *Nabucco,* which was being given in our town by a very good, very urban, touring company for one night. Dana's choir director was a friend of the musical director of the company from *their* days in graduate school. The text of the chorus had to do with the Hebrews sitting themselves down by the waters of Babylon and weeping. Dana sang it every day, but in Italian. It doesn't sound as depressing in Italian as it does in English.

The second element was our summer house, which we had purchased the fall before, in a fit of response to autumnal color. It is in the mountains not far from where we live. Since buying it, we have also bought a well, a lot of plaster, a coat of exterior housepaint, a heavy-duty lawn mower, a set of house jacks, and a wildflower book. We have identified forty-two different species of wildflowers in the area around the house alone.

The third element was that Dana fell in love with one of her fellow singers, or maybe it was the musical director. She doesn't know that I know that this was an element.

Not too long ago, the single performance of the opera *Nabucco* came and went. Leah stayed home, screaming, with the babysitter. Lizzie and Stephanie went along. I paid attention to the music most of the time, and the part that Dana sang about sitting down beside the waters of Babylon was very pretty, to say the least. I closed my eyes, and there were certain notes that should not have ended, that should be eternal sounds in the universe. Lizzie sat in the front seat and fell asleep on the way home. Stephanie leaned against Dana in the back seat, and also fell asleep.

In the midst of all this breathing, still dressed in her Old

Testament costume and with her hair pinned up, Dana said, "I'll never be happy again." I looked at her face in the rearview mirror. She was looking out the window, and she meant it. I don't know if she even realized that she had spoken aloud. I drove into the light of the headlights, and I didn't make a sound. It seemed to me that I didn't have a sound to make.

When we got home, Leah was still awake. She was thrilled to see me, and while Dana put the others to bed and changed her clothing, I sat next to Leah's crib and held her hand while she talked to me. She talked about the moon, and her books, and her Jemima Puddleduck doll, and something else unintelligible. She perused my face for signs of pleasure. Sometimes she made gestures of ironical acceptance, shrugs of her little baby shoulders. Sometimes she sighed, as if she didn't quite understand how things work but was willing to talk about it. Are these imitations of our gestures? Or does the language itself carry this burden of mystery, so that any speaker must express it?

My eyes began to close, but Leah wasn't finished for the night, and when I slid down the wall to a reclining position, she insisted that I sit up again. It was nearly one by this time. Saturday night. I had root-canaled two, and drilled and filled two, and cleaned two more a very long time before. One of them had insisted upon talking about her sister, who had cancer of the jaw. I had been arduously sympathetic, because, of course, you must. The room was dark and filled with toys. The baby was talking. The moon shone in the window. That was the last real peace I had.

Teeth outlast everything. Death is nothing to a tooth. Hundreds of years in acidic soil just keeps a tooth clean. A fire that burns away hair and flesh and even bone leaves teeth dazzling like daisies in the ashes. Life is what destroys teeth. Undiluted apple juice in a baby bottle, sourballs, the pH balance of drinking water, tetracycline, sand in your bread if you were in the Roman army, biting seal-gut thread if you are an Eskimo woman, playing the trumpet, pulling your own teeth with a pliers. In their hearts, most dentists are certain that their patients can't be trusted with their teeth, but you can't grieve for every tooth, every mouth. You can't even grieve for the worst of them; you can only send the patient home with as many of the teeth he came in with as possible.

After a while, Leah's eyes began to take on that stare that is preliminary to sleep, and her remarks became more desultory. She continued to hold my hand. I thought about the Hebrews sitting down beside the waters of Babylon, and I began to weep, too, although as quietly as possible. I didn't see how I was going to support the total love of one woman, Leah, while simultaneously relinquishing that of another, Dana. I wasn't curious. I said my prayer, which was, "Lord, don't let her tell me about it," and shortly after that I must have fallen asleep, because the next thing I knew it was morning and I had a crick in my neck from sleeping by the window all night.

I crawled over to the half-open door and slithered through, so as not to awaken Leah. I expected to be alone, but I found Dana in her robe at the table. She was eating cold pizza. Her hair was standing up on one side, and she hadn't managed to get all the makeup off from the night before, so there were smudges around her eyes and her lips were orange. I said, "What time is it? You look terrible." She gave me a stricken look and said, "I can't believe it's over. It was so beautiful. I could sing it every night forever."

"Well, you'll sing other things." I must have sounded irritable, when I meant to sound encouraging.

"I don't want to sing other things." She sounded petulant, when she must have meant to sound tragic. I have found that there is something in the marriage bond that deflates every communication, skews it toward the ironic middle, where man and wife are at their best, good-humored and matter-of-fact. But maybe there are others who can accommodate a greater range of exhilaration and despair. Tears came into her eyes, and then began running down her cheeks. I sighed, probably sounding long-suffering, and sat down beside her and put my arms around her. Sitting down, it was awkward. I cast around for something to say. What I hit on was this: "Mrs. Hilton needs to go to a gum specialist. I scaled her yesterday for an hour, and she is exposing bone around the second and third molars."

"Have I worked on her?"

"Curly red hair, about thirty?"

"Eight-year-old X-rays of impacted wisdom teeth?"

"Won't have them out till they hurt."

"I had her. I didn't think her gums were that bad. She could go to Jerry."

"No dental insurance. Practically no money, I gather."

Dana sighed. "Lots of kids, I bet."

"Five. Sometimes she brings the eighteen-month-old and the three-year-old."

"Yeah." Now the tears really began to roll down her cheeks, and she closed her eyes tight to stop them. I had only meant to bring up a mouth, not a life. I held her tightly and repeated my prayer, and it was answered, because although she heaved a number of times, and held her breath as if about to say something, she never did.

Not long after, Lizzie and Stephanie appeared on the scene, the markers came out, the demands for paper, cereal, bananas, and milk went up, and the television went on. Lizzie and Stephanie go head to head on the drawings. Lately, Lizzie's have a lot of writing on them. Wherever the sky would ordinarily be are Lizzie's remarks, in blue, about what the figures are doing. Stephanie can't write yet, but she pays attention. Her skies are full of yellow stars. Dana went into the kitchen and sang her song about the weeping of the Hebrews while dishing up red bowls of Cheerios and bananas. Easter was coming up, and it occurred to me that the choir might go on to something less passionate, but I couldn't imagine what it would be. They would certainly go on to fewer rehearsals every week—maybe only one.

Leah was still asleep. I remembered that I was still in my opera clothes, as formal as we get where I live, which was khaki pants, light blue shirt, sweater vest. Dana came through the dining room, and when I went up to the shower, she was already there, stepping out of her underpants with a sigh. Her breasts are wrinkled and flat from six years of nursing, but the rest of her is muscular and supple. I said, "May I join you?" Her eyes lifted to my face. It seems to me that they are very beautiful: pale, perfect blue, without a fleck of brown or green. Constant blue. Simultaneously deep-set and protuberant, with heavy, wrinkled lids. Her mother has the same eyes, only even older and therefore more beautiful. I don't know what I expected her to say. She always says yes. Now she said, "Sure." She smiled. She got out another towel. I turned on the water, got in first, and moved to the back of the tub. I reached out my hand and helped her in. We got wet, and soaped each other. She was businesslike about it, but friendly. I tried to be the same way. We talked about nitrous oxide, as I remember. We washed our hair, and she washed her face two or three times, asking each time whether the black was off her eyes.

I could not stop looking at her eyes. I wondered if the object of her affections had noticed them yet, in the sense of knowing what he was seeing rather than simply feeling the effect they had on him. She turned her back to me and bent her head under the shower, and I wondered the same thing about her back and shoulders, about the way her neck drops into her shoulders without seeming to spread, like a tulip stem.

Does he appreciate the twist of her wrist when she is picking up little things, the graceful expertise of her fingers working over that mouth, whatever mouth it is? I wondered whether the object of her affections, in fact, was the meditative sort, who separates elements, puts one thing down before picking up another, had it in him to have ever been a dentist, a mere dentist, that laughing stock of the professional community. Every time she saw me looking at her, she smiled, and every time I seemed to be doing something else, she sighed. I said, "Perk up, Dana. There's always more music."

"It's a waltz. That's what's so tragic about it. You could dance to it, but you can't." She got out, saying, "There's Leah." I rinsed off hurriedly, and wiped myself down while going to Leah's room. She doesn't like to be kept waiting. She was lying on her back with her feet up on the end of the crib, calling, "Daddy! Dave! Daddy!" When she saw me, she smiled and rolled over, noting with pleasure, I suppose, the wet hair, the dripping chest, the towel, the hurry, all the signs that I had been subdued once again.

I lifted her, stripped her of wet clothes, and wiped her off with my towel. She went to the chest of drawers. I opened the bottom one for her. She chose red shorts, green slacks, and two shirts. I chose a pair of underpants and a pair of socks. She put everything on cooperatively, then admired the effect for a moment or two. I was talking the whole time: "Good morning, sweetheart! How did you sleep? What a pretty girl! Ready for breakfast? How about some Cheerios with bananas?" The usual paternal patter. I carried her downstairs, the towel wrapped around my waist, her hands upon my shoulders and her gaze upon my face. We will never know what she sees there until she finds it again, I suppose, in the face of some kid twenty years from now.

Dana was getting ready to go out. She glanced at me, and said with due formality, "I'm going to the store for milk and the newspaper. Who wants to come along?" But they were all in their nightclothes, except Leah, and so she got away without a single one of them. She looked at me and also said the right thing, "Back in a flash. Anything you want special?" I shrugged. She left. I went into the kitchen and sliced a banana with one hand, laying it on the counter and chopping at it with the paring knife, because Leah wouldn't let me put her down. Then I unscrewed the cap of the milk with one hand, poured the Cheerios with one hand, kissed Leah, and carried her to her high chair, where she consented to be put for the duration of her meal. Dana had not asked me where I spent the night, although she must have noticed that I wasn't in bed with her.

She was not back in a flash, which has to be interpreted as twenty-five minutes or half an hour—seven minutes each way to the store, and then a generous ten for milk and newspaper. It took her an hour, and she came back much more serene than she had been since dinner the night before. She carried in her bag, said, "I got doughnuts for good girls. It's a lovely day out!" and sped into the kitchen. Oh, she was happy, happy, happy, but not exhilarated, not anything blamable or even obvious. She was simply perfectly calm, full of energy, ready for the day. No sighs. No exertion of will. I wondered if he lived nearby, but then I made myself stop wondering about him even before I might start. Leah was standing beside me, and I reached down and swung her into my arms, buried my fatal curiosity in her fleshy, baby smell.

It was a lovely day, and we decided upon a spur-of-the-minute trip to the house, to admire the plaster and the running water and to picnic on the front deck. Lizzie and Stephanie thought it was interesting that you could have a picnic at a house where there was a refrigerator and a stove, and viewed the whole plan as another example of Dana's peculiar but always instructive way of looking at things. Dana let Lizzie pack the food and Stephanie pack the toys, of which there have to be enough not only for everyone to have something to play with every moment of the trip but also to look at, consider, and disregard. It was fine with me. Dana seemed to me to be sort of like a hot-air balloon. The more weight we could hang on her, in terms of children, houses, belongings, foodstuffs, office equipment, and debts, the harder it would be for her to gain altitude.

The children sat behind us and Dana sat beside me, with her feet on the lunch basket. My strategy was to talk about patients all the way, both to remind her of what we shared and to distract her from her sadness, which sprouted as soon as we passed the city limits and grew with every mile we drove. The older children played together nicely. Lizzie, in fact, read Stephanie *Green Eggs and Ham,* and Leah was generally cordial, allowing Dana to both talk to her and give her pieces of apple. When the apple was gone, Dana tentatively reached out her hand, as she had done often in the past, and Leah took it and held it. I drove and talked.

I have found that it is tempting to talk about every minute of the past six weeks as if the passing of every minute were an event, which was what it seemed like. I remember that car ride perfectly—the bright, early spring sunlight flooding all the windows; my own voice rising and falling in a loquacious attempt at wit, concern, entertainment, wooing; my repeated glances at her profile; the undercurrent in all my thoughts of how is she now? And now? And now? As if she were in some terminal condition.

But it was only a car ride, two hours into the country, "a dentist" with "the wife" and "the kids." It could have been 1950. I remember thinking that then, and wishing that it were —some confused thought about the fidelity of our mothers' generation, or barring the truth of that, that at least whatever it was that was present would be thirty-five years in the past, if it had taken place in 1950. Well, as I say, every minute had its own separate identity.

Some nights later, we were lying in bed after making love and I was nearly asleep. Her voice rose out of the blackness of coming somnolence like a thread of smoke. She said, "I wish we were closer." Although I was now wide awake, I maintained my breathing pattern and surreptitiously turned my chest away from her, as if in sleep, so that she couldn't hear my heart rattling in its cage. Now she would tell me, I thought, and then we would have to act. I let out a little snore, counted to twenty, and let out another one. After a minute or so, when my heart had steadied, I turned, also as if in sleep, and threw my arm over her, and hugged her tightly, as if in sleep. My nose was pressed into the back of her neck. She said, "Dave? David? Are you asleep already?" Then she sighed, and we lay there for a long time until the muscles at the back of her neck finally relaxed and she began to snore for real.

I don't know when she saw him, but I know that she did, because sometimes her sadness was cured. A long time ago, before she joined the choir, when Leah was still nursing five or six times a day, she read a book by some Middle European writer about a man who had both a wife and a mistress. I remember the way she tossed the book down and said, "You know, I always think of men who have wives and mistresses as having everything, but of women who have husbands and lovers as simply being oversubscribed." Then she laughed and went on: "I mean, where would you fit it in? Would you phone him from the grocery store with two old ladies behind you waiting to call the car service and two kids screaming in the basket?" So where did she fit it in? She was always at home when she was supposed to be. She was always in bed with me all night. She never canceled an appointment with a patient. Sometimes she was late coming home from choir practice, once a week, but she had been late in the past, and she was never more than half an hour late. But sometimes she was desperate with sadness and sometimes she was fine, and these states of mind didn't have a thing to do with me, or our household, or the office. And in addition to that, she denied that they even existed, that she was ever in turmoil or that she was ever at peace. I don't mean to say that we spoke of them. I wouldn't have allowed that under any circumstances. But she would catch me looking at her, and she would stare at me with that same stare I remembered from dental school, defiant, daring me to have any opinions about her at all.

I should say that it didn't take long for Lizzie to realize that something was up. Lizzie's situation as the oldest and her observant character make her the point man most of the time, and a lot of our battles have been fought in her digestive tract over the years. The pediatrician, whom I like a lot, does not always go for the psychosomatic explanation. In the case of Lizzie's stomach, he suggests that some children simply suffer more intense peristaltic contractions than others. Any food triggers digestion, which may or may not be painful. And it is certainly true that Lizzie has stomachaches all times of the year, all seasons of the spirit, and also tends to throw up a lot, as does Dana's sister, Frances. It has been routine on every car trip for thirty-seven years for whoever is driving Frances to pull over so that Frances can give her all on the side of the road. It is a family joke, and Frances doesn't get a lot of sympathy for it. Ditto Lizzie. Nature or nurture? My observation is that parents believe religiously in nature, while the hidden forces that are acting to deform the plastic child are glaringly apparent to any college psych major. At any rate, Lizzie woke up every morning of the week after our trip into the country with a raging bellyache and an equal determination not to go to school, but to stay home and keep her eye on the domestic situation.

Each morning I carried her to school in tears, deposited her in the arms of Mrs. Leonard, brushed off her clutching hands, and turned on my heel to the screams of "Daddy! I

need you! I need to be with you!" School, though she always
settled down to her work at once, didn't make her forget my
betrayal, and explanations, about how sometimes when mommies and daddies argue it makes the children feel bad, did not
convince her that she wasn't actually sick. We took her temperature morning and night, promising that if it went up so much
as a degree she could stay home.

I took her to the pediatrician, who put his arm around her
and said that sometimes when mommies and daddies argue it
makes the child feel bad. He also felt her stomach and checked
her ears and throat, but she wasn't convinced. I tried to explain to him, because he is rather a friend, and certainly a
fellow in the small professional community of our town, that
we weren't exactly arguing, but his gaze—warm, sympathetic,
resigned—flickered across my face in disbelief. Here was the
child, her stomach, her panicked look, the evidence of forces
at work. He said, "The stomach problem she's always had is
going to be the focus of all her uneasiness. Some kids get
headaches. Some get accident-prone. Every feeling is in the
body as well as in the mind." His voice kept dropping lower
and lower, as if he didn't know how to speak to me, a medically
trained white male, and it's true, I was rather resentful. More
resentful of him than of Dana or the Other. Maybe he was the
Other. I wanted to punch him out.

Instead, I took Lizzie to the grocery store and let her pick
out dinner. Canned corn, mashed potatoes, pork chops, orange sherbet. Not what I would have chosen, personally. Then
I took her home and let her eat a Hershey bar and watch *The
Pink Panther* until it was time for Stephanie to come home.

When Stephanie came home, I noticed for the first time
that she had her own uneasiness. She wouldn't look at me or
come in the house. She dropped her school bag without showing me any papers, and went outside to play on the swings. A

few minutes later she saw that one of her kindergarten friends down the street had gotten home as well, and she came and asked to go there, although this is not a friend she particularly likes, and she stayed for the rest of the afternoon, and then called to ask if she could eat dinner there. I suspect that what she would really have liked to do was move in there.

Lizzie began to cry, because Stephanie didn't want to play with her, and then we had an argument about whether Stephanie loves her or not, and then I sent her to her room, and then I went up and explained to her that people have to want to play with you on their own, you can't make them, and they can't make you, either. Then I recalled examples of Lizzie not wanting to play with Stephanie, which she denied, and then I gave up, and then I went over to the preschool, leaving Lizzie by herself briefly, and picked up Leah, who, I was told, had put on her shoes and socks all by herself. She was very proud. I was, too.

Since the onset of Leah's infatuation, we had gotten into the habit of dividing the evening's tasks child by child. Dana would serve Lizzie and Stephanie and I would serve Leah. That is how it presented itself to me, although, of course, Lizzie and Stephanie had table setting and clearing to do, and were subject to discipline and the apparent dominance of the parental committee. In view of my determination not to have anything irrevocable communicated to me, this was a pretty good system, and one that I clung to. On this particular day, Dana was feeling rather blue. There was some despairing eye contact across the living room and across the kitchen. I took Leah and went out for beer, lingering over the magazine rack and talking at length with a patient I encountered about real estate taxes. I stayed away for an hour. I missed Dana terribly and only wanted to go home.

The next day at the office I missed her, too. She was right in the next room. I should say that in addition to being dentists, parents, home owners, musicians, and potential or actual adulterers, Dana and I are also employers of four people—two dental assistants and two receptionists—and office society is nearly as complex as domestic society, with the added temptation to think, unjustifiably in my experience, that it can be tinkered with and improved by a change of personnel. The receptionists are Katharyn and Dave, eight to one and one to six, six bucks an hour, and the assistants are Laura (mine) and Delilah (Dana's), eight to two and noon to six, fifteen bucks an hour. Our receptionists are always students at the university, and turn over about every two and a half years. Laura has been my assistant for five years, and Delilah came last year, replacing Genevieve. Both, as I said before, have sets of twins: Laura's fraternal, twelve years old, and Delilah's identical, four years old. Laura and Delilah also have pension plans, so, of course, we are also a financial institution, with policy decisions and long-term planning goals and investment strategies. Dave is a flirt. For convenience, he is known as "Dave," while I am known as "Dr. Dave," even, at the office, to Dana. Dana is know as "Dana." Katharyn has been engaged for three years to an Arabian engineer she met during her freshman year. Laura is divorced, edgy, bossy with the patients. Delilah is rounded, soft, an officer in the local Mothers of Twins club, which Laura has never joined. Dave flirts more with Laura than he does with Delilah, which raises the friction potential in the office about twenty-five percent. On the other hand, he is a terrific receptionist—painstaking, well organized, canny about a patient's fear of dentists. He has a sixth sense about whom to call the day before the appointment, and how to say, "We'll be expecting you, then," so that the patient doesn't dare "forget." He also does the books, so we have been able to let the bookkeeper go. He is graduating next December, a dark day.

I am so used to Laura by now that I don't know what to say about her. She has a raucous, smoke-coarsened, ironic voice, which she uses to good effect in lecturing the patients about dental hygiene. "What is this, you don't floss? You want your gums to turn to cotton candy? Believe me, if you sat in this chair and watched what comes through the door every day, you wouldn't be so optimistic. Take this. I'm going to show you." We have never talked about anything but business. Of Delilah I don't know much. She and Dana talk a lot, it seems to me, and for a long time this whispery murmur from the next office has been a kind of comforting white noise at the end of my workday. During the week, after the opera, it falls silent. Dana doesn't have much to say, or rather, what she has to say cannot be said, so she says nothing. I look blankly out the window between patients. I am sure that behind the wall Dana is doing the same thing.

What did I think I was doing on that first day of dental school? Why did I choose to pour the formless me into this particular mold? I hadn't known any dentists except the ones who worked on my own teeth. They didn't strike me as romantic figures. I was, and still am, rather struck by the mystery of teeth, of their evolution and function, of the precisely refined support system in the gums and jaws that enables a person, every person just about, simply to chew. Senseless, mindless objects, teeth, two little rows of stones in the landscape of the flesh, but as sensitive, in their way, as fingertips or lips.

I also felt the mystery of building houses back then—the way lengths of wood, hammered together with lengths of steel, created a space that people either wanted or didn't want to be inside of. I thought of architecture, but architecture was making pictures, not making buildings. Most of my fellow biology majors went to medical school or botany school or zoology school. When I considered doctoring, I used to imagine a giant body laid open on the operating table like a cadaver, but alive, and myself on a little diving board above it, about to somersault in. Not attractive. And I didn't want to spend the rest of my life fighting with some university administration about the age of my lab equipment.

This *is* what I saw myself doing: sitting here, my back hunched, the office cool and clean, the patient half asleep. I am tinkering. Making something little. But perhaps making little things belittles the self. I've noticed at conventions that dentists argue about details a lot. I wish my wife loved me. I wish her constant blue eyes would focus on me with desire instead of regret. I wonder if I haven't always been a little out of the center of her gaze, a necessary part of the life she wants to lead, but a part, only a part.

That was a Friday. The last day of a long, trying week. I suspect that Dana and I measured our time differently that week. For her, maybe, the time fell into blocks of unequal length, pivoting about the minutes she spent wherever, wherever it was that she managed to see him. My week, of course, was more orderly, and it was primarily defined by those trips with Lizzie to school each morning and lying in bed with Dana each night, wide awake and pretending to be asleep so that she wouldn't speak to me. She was, I should add, restless all week. Once, she got up at three and did something downstairs until five-ten, then she came back to bed and went back to sleep. My mother used to look at us severely if we complained of not sleeping and say, "So what have you got a guilty conscience about?"

On Friday the children fell into bed at eight o'clock, practically asleep already. Dana sat knitting in front of the TV. There was an HBO showing of *Tootsie*. I went in and out, longing to sit down, unable to. Every time I went into the living room, I peered at Dana. She seemed remarkably serene, almost happy. I decided to risk it and sat down beside her on the couch. She glanced at me and smiled, pulled her yarn out of the skein with a quick, familiar snap of her wrist, and laughed at the place in the movie where Terri Garr stands up screaming. I settled into the cushions and put my arm around her shoulders. It was tempting, very tempting, not to know what I knew, but I knew that if I relaxed, she would tell me, and then I would really know it. She said, "Hard week, huh?" She sighed. I squeezed her shoulder.

"Leah doesn't make it easy, does she?"

"What if she's like this forever?"

"Remember when we used to say that about Stephanie? When she was waking up and screaming three or four times every night?"

"Do you think that was the worst?"

"It was pretty bad when Lizzie swallowed that penny."

"But that night when I had to stay in the hospital with her, I didn't dare think it was bad at all. All those babies in the otolaryngology ward were so much worse." She bit her lip, looked at the movie, turned her work, looked at me. "You know," she said, "you scare me a little. You always have. Isn't that funny?"

I thought, Compared to whom? But I said, "I don't believe you."

"It's true. You don't smile much, not the way most people do. You have this way of letting your gaze fall upon people when they attract your attention, but not smiling, not reassuring them in any way that you aren't judging them. And you're awfully tall."

"Awfully?"

"Well, it's not awful, I mean. That's just an intensifier. But you're a lot taller than I am. I don't think about that much, but you must be eleven inches taller than I am."

"But you've been married to me for ten years. How can you say that I scare you?"

"Remember how you used to sit me on the handlebars of your bike and coast down Cloud Street? How can I say that you don't scare me, after that?"

"Well, back then I was trying to scare you."

"Why?"

"Because you scared me. You scared everybody. You were so fucking smart."

She laughed. She turned her work. She said, "Dave, do you like me?"

I wanted to groan. I said, "I love you."

"But do you like me? If you weren't sleeping with me, would you want to talk to me and have lunch with me and stuff like that?"

"Sure."

She sighed. "But do you think that we're friends?"

"Sure."

She looked at me, and sighed again.

"Why are you sighing?" This was risky, and could have led to anything, but the temptation to comfort your wife, if you love her, is a compelling one in my experience.

She thought for a moment, then looked at me and said, "I don't know. Life. Let's go to bed." She put down her knitting, turned off the light and the television, and led me by the hand up the stairs. She took off my shirt and my pants. Reached up to my awfully tall shoulders and ran her fingers across them. I undid the tie of her robe and cupped her breasts in my hands. She ran her hands down my chest, exploring, trying me out, looking at me again, over her shoulder in a way. I'm not going to say that I could even begin to resist.

I am thirty-five years old, and it seems to me that I have arrived at the age of grief. Others arrive there sooner. Almost no one arrives much later. I don't think it is years themselves, or the disintegration of the body. Most of our bodies are better taken care of and better-looking than ever. What it is, is what we know, now that in spite of ourselves we have stopped to think about it. It is not only that we know that love ends, children are stolen, parents die feeling that their lives have been meaningless. It is not only that, by this time, a lot of acquaintances and friends have died and all the others are getting ready to sooner or later. It is more that the barriers between the circumstances of oneself and of the rest of the world have broken down, after all—after all that schooling, all that care. Lord, if it be thy will, let this cup pass from me. But when you are thirty-three, or thirty-five, the cup must come around, cannot pass from you, and it is the same cup of pain that every mortal drinks from. Dana cried over Mrs. Hilton. My eyes filled during the nightly news. Obviously we were grieving for ourselves, but we were also thinking that if *they* were feeling what *we* were feeling, how could they stand it? We were grieving for them, too. I understand that later you come to an age of hope, or at least resignation. I suspect it takes a long time to get there.

On Saturday, Dana asked me to take the children up to the house in the country and maybe spend the night. The beds, she said, were made. There was plenty of firewood. We would, she said, have a good time. She would join us for dinner, after the Saturday-morning office hours. It was very neatly done. I said, "Maybe that's a good idea. But you could take them and let me do the morning work." Her face fell into her shoes. I said, "No, I would like to go into the country, I think."

It was another sunny day, but cold. Each child was bundled against the weather, her coat vigorously zipped, her hat pulled down over her ears with a snap, her mittens put on and tucked into her sleeves. To each one, Dana said, "Now you be nice to Daddy, and don't make him mad, okay? I'll finish my work and come for dinner, so I will see you very soon. Tonight we'll have a fire in the woodstove and make popcorn and have a good time, okay?" And each child nodded, and was hugged, and then strapped in. Leah sat in front, eyeing me with pleasure. We drove off.

I couldn't resist looking at Lizzie and Stephanie again and

again in the rearview mirror. They were astonishingly graceful and attractive, the way they leaned toward each other and away, the way their heads bent down and then popped up, the way their gazes caught, the way they ignored each other completely and stared out the windows. The pearly glow of their skin, the curve of their cheeks and foreheads, the expressiveness of their shoulders. I felt as if I had never seen them before.

After about an hour, Lizzie began feeling anxious. She asked for milk, said she was hot, subsided. Stephanie sat forward and said, "Is the pond still frozen, do you think? Can we slide on the pond?"

"I don't know. We'll see."

"Daddy, my stomach feels funny." This was Lizzie.

"You shouldn't have drunk so much milk."

"I didn't. I took three swallows." Then she panicked. "I'm going to throw up! Stop! I'm going to throw up!"

"Oh, God," said Stephanie.

"Oh, God," said Leah, mimicking her perfectly. I pulled over. Lizzie was not going to throw up, but I got out of the car, opened her door, took her to the side of the road, bent over her, holding her forehead in one hand and her hair in the other. All the formalities. Her face turned red and she panted, but though we stood there for ten minutes, she neither gagged nor puked. I felt her body stiffen, and we straightened up. There were tears in her eyes, and she said petulantly, "I was going to."

"I know. It's okay."

But it wasn't okay with Stephanie. As soon as I pulled onto the highway again, she said, "I don't see why we always have to stop. She never does anything."

"I was going to."

"You were not."

"How do you know? I was."

"Were not."

"Stephanie—" This was me. I looked in the rearview mirror. Stephanie's tongue went out. Leah said, admiringly, "Stephanie—" The argument subsided, to be resumed later. They always are.

Now Lizzie said, "Why are we going to the house? I don't want to go. We went there last week."

"Me, neither," said Stephanie. "I was going to play My Little Ponies with Megan." She must have just remembered this, because it came out with a wail.

"It'll be fun," I said, but I wasn't as convincing as Dana, who must have cast a spell to get us to leave, because I didn't want to go to the country, either. I glanced at my watch. It was ten o'clock. We could have turned around and been home before lunch, but we didn't. There was no place for us there. At the next K-Mart, I turned into the parking lot with a flourish and took them straight to the toy department.

After the dinner that Dana missed and the bedtime she failed to arrive for, I turned out all the lights and sat on the porch in the dark, afraid. I was afraid that she was dead. I wished she had a little note on her that said, "My family is at the following telephone number." But, then, a note could be burned up in the wreck, as could her purse, the registration to the car, all identifying numbers on the car itself. Everything but her teeth. I imagined myself telling the children that she had gone off with another man, then some blue-garbed policeman appearing at the office this week or next with Dana's jaw. I would recognize the three delicate gold inlays I had put there, the fixed prosthesis Marty Crockett did in graduate school, when her tooth broke on a sourball. I would take her charred mandible in my hand and weigh it slightly. Would I be sadder than I was now?

Headlights flared across the porch and she drove up with a resolute crunch of gravel. The car door opened. She seemed to leap out and fly up the steps, throw open the door to the dark house, and vanish. She didn't see me, and I didn't say a word. I saw her, though. I saw the look of her face as if my eyeballs were spotlights. She was a soul desperate to divulge information. I got up quietly and walked down the steps, avoiding the gravel, and tiptoed across the front meadow to the road.

So how does the certainty that your wife loves another man feel? Every feeling is in the body as well as in the mind, that's what he said. But the nerves, for the most part, end at the surface, where they flutter in the breezes of worldly stimulation. Inside, they are more like freeways—limited access, running only from major center to major center. I have to admit that I don't remember much Gross Anatomy, so I don't know why it feels the way it feels, as if all your flesh were squeezing together, squeezing the air out of your lungs, squeezing the alveoli so they can never inflate again. More than that, it is as if soon there might be no spaces left inside at all, no conduits for fluids, even. Only the weight of solid flesh, the conscious act of picking up this heavy foot, and then this heavy foot, reaching this cumbersome hand so slowly that the will to grasp is lost before the object is touched. But when the light went on and the door opened, and Dana peered into the darkness, I jumped behind a tree as sprightly as a cricket. Every feeling is in the mind as well as in the body. She went back into the house. The light on the stairs went on, then in the upstairs hall, then in the bathroom. A glow from the hall shone in each of the two children's rooms, as she opened their doors to check on them, then the window of our room lit up. It seemed to me that if I could stay outside forever she would never tell me that she was going to leave me, but that if I joined them inside the light and the warmth, the light and warmth themselves would explode and disappear.

I went around the side of the house, placed myself in the

shadow of another tree, and watched the window to our bedroom. The shade was drawn, and I willed Dana to come and
put it up, to open the window and show me her face without
seeing me. She has a thin face, with high, prominent cheekbones and full lips. She has a way of smiling in merriment and
dropping her eyelids, before opening her eyes and laughing.
In dental school I found this instant of secret, savored pleasure
utterly beguiling. The knowledge that she was about to laugh
would provoke my own laughter every time. I wonder if the
patients swim up out of the haze of nitrous oxide and think that
she is pretty, or that she is getting older, or that she looks
severe. I don't know. I haven't had a cavity myself in fifteen
years. Laura cleans my teeth twice a year and that's it for me.
The shade went up, the window opened, and Dana leaned out
and took some deep breaths. She put her left hand to her
forehead and said, in a low, penetrating tone, "Jesus." She
sighed deep, shuddering sighs, and wrapped her robe tightly
around her shoulders. "Jesus," she said. "Oh, Jesus. Jesus
Christ. Oh, my God." I had never heard her express herself
with so little irony in my whole life. A cry came from the back
of the house, and she pushed herself away from the window,
closing it. Moments later, the glow from the hall light shone
in Leah's room.

Now I went back to where I had been standing before. The
windows in the children's rooms faced north and west, and
hadn't received their treatments yet, so everything Dana did
was apparent in an indistinct way. She went to the crib and
bent over it. She stood up, and bent over it again. She held out
her arms, but Leah did not come into them. I could hear the
muffled staccato of her screams. Dana stood up and put her
hands on her hips, perplexed and, probably, annoyed. There
was a long moment of this screaming; then Dana came to one
of the windows and opened it. She leaned out and said, "David
Hurst, goddamn you, I know you're out there!" She didn't see

me. She turned away, but left the window open, so I could hear Leah shouting, "No! No! Daddy! Daddy!" Now the glow of the hall light appeared in the windows of Lizzie and Stephanie's room, and then Lizzie appeared next to Dana. Dana bent down and hugged her, reassuringly, but the screaming didn't stop. At last, Dana picked Leah up, only with a struggle, though, and set her down on the floor. I didn't move. I was shivering with the cold, and it took all my will not to move. It was like those nights when Stephanie used to wake up and cry. Each of us would go in and tuck her in and reassure her, then go out resolutely and shut the door. After that we would lie together in bed listening to the cries, sometimes for hours. Every fiber in your body wants to pick that child up, but every cell in your brain knows that if you pick her up tonight, she will wake up again tomorrow night and want to be picked up. Once, she cried from midnight until about seven in the morning. The pediatrician, I might add, said that this was impossible. You could say that it is impossible for a man to pull all of his own teeth with only the help of a few swallows of whiskey. Nothing is impossible. I know a man who dropped his baby in her GM Loveseat down a flight of stairs. Having carried that burden uncountable times myself, having wrapped my arms and my fingers tightly around that heavy, bulky object, I might have said that it was impossible for a father to drop his child, but it happened. Nothing is impossible. And so I didn't move.

Stephanie got up and turned on the light in her room. Dana turned on the light in Leah's room. Soon there were lights all over the house. After that, the light of the television, wanly receiving its single channel. I saw them from time to time in the downstairs windows, Dana passing back and forth, pausing once to clench her fists and shout. What she was shouting was "So shut up, just shut up for a moment, all right?" A sign that she has had it. They always shut up. Then she opens her fists and spreads her fingers and closes her eyes

for a moment and takes a deep breath and says, "Okay. Okay."
She went out of view. The light went on in the kitchen, and she
reappeared, carrying glasses of milk. She went away again. She
reappeared carrying blankets and sleeping bags. Then they all
must have lain down or sat down on the floor, because all I saw
after that was the wall of the living room, with half a Hundert-
wasser print and the blue of the television flickering across it.
I looked at my watch. It was a quarter to two.

At two-thirty, lights began going out again, first in the
kitchen, then the dining room. The television went off. Dana
passed the window, carrying a wrapped-up child, Leah, because that was the room she went into. She went to the window
and closed it. Then she carried up Lizzie and Stephanie, one
at a time. Don't stumble on those blankets going up the stairs,
I thought. The living room light went out. The hall light. The
bathroom light. The light in our room. It was three by now.
The house was dark. I imagined sleep rising off them like
smoke, filtering through the roof and ascending to the starry
sky. I stayed outside. The sun came up about six. I went inside
and made myself a big breakfast. I sat over it, reading the
paper from the day before, until nearly eight-thirty, when
Dana came down. She was furious with me and didn't speak.
I estimated that her pride might carry us through another
three or even four days without anything being communicated.

I got up and walked out, leaving all the dirty dishes. Was
I furious with her? Was that why I had taken this revenge? In
the interests of self-knowledge, I entertained this possibility.
Ultimately, however, I didn't care what my motives were. The
main thing was that I had invested a new and much larger sum
in my refusal to listen to any communications from my wife,
and I saw that I would have to protect my investment rather
cannily from now on.

For someone who has been married so long, I remember

what it was like to be single quite well. It was like riding a little moped down a country road, hitting every bump, laboring up every hill. Marriage is like a semi, or at least a big pickup truck jacked up on fat tires. It barrels over everything in its path, zooming with all the purpose of great weight and importance into the future. When I was single, it seemed to me that I made up my future every time I registered for classes. After I paid my fees, I looked down at that little $4,000 card in my hand and felt the glow of relief. It was not that I was closer to being a dentist. That was something I couldn't imagine. It was that four more months of the future were visible, if only just. At the end of every term, the future dropped away, leaving me gasping.

Dana, however, always had plans. She would talk about them in bed after we had made love. She talked so concretely about each one, whether it was giving up dentistry and going to Mazatlán, or whether it was having Belgian waffles for breakfast, if only we could get up two hours hence, at five-thirty, in time to make it to the pancake house before our early classes, that it seemed to me that all I had to do was live and breathe. The future was a scene I only had to walk into. What a relief. And that is what it has been like for thirteen years now. I had almost forgotten that old vertigo. I think I must have thought I had grown out of it.

The day after I stayed up all night, which I spent working around the country house, clearing up dead tree limbs and other trash, pruning back this and that, the future dropped away entirely, and I could not even have said whether I would be at my stool, picking up my tools, the next morning. The very biological inertia that propelled me around the property, and from meal to meal, was amazing to me. I was terrified. I was like a man who keeps totting up the days that the sun has risen and making odds on whether it will rise again, who can imagine only too well the deepening cold of a sunless day. I gather that I was rather forbidding, to boot, because everyone stayed away from me except Leah, who clambered after me, dragging sticks and picking up leaves, and keeping up a stream of talk in her most man-pleasing tones.

Dana supported her spirits, and theirs, with a heroic and visible effort. They drove to one of the bigger supermarkets, about twenty miles away, and brought everything back from the deli that anyone could possibly have wanted—bagels, cream cheese mixed with lox, cream cheese mixed with walnuts and raisins, French doughnuts, croissants with chocolate in them, swordfish steaks for later, to be grilled with basil, heads of Buttercrunch lettuce, raspberry vinegar and olive oil, bottles of seltzer for Lizzie's stomach, *The New York Times,* the Chicago *Tribune,* for the funny papers. She must have thought she could lose herself in service, because she was up and down all day, getting one child this and another child that, dressing them so that they could go out for five minutes, complain of the cold, and be undressed again. She read them about six books and fiddled constantly with the TV reception. She sat on the couch and lured them into piling on top of her, as if the warmth of human flesh could help her. She was always smiling at them, and there was the panting of effort about everything she did. I wondered what he had done to her, to give her this desperation. Even so, I stayed out of the way. Any word would be like a spark in a dynamite factory. I kept Leah out of her hair. That is what I did for her, that is the service I lost myself in.

At dinner, when we sat across from each other at the old wooden table, she did not lift her eyes to my face. The portions she served me were generous, and they rather shamed me, as they reminded me of my size and my lifelong greed for food. I complained about the fish. It was a little undercooked. Well it *was* a little undercooked, but I didn't have to say it. That was the one time she looked at me, and it was a look of concentrated annoyance, to which I responded with an aggressive stare. About eight we drove back to town. I remember that drive perfectly, too. Leah was sleeping in her car seat beside me, Lizzie was in the back, and Dana had Stephanie in her car. At stoplights, my glances in the rearview mirror gave me a view of her unyielding head. At one point, when I looked at her too long and missed the turning of the light, she beeped her horn. Lizzie said that her stomach hurt. I said, "You can stand it until we get home," and Lizzie fell silent at once, hearing the hardness in my voice. It was one of those drives that you remember from your own childhood and swear you will never have, so frightening, that feeling of everything wrong but nothing visibly different, of no future. But of course, there is a future, plenty of future for the results of this drive to reveal themselves, like a long virus that visits the child as a simple case of chicken pox and returns over and over to the adult as a painful case of shingles.

I should say that what I do remember about Dana, from the beginning, is a long stream of talk. I don't, as a rule, like to talk. That is why I preferred those rubber dams. That is why I like Laura. Dana is right, people who don't talk and rarely smile seem threatening. I am like my mother in this, not my father, whose hardware store was a place where a lot of men talked. They wandered among the bins of traps and U joints and washers and caulk, and they talked with warmth and enthusiasm, but also with cool expertise, about the projects they were working on. My father walked with them, drawing them out about the details, then giving advice about products. When my father was sick or out of town, my mother worked behind the counter and receipts plummeted. "I don't know"—that's what she answered to every question. And she didn't. She didn't know what there was or where it might be or how you might do something. It was not that she didn't want to know, but you would think it was from the way she said it: "Sorry, I don't know." Snap. Her eyelids dropped and her lips came together. I suspect that "I don't know" is the main sentiment of most people who don't talk. Maybe "I don't know, please tell me." That was my main sentiment for most of my boyhood. And Dana did. She told me everything she was thinking, and bit by bit I learned to add something here and there. I didn't know, for example, until the other night that I don't smile as much as most people. She told me. Now I know.

What is there to say about her voice? It is hollow. There is a vibration in it, as of two notes, one slightly higher than the other, sounding at the same time. This makes her singing voice very melodious, but the choir director doesn't often let her sing solo. He gives someone with purer tones the solo part, and has Dana harmonize. These small groups of two or three are often complimented after the choir concerts. It is in this hollow in her voice that I imagine the flow of that thirteen-year stream of talk. She is a talker. I suppose she is talking now to him, since I won't let her talk to me.

Monday night, after a long, silent day in the office to the accompaniment of extra care by the office staff that made me very uncomfortable, we went to bed in silence. She woke up cursing. "Oh," she said, "oh shit. Ouch." I could feel her reaching for her feet. When we were first married, she used to get cramps in her insteps from pointing her toes in her sleep. Some say this is a vitamin deficiency. I don't know. Anyway, I slithered under the covers and grabbed her feet. What you do is bend the toes and ankles back, and then massage the instep until the knot goes away. Massage by itself doesn't work at all; you have to hold on to the toes so that they don't point by mistake, for about five minutes. I did. She let me. While I was holding on to her feet I felt such a welling up of desire and pain and grief that I began to heave with dry sobs. "Dave," she said. "Dave." Her hollow voice was regretful and full of sorrow. In the hot dark under the covers, I ran my thumbs over her insteps and pushed back her toes with my fingers. Your wife's feet are not something, as a rule, that you are tactilely familiar with, and I hadn't had much to do with her feet for eight or nine years, so maybe I was subject to some sort of sensual memory, but it seemed to me that I was twenty-five years old and ragingly greedy for this darling person whom I had had the luck to fool into marrying me. Except that I wasn't, and I knew I wasn't, and that ten minutes encompassed ten years, and I was about to be lost. When the cramps were out of her feet, I knelt up and threw off the covers, and said, "Oh, God! Dana, I'm so sorry I'm me!" That's what I said. It just came out. She grabbed me by the shoulders and pulled me down on top of her and hugged me tightly, and said in a much evener voice, "I'm not sorry you're you."

And so, how could she tell me then? She couldn't, and didn't. I think she was sorry I was me, sorry that I wasn't him in bed with her. But when husbands express grief and fear, wives automatically comfort them, and they are automatically comforted. Years ago, such an exchange of sorrow would have sent us into a frenzy of lovemaking. It did not this time. She held me and kissed my forehead, and I was comforted but not reassured. We went back to sleep and got up at seven to greet the daily round that is family life. Zap, she used to say, there goes another one.

I was worried about her and she was worried about me, and that was an impasse that served my purposes for most of that week. God knows what the bastard was doing to her, but she was very reserved, careful, good, and sad. She went to the grocery store a lot. Maybe she was calling him from there, standing in the phone booth with two children in the basket and a line of old ladies behind her waiting to call the car service.

Each of my children favors one sense over the other. Lizzie has been all eyes since birth. We have pictures of her at nine days old, her eyes focused and glittering, snapping up every visual stimulation. She is terrific at finding things, and has been since she could talk. It took us awhile to believe her, but now we believe her every time. She doesn't stare, either. She glances. She stands back and takes in wholes. It seems to me that her eyes are the source of her persnickety taste and her fears. She simply cannot bear certain color combinations, for example. They offend her physically. Likewise, what she sees is far away from her, out of her control, and so makes her afraid. She rushes in, gets closer, so that she can look more carefully. But it is hard for her to reach out and touch or rearrange. Fear intervenes. She only looks, she feels no power.

Stephanie is the wild beast who is soothed by music. She has always heard things first, looked for them second. She often looks away from what she is paying attention to, making her seem evasive, but really she is listening. She is the only child I've ever known who doesn't interrupt. I don't even know if she listens to words as much as to tones, to the rhythms of sentences and the pitch of voices. Will she be a musician? She likes music. But she likes the sound of traffic, too, and the sound of cats in the backyard, and the cries of birds and the rustle of leaves. She simply likes the way the world sounds, and she listens to it. She comes closer than Lizzie does, but she doesn't seem to respond to what goes in at all, except with a single, final look, to make sure, maybe, that what is heard has a source. Then she backs away. Is she the one I should worry about?

Leah sat up at five months and reached for the toys that were in front of her. It took her another five months to crawl. Yes, she was big and fat, but more than that, she was satisfied. Her hands were huge, and she could hold two blocks in each of them when she was six months old. Hand to mouth. You couldn't keep anything out of her mouth. Now it seems as though she doesn't recognize anything without touching it.

She runs her hands over my face. She holds on tight. She snuggles. Standing in front of a table of toys, she is as satisfied as a human can be, and she has stretches of concentration that Lizzie and Stephanie don't begin to match, although they are five and three years older than she is. If you distract her, she looks drugged for a moment. Drugged by touch.

And so I have three separate regrets. What does Lizzie see? What does Stephanie hear? What unsatisfied, yearning tension does Leah feel in my flesh when she snuggles against me and puts her hands on my shoulders? There is no hiding from them, is there? And there is no talking to them. They don't understand what they understand. I am afraid. I should call the pediatrician, but I don't. I think, as people do, that everything will be all right. But even so, I can't stop being afraid. They are so beautiful, my daughters, so fragile and attentive to family life.

I wish they were boys and completely oblivious, as I was. I could not have said, before I met Dana, whether my parents' marriage was happy or not. I didn't know. She told me. She said, "Your parents are so dissimilar, aren't they? I mean, your father is sociable and trusting and all business, and your mother just doesn't know what to make of things, does she? They are a truly weird combination." We were twenty-two. She had spent her first half hour with them, and this was what she came out with, and that is what I have known about them ever since.

The next day a new patient came in, a heavyset, pugnacious man about my age. I poked around in his mouth and said, "Besides your present cavities, you have some very poorly filled teeth here." He sat up and looked at me and said, "You know, I've never been to a dentist who thought much of what was done to your teeth before him. And I'll say this, you'd better be cheap, because five years from now, some guy's going to tell me he's got to redo all your work, too." He sat back and looked out the window for a second, but he must have thought that the ice was broken, because he started right in again. "Doctors never say boo about what they see. I mean, some guy could cut off your healthy leg and leave the bad one, and you wouldn't get another doctor to admit the guy had made a mistake."

"Hmm," I said.

"I don't know," he said. "Things are more fucked every day."

"Open, please," I said.

"I mean, I don't know why I'm sitting here having my teeth fixed. It's going to cost me a lot of money that I could spend having the other stuff fixed. By the way, don't touch the front teeth. I play the trumpet, and if you touch the front teeth, then I'll have to change my embouchure."

I said, "Open, please."

"Well, I'm not sure I want to open. I mean, if you don't do anything, then I can spend my money on therapy or something that might really improve my life."

"We do ask patients to pay for appointments they don't keep. If you're uneasy about the discomfort, we have a lot of ways to make sure—"

"Hell, I don't care if it pinches, like you guys all say. I don't care if it hurts like shit. I just want to feel I'm not wasting my time."

"Proper dental care is never a—"

"My wife made this appointment for me. Now I've lost my job, and she's kicked me out. But she sent me this little card, telling me to go here, and I came. I mean, I can't—"

"Mr. Slater, please open your mouth so that we can get on with it."

"I can't believe she kicked me out, but I really can't believe she cares whether or not I go to the dentist."

"I don't know, Mr. Slater. But you are wasting my time and yours, too."

"Didn't you say you'd get paid anyway?"

"That's our policy, yes."

"How long does it take you to fill a couple of teeth?"

"About half an hour."

"Then just let me talk. I'll pay you."

"I don't like to talk, Mr. Slater," I said. "I'd rather fill teeth."

"But I'll pay you the money I should be paying a psychiatrist."

I put down my mirror and my probe. Dana passed the door and glanced in, curious. Her eyes left an afterimage of blue. Slater said, "That your wife?"

"What do you want to talk about, Mr. Slater?"

He sat back and deflated with a big sigh. He looked out the window. I did, too. Finally, he said, "Hey, I don't know. Go ahead and fill a couple of teeth. You're probably better at that anyway."

"That's what I'm trained to do, Mr. Slater."

He made no reply, and I filled two molars, right lower. He didn't speak again, but every time I changed my position or asked him to do something, he fetched up a bone-quivering sigh. His front teeth, I should say, were a mess. A brittle net, crooked, destined for loss. He left without speaking to me again, and paid with his MasterCard.

After he left I wanted him back. I wanted the navy-blue collarless jacket that he wouldn't take off, I wanted the Sansabelt slacks that stretched tight over his derriere. I wanted the loafers. I wanted him to tell me about his wife. He didn't smile much. He had a rough way of speaking. He was tall and not a pleasant man. It seemed to me that I could have drilled his teeth without novocaine, man to man, and it would have relieved us both.

He was with me all the rest of the afternoon. I imagined him leaving the office when I did. I imagined how he would walk, how he would get in his car, how he would drive down the street—thrusting and pugnacious, jamming the pedals, hand close to the horn all the time. Grief, I saw, had loosened him up, as if at the joints, and up and down his vertebrae. He had become a man who would do or say anything, would toss back his head or fling out his arms in a gesture impossible before. He wouldn't leave me alone. I felt bitterly sorry for him all afternoon. It seemed to me that his fate would be an ill one, and mine, too. All of our fates.

By the time Dana came home, I couldn't stop doing things as Slater might have done them. I was talkative and aggressive. I put my hands on her shoulders and turned her around so that she would look at me. I wandered around the kitchen, opening cupboards and slamming them shut. I talked about all of my patients except Slater at boring length. My voice got loud. Dana shrank and shrank. At first she laughed; then, with a few sidelong glances in my direction, she began to scuttle. I wondered if Slater's wife was just then doing exactly the same thing. But she wasn't. She had kicked him out, and I could certainly see why. Finally I stopped. I just stopped where I was standing, with my mouth gaping open, and Dana and I traded a long glance. I said, "What time is dinner?"

"About half an hour. Dave—"

"I'm going out. I'll be back, okay?" Slater wouldn't have asked in that way for permission. Neither would Dave Hurst, a month ago. I slammed out the back door and got into the car.

After I left Dana, Slater left me, and Dana joined me. I had hardly seen her back at the house, the whole time I was hovering around her, but now I could practically smell her, feel the vigor of her presence. As a rule, I don't know what she looks like. I don't think I have known, since the beginning, before everything about her looks became familiar to me, and saturated with feeling. As I drove along in the car, a picture of what she looks like came to me for the first time in years. And I thought, She is pretty, but she is getting a little prim-looking, with her gold button earrings and the gold chains around her neck. She wears neat blouses in the office, even now, in the midst of passion. And as this picture came to me, it also came to me that this passion was unbearable to her, and that the only way she knew to make it bearable was to pour herself into it as well as everything else, the way she has always done. I stepped on the gas, and soon I was streaming down the inter-state at 92 miles per hour. "Lord," I said, "let me fly. Give me that miracle to ease this pain." I pushed the car up to 100. I hadn't had a car into three figures in seventeen years, since Kevin Mills let me gas his father's Oldsmobile 98 up to 115 the summer after we graduated from high school. I went fast, but I didn't fly. Instead, I thought of my children and turned back at the next exit. I realized that the object of Dana's affections had refused her.

At the dinner table, Slater invaded me again. I was cutting Leah's meat and she was complaining that the pieces were too large, so I cut them and cut them until they were nearly mush. Then she said, "I don't like it." I sat back and looked at her, then around the table at the others, and it seemed to me that I was Slater, visiting for dinner. The woman was blond, sort of pretty and nice enough, I thought, but her children were horrible, the oldest sullen and suspicious—clank, clank-clank went her knife and fork on the plate—the next one an oblivi-ous blonde, masticating her food with annoying languor, and the third irritable and squawking. At last, inevitably, Leah smacked her bowl and it landed upside down on the floor. As Slater, I waited for their mother to do something about it. As my wife, Dana looked at me expectantly. Leah looked at me expectantly. I pretended to be their father. I jumped up and grabbed Leah out of her chair, and said in gruffish tones, "That's enough. I'm putting you into your bed." And I carried her upstairs. The windows were dirty and the sills needed vacuuming, and there were toys all over the floor of the child's room. The responsibility for all this seemed put upon me, and I stomped down the stairs, shouting, "Be quiet! Stop yelling! You can come down in five minutes."

"Dave," said Dana.

I answered to this name.

"I don't think you should shout at her like that."

"Somebody has to. Maybe nobody has enough. You don't. What the fuck is going on around here?"

Dana looked up fearfully. "Nothing. Nothing is going on, just everything the same. Why don't you sit down and—"

Now I really was Slater. "Everything's more fucked every day."

Lizzie and Stephanie had put down their forks and were staring out at me from under their foreheads, as if they couldn't take the full blast of me in their faces, but couldn't resist a look.

Dana said, "Why are you like this? Why are you so angry all the time? It's unbearable."

"I'm not angry all the time! I'm not really angry now."

"Listen to yourself! Can't you hear what you're saying?"

"But it's true, things are more fucked every day! Every day! Every day is worse!"

"No, it isn't! It isn't. Don't say that. I won't listen to that! You've always said that! I hate it."

"I have not always said that. I just realized it today."

"You have." She burst into tears. I was bitterly hurt and angry. Her greatest lifelong sin seemed to me to be that she didn't agree with me about the way the world is. I thought, I could accept anything else, let her love him, let her fuck him, let her talk to him forever, but give me this little agreement that I've never had before. I said, or rather shouted, "Admit that I'm right. Admit that every day is worse!"

"I won't!"

I could kill you, I thought.

"What did you say?"

"I didn't say anything."

"You said you could kill me." I looked into each horrified face and saw that I had said it, or Slater had said it. I groaned. "I didn't mean to say it."

"But you thought it."

"I can't control my thoughts."

"You thought you could kill me."

"I don't know what I thought. I thought a lot of things. I think all the time." I sat down and looked first at Lizzie and then at Stephanie, and I said, "A person can think anything that they want, because there is no way to make yourself not think things. But you don't want to do everything you think. I'm sorry. I think I'll go out for a little while." And then Slater and I slammed out of the house and got in the car again, although my father always used to say, in every crisis, "At least don't get in the car." And he never did.

Slater kept wanting to stop at a bar. Or at a gas station to pick up a couple of six-packs. Dave didn't think this was an especially good idea, but he did think he deserved something. What Dave really thought was that a responsible professional man, owner of two homes, employer of four persons, parent of three daughters, and lifelong meditative personality ought to be able to control himself. He also thought that his wife, a responsible professional woman, and ditto ditto ditto, if not ditto, ought to have been able to control herself, too. We stopped, Slater and I, at a rest area about thirty miles up the interstate, and there, without the benefit of a six-pack, we stood back from the road in the gloom of a chilly night and we screamed and screamed and screamed. After screaming, while noticing that we had screamed our throat into raw throbbing, we noticed the stars. They lay across the dark blue sky like sugar and diamonds sprinkled together. And Lord, how they shamed the flesh.

In the exhausted backwash of all this verbalizing, I realized that my plan not to be communicated with was at greater risk than ever, because I had made myself so unpleasant that it was likely she would flee to him, or at least flee from me at whatever cost. In fact, my success now rested with his resolution not to have her. Only with that. I wondered what it was about her, her circumstances or her person, that gave him pause. Or maybe it was her intrinsic passion. Maybe he had thought he saw in her cool blondness some sort of astringent distance, and now he saw that between Dana and a desired object there was no distance allowed at all. Maybe he was dazzled by the neat blouses and the deft workmanship into not seeing the defiant, greedy stare. Maybe he saw only the established dentist, not the determined dental student, the stainless-steel blonde in the doorway of the classroom, radiating tensile strength like heat. Appearances aren't deceiving, I think, but you have to know where to look.

I should say that it was hard for me not to see her as a dramatic figure. I always had seen her that way. Maybe, in fact, he only viewed her as something of a bore, a little thing, a mere woman passing through his life. I don't know. I never even saw him. I got home about twelve and sneaked into bed. Dana was already asleep. There is something I have noticed about desire, that it opens the eyes and strikes them blind at the same time. These days, when I lie awake at night and think about those early spring weeks, the objects of the world as they were then appear to me with utter clarity. Edges sharp, colors bright, movements etched into the silvery mirror of light and air. When I used to think of the word *confusion*, I would think of a kind of gray mist, but that is not what confusion is. Confusion is perfect sight and perfect mystery at the same time. Confusion is seeing without knowing, as if the optic nerves were still attached but the hemispheres of the brain were parted. Desire is confusion vibrating in the tissues.

Confusion and desire also include the inability to keep quiet. One of the things I remember with embarrassing clarity is all the talking I did, all the statements I made about every possible thing. They were all assertions, bombast, a waste of breath. Could I have shut up? The world was beautiful during those weeks—chill, sunny, gold-green, severe undecorated shapes of mountains, tree limbs, stones, clouds, floating together and together in a stream of configurations as the eye rolled past them. If I had it again, I would look at it better.

About this time we had what Dana would call "an early warning." News of the impending disaster came first to Laura, through her cousin in California, then to Dave from his mother two states away. Vomiting, high temperatures in both children and adults, lethargy, sore throat, possible ear complications. Dana told Dave to rearrange our schedules for about a week, so that the illness could pass through the body of the family with as little disruption as possible. It isn't unusual—the note from the school nurse reporting a case of chicken pox, the patient confiding, just before he opens his jaws, that he is feeling a little woozy, and then he leans back and out it comes, the miasma of contagion. Once each winter, if we are lucky, twice if we are not, the great family reunion that is the flu, or strep throat. The family patients have their characteristic styles of illness, and Lizzie is truly the worst, since she can't stand discomfort but fights the medicine. Dana is hardly any better, and seems to get a certain amount of relief from simply cursing, which doesn't give the rest of us any relief at all. And me? Dana says that I am the one who haunts the house with a martyred air. I ask for a glass of orange juice, she says, and then, before she has a chance to get it, I turn up beside the refrigerator, wounded to the quick by her failure of care, and pour it myself. Yes, yes, yes. I wasn't eager, given our circumstances, to take on this flu.

The patients, now transformed into vectors, came without cease. I leaned over them. I picked up one instrument at a time and set each down. I wanted to be careful and not angry. I wanted, in fact, not to be myself, but I didn't want to be Slater, either. None of the patients really replaced him in the chair, though, and when Dana passed the door, or spoke in the outer office, his ears pricked with that sleazy curiosity of his. "That your wife?" he kept saying. My private revenge against him was that I knew that his front teeth were going to disintegrate, and that his embouchure wouldn't be his for long, no matter what. Slater was an insensitive fellow, though, and didn't care what I knew. He also wanted to sit sullenly in the office and eat steak subs with cheese and drink coffee every day for lunch. Dana wasn't the only staff member pretty fed up with him. Laura didn't like his manner at all, and Delilah just stayed away. Only Dave didn't seem to notice.

Anyway, during those lunch hours, Slater and I were locked in argument. It was not that we couldn't agree what to do. Neither of us knew what to do. Our concerns were more abstract. I wanted to find reasons for my feelings. It would have relieved me to know, for instance, that steak, cheese, and coffee were biochemical poisons that were deepening my anxiety. Slater had never seen anything, heard anything, or felt anything. Slater had no receptors, only transmitters. He wanted to shout and drive and drink and blow his trumpet. He was marvelously contemptuous of every thread I wanted to look at. What good had it done me, all these years, Slater declared, to pick up one tool at a time? Income, I said, look at my income, look at what people think of me. People, said Slater, think nothing of you. You are just a dentist, another white coat, another small thing. Every day you sit at your stool fashioning things in people's mouths, and then they close their mouths and stand up, and more than anything they want to forget you, and your work never sees the light of day.

But you, I said, you know nothing, you stumble through your life without a first notion, pressing yourself and your breath and your music into the world. What good has it done you, Slater, to consume without thought and express without consideration? No good, said Slater. No good. But I know that it does me no good, and you don't even know that.

And then I sit with my head against the wall, waiting for the next patient, and I can hardly move or breathe, and when the tears begin rolling down my cheeks, I just turn my head toward the window, I don't even wonder why they have come or how I might dismiss them. I hear Dana's step pause beside the door, the step of her $120 Italian high heels, for she is very particular about elegant shoes. I can imagine the flash of her curious blue eyes, but she says nothing, and when Delilah speaks from the other office, she turns and goes out, and both Slater and I feel gaspingly sorry for ourselves. There is nothing meditative about it.

This went on until about Thursday. On Thursday, everyone in the family woke up at a quarter to nine from a sleep that could have been drug- or enchantment-induced. There was no possible consideration of anything except clothing, breakfast, and the fact that the girls were already late for school. Even Lizzie was so somnolent that she gave no thought to the embarrassment of walking into the classroom late. She lifted her arms to receive her sleeves and opened her mouth to receive her Cheerios, and Stephanie wandered around the bathroom as if she didn't know what she was doing there, and Leah let Dana dress her without a word of protest. Dana kept making toast. I kept eating it. It was buttery and delicious. She wouldn't let us hurry. She called the office and said I was busy and would be an hour and a half late, then she called the school and said that the girls would be there in time for recess. She was sleepy, too, and wandered from bathroom to bedroom half-dressed, looking for articles of clothing that were right under her nose. At ten-thirty we took Leah early to day care and went to the office together, where Dana worked on the patients I had stood up. I don't think I thought of Slater or the Other or the crisis of my marriage until well into the second patient, and then the patient's malocclusion seemed more immediate, and, even, more interesting. Delilah had brought daffodils from her garden and set them on Dave's desk, and so the day had a refrain, "Aren't those lovely flowers!"

When I used to work construction, my boss would tell me about the seventeen-inch rule. The seventeen-inch rule has to do with the construction of staircases. If you add together the width of the tread and the height of the riser, they should come out to seventeen inches. If they do, the step will meet the foot. If they don't, the foot will stumble. Sometimes, if he had a remodeling job in an old house, I would check out the seventeen-inch rule, and it was always true. The effort of steps that were too steep or too shallow was always perceived by the knees and the tendons, if not by the brain. And so I would say that we had a seventeen-inch day. Patients came on time and opened calmly. Teeth nearly drilled themselves, or jumped out into my hand. Dana and Delilah chattered and murmured in the next office. Laura and Dave teased each other. At lunch, Dana and I found ourselves on the back step of the office, facing the alley, eating peanut-butter sandwiches with raspberry jam and drinking milk. Our shoulders touched. She said, "You know, I think Leah told her first joke today."

"What was that?"

"Well, she was making claws with her hands, and roaring, the way she does, and I said, 'What's the name of your monster?' and she looked at me and said, 'Diarrhea.' And then she grinned."

We laughed and our shoulders bumped.

"Do you want the last bite of this?" She held out a piece of her sandwich.

I nodded and opened my mouth. She put it in. I chewed it. We got up and went inside. An hour and a half later I was finished for the day and half expected to be met by Slater on the steps of the office, but the coast was clear. I took out my list of errands and purchases and walked toward downtown. Everything was on sale, including a very nice blue-and-green-plaid Viyella shirt, 16–35, $16 marked down from $50. I put it on in the store, something I never do. As a rule I let new clothes sit in the closet for weeks before wearing them. I kept walking, looking at yards and houses and daffodils and crocuses, and felt that spurious permanency that comes with the sense of true peace. For dinner I bought boned chicken breasts and frozen pesto sauce. Dana came home and made fresh noodles.

Leah sat between Stephanie and Lizzie on the couch and they played this game: Lizzie would take Leah's face between her two palms and say, "Say yes, Leah," and then she would nod Leah's face up and down. Then Stephanie would take Leah's face from the other side and say, "Say no, Leah," and turn her head gently from side to side. None of the three could stop laughing, the two older girls from the sight of it, and from the feeling of their own power, and Leah, perhaps, from the pleasure of their attention, or perhaps from the rattling perspective shifts she experienced as they manipulated her head. I said, "Careful of her neck." But they were, without my saying anything. I pretended not to be watching them, but really I was transfixed by the passing of that baby head from hand to hand, by the way Lizzie's and Stephanie's fingers spread and flexed, by how strong their hands were with all their childish pudginess, and by how unconscious they were and yet how sensitive. I went into the kitchen. When I came back a few minutes later, the big girls were at their pictures and Leah was coloring her fingernails with a blue marker. I opened my mouth to remind her not to write on her skin, but before the first word was out, she had drawn a line from her ankle to her diaper. She looked up at me. I said, "That's naughty. Don't write on yourself." She knew I would say it, and I did. She refrained from writing on herself then as a formality until I left the room.

These are the trivia of family life, what the children do and say, how the fragrance of dinner wafts through the house, a view of the yard through the glass of the front door, the border collie across the street barking at the UPS man, a neighbor who has been hardly noticed these last weeks bringing the packets of seed you ordered together, looking at you quizzically and with concern, then turning away, making a joke upon herself. One by one they come upon the senses, charge along the neurons, leap the synapses, electrify the brain, and there is a moment, a moment of a specific duration which I don't remember, before the synapses jam, when the ear hears, the nose smells, the eyes see, the fingers sense the cool smooth foil of the seed packets.

We ate dinner.

We watched *Family Ties,* then *Cheers.* We put the children to bed and watched *Hill Street Blues.*

Dana was sitting beside me on the couch. She yawned and turned toward me. I saw my face in the pupils of her eyes, then I saw that she was smiling. She said, "I can't believe I'm so tired. Are you going to sit up?"

I was, and I did, alone in the silent living room, with the lights off and a beer warming in my hand. It seemed to me that the unexpected peace of the day had left me dizzy with pleasure, such pleasure that its prospective loss made my stomach queasy. Feelings are in the body as well as in the mind, is what he said. I lay back on the carpet, on the floor of the organ that was my house, and felt my family floating above me, suspended only by two-by-fours as narrow as capillaries and membranes of flooring. My pulse beat in my ears and the walls of the house seemed to throb with it. I closed my eyes and took some deep breaths. From China, from California, state by state, patient by patient, the flu had arrived.

I wonder if it is possible to prepare yourself for anything. Of course I lay there, saying, This is the flu, it isn't supposed to last more than two or three days, I should find the Tylenol. In the moment I didn't feel bad, really, a little queasy, a degree feverish. The disease wasn't a mystery to me. I know what a virus looks like, how it works. I could imagine the invasion and the resistance. In fact, imagining the invasion and the resistance took my attention off the queasiness and the feverishness. But when I opened my eyes, and my gaze fell upon the bookcases looming above me in the half-light, I shuddered reflexively, because the books seemed to swell outward from the wall and threaten to drop on me, and my thoughts about the next few days had exactly that quality as well. I did not see how we would endure, how I would endure.

There are many moments in every marriage that are so alike that they seem to be the same moment, appearing and vanishing, giving the illusion of time passing, and of no time passing, giving the illusion that a marriage is a thing everlasting. One of these recurring moments, for Dana and me, has always had to do with getting ready—finding a clear position to take up before the avalanche of events, like semester exams, births, vacations. Perhaps we practiced for this every night that we coasted down Cloud Street on my bike. That hill was not only long, it curved sharply to the right and had three steep dips. I suppose, looking back, that the precipice, such as it was, lasted seven or eight blocks before flattening out. Dana's apartment was about a block and a half from the top of the hill, and the first night I took her out I was so exhilarated that I put my feet on the handlebars of my bike and coasted all the way to the stoplight, eleven blocks from Dana's house.

The next time we went out, I suggested that we coast down it together. I remember the way that her eyelids snapped open at the idea and her stare locked into mine, but it took her only a second to say yes, and then we had to do it. I said, "Sit on the handlebars, then," and she did. She put her hands in front of mine, balanced with the small of her back, and looked straight ahead, straight at the first dip, and I thought, We are going to die now. I settled the bones of my ass on the seat and tightened my fingers on the grips. I pushed off and pedaled. I did not want to drift into it, whatever it was, I wanted to pump into it. It was agony. The bike was surprisingly front-heavy. I could hardly manage the dips, and skidded dangerously to the left when the right-hand curve came up. Our weight carried us a block past the stoplight, which, fortunately, was green.

After we had stopped, we didn't even speak about it, but resumed our conversation about dental matters while walking the thirteen blocks back up the hill. This time we didn't stop at Dana's house, but climbed to the top, where I stood holding the bike while she hoisted herself on. Looking back, it is that moment I remember, that recurring moment, always the same, of her hands and her thighs and her back, their stillness, the lifting of my foot onto the right pedal. Taking a clear position. I wonder why she trusted me so. I do not discount the possibility of simple stupidity.

Now, the flu. Three steep dips and a sharp curve to the right. People without children don't begin to know the test that these illnesses present. But there was no clear position to be taken, and no one to take it with. I lay on the floor until about three, when I went upstairs and puked into the toilet. Then I lay in the hallway outside the bathroom, shivering with fever and waiting to puke again. At six, Dana found me, gazed down with a knowing look, and went to find the seltzer, the Tylenol, the thermometer, the cool washcloth, my pajamas, a pillow so that I could remain in the hallway, where I found a kind of solitary and rigorous comfort. The children thought it was very peculiar and amusing to step over me. I was too dizzy to care.

They abandoned me. The children went to school and day care without a backward look; Dana went early to the office to take care of my patients, with only a shout from the front door that she was leaving now, would I be all right? I got my own juice, my own blanket, drew my own bath, because it seemed as if that would ease the aches and pains. I did everything for myself, because they were all off, doing as they pleased, healthy and happy. I could see out the window that it was a beautiful day, and I imagined them all dazed by the sparkle of the light, on the street, on the playground, all thoughts of me blasted out of them. Lizzie would be working in her reading workbook, Stephanie drawing pictures of the family, Leah making turtles out of egg cartons and poster paints, Dana mixing up amalgam on her tray, all of them intent only on their work, no matter how much I might think of them. Just then the phone rang, and it was Dave. He said, "Dana wanted me to call and ask if you needed anything." I said, "No. I just took some Tylenol." After that I got into the bathtub and floated there for an hour, resenting the fact that I had left my juice next to the telephone in the bedroom. Drying myself, I was dizzy again and nearly fell down. I entertained myself with thoughts of hitting my head on the bathtub and suffering a subdural hematoma; then I staggered into the bedroom and fell across the bed, already mostly asleep. Three hours later, I resurrected. I was clear-eyed, cool, happy. The forces of resistance had won an early victory.

Lizzie threw up for the first time while she was watching *The Flintstones* and eating her Hershey bar. She made it to the front hallway, but not to the bathroom. Stephanie was not sympathetic. Leah, carrying her Play Family garage from the living room to the kitchen, could not be prevented from stepping in it. Lizzie had already fled upstairs, Stephanie was hiding her nose in the sofa cushions, and Leah's wet bare footprint followed her into the dining room. I went for paper towels and a bucket, and I heard Lizzie, panicky, shouting from upstairs, "Daddy! Daddy!" She stumbled from somewhere above my head to somewhere else, and began to retch again. Just then, mop in one hand and bucket in the other, I felt all the grief of the last weeks drain away, to be replaced, not by panic, but by order. I caught Leah, wiped her foot off, and spread some paper towels over the mess in the hall. Then I went to Lizzie, who was draped over the toilet, and carried her into her bedroom, where I laid her on her bed, undid her clothes, and surrounded her with towels. Her face was red and soaked with tears, and I thought, I can't help you. I wiped her face with a cool washcloth, and then Stephanie shouted from downstairs, "She's going to get in it! She's getting near it! Daddy! Daddy!"

Lizzie said, "Don't go away."

That was the beginning.

What is it possible to give? Last fall I was driving to the office in a downpour, and I saw a very fat woman cross the street in front of the bus depot and stick out her thumb. No raincoat, no umbrella. I stopped and let her in. The office was about three blocks down, but I thought I would drive her wherever she needed to go in town. She said she was going to Kinney, a town about ten miles east, and it occurred to me simply to drive her there. She was wearing cloth shoes and carrying all her belongings in a terry-cloth bag. I don't think I answered, but she spoke anyway. She said, "My husband works out there. I just got in from California, after two months, and the whole time he was sending me these postcards, saying, Come back, come back, and so I bought my ticket." She fell silent. Then she looked at me and said, "Well, I called him up to say I'd got my ticket, and he said right there,

'Well, I want a divorce anyway.' So here I am. He works out there."

I said, "Maybe you can change his mind."

"I hope so. She works out there where he works, too. I want to get to them before they get into work. If I can't change his mind, I'm going to beat him up right there in the parking lot." She looked at me defiantly.

I said, "Why don't I drop you at the Amoco station at the corner of Front Street? You can stand under the awning, and there ought to be a lot of people turning toward Kinney there."

"Yeah."

After I got to the office, I thought maybe I could have bought her an umbrella, but I didn't go out and get her one, did I? It perplexes me, what it is possible to give a stranger, what it is possible to give a loved one, the difference between desire and need, how it is possible to divine what is helpful. I might say that I would give Dana anything to insure her presence in our house, our office, our family, but in saying this I have only traded the joy of giving for the despair of payment. I went downstairs and cleaned up the mess, then I went back upstairs and wiped Lizzie's face again with a newly wrung-out washcloth. If you stimulate the nerve endings in a pleasurable way, the neurons are less capable of carrying pain messages to the brain, and the brain is fooled. Dana was an hour late from work.

I should say that Lizzie heaved twelve times in four hours, so much that we were forcing ginger ale down her throat so that something, anything, could come back up. And she was fighting every drop, and screaming in panic, and throwing herself back and forth among the towels on her bed. We didn't have dinner, of course, but we did laundry, all the nightgowns, all the sheets, all the towels. About eleven, Dana said, "You're better," as if she had just noticed.

"Thirteen hours, normal to normal in thirteen hours."

"That's something, anyway."

"Not a basis for confidence, though."

She pursed her lips. "I wish you weren't always so pessimistic."

"As long as this lasts, why don't we avoid talking about how we always are?"

"Okay, but no sarcasm, either."

"A deal." We shook hands. Lizzie threw up four more times before morning, then six times on Saturday. When I called the pediatrician for a little reassurance and told him she had thrown up twenty-two times, he said, "That's impossible."

Dana says that they are formed at birth, and that they spend their whole childhoods simply revealing themselves. With a sort of arrogance that you might say is typical of her, she says that she knew all this in advance, as soon as she laid her mother's hands on them, that Lizzie did not care to snuggle, that Stephanie's neonatal thoughts were elsewhere, that Leah wanted to melt into the warmth of Dana's flesh. Some people cannot, will not be comforted. Lizzie is this way. She tosses off the covers and complains of the cold. Her joints ache, and she won't take the medicine. A swallow of seltzer gives her mouth such cool pleasure that she won't take another. She writhed about among the towels, needing and fighting sleep, and I sat near her, sometimes smoothing her forehead with the wrung-out washcloth, and contemplating her doom in much the same way that you contemplate their future glory when they do well in school or learn to read at three and a half. Then she fell asleep about ten and slept all night, not doomed, but saved one more time.

Dana lay next to me in a snore, and I thought of the soul, nacreous protoplasm, ringed in the iron of the self, weak little translucent hands on the bars, pushing, yanking, desperate for release. The moonlight stood flat in the window glass, as if caught there, and I turned and pressed myself against the warmth of my disappearing wife. Leah awakened at four. She would consent to be held only by me, and there was no sitting down allowed, only walking. A torture, in the middle of the night, that could have been devised by the KGB.

That was Sunday, the resurrection of Lizzie and the marathon of Leah, kitchen, dining room, living room, an endless circle. Sometimes Dana handed me food and drink, as in the old Kingston Trio song about the fellow who got stuck on the MTA. Dana kept putting on records, to keep me occupied, and sometimes she took Leah from me, but the screams were unrelenting. Sometimes I put her down in her bed, when she seemed to be asleep, but she always woke up and called out for me. Sometimes I staggered under the weight. Sometimes I got so dizzy from the circling that I nearly fell down. I had a chant: Normal to normal in thirteen hours. Maybe it was a prayer.

For dinner Lizzie and Stephanie wanted pizza. I circled. Leah's head rested back on her neck against my shoulder. Her mouth was open and her eyes were closed. One arm was tossed around my neck and her fingers hung in the collar of my shirt. From time to time I sat down in the rocking chair (this was always accompanied by a groan of protest from Leah) and rocked until the protests grew unbearable. The pizza came and Lizzie didn't want any. Stephanie ate only a single piece, because Lizzie pointed out to her that mushrooms had been put on by mistake. Dana screamed at them, threw away all the rest of the pizza, said we would never order another one, and sent them to their rooms; then she flopped on the couch, ashamed and unhappy, and followed me with her gaze while I circled the downstairs.

She said, "You're such a hero. I can't believe it."

"What else is there to do?"

"Yes, but you don't even seem to want to strangle every one of them. I do. Put us all out of our misery."

I headed for the kitchen and returned. "Are you miserable?"

Her eyes lifted to mine. She said, "I expect to be." I stopped walking and looked at her, then started again. She looked away and shrugged. "The flu always hits me like a ton of bricks."

"I didn't have it too badly. Maybe this one is worse for children than adults."

"But you never really get sick. I always think there's a kind of purity about you. Untouched. You remind me of some kind of flower."

"A flower?"

"I don't mean that you aren't masculine. You know that. I don't know." She looked out the window, speculating. "You know when you lean down and look right into a tulip? You know the way the petals look thick with color, but thin with light, permanent and delicate at the same time?"

"I suppose."

"That makes me think of you. Always has."

"Do you think of me?"

She looked back at me. She smiled slightly and said, "I have been lately, for some reason."

"Dana—"

"I better go and release them from bondage, or they'll be furious for the rest of the night." And then the whirlwind swept us up again.

However the flu took Leah, with nausea she couldn't puke out or give voice to, with aches and pains, with lethargy, it took her for three days, and I walked her for most of those three days. At first I was tired and bored; she was heavy, and the urge to put her off was more pressing than hunger, more like a raging thirst. I would panic at the thought of the hours, even the minutes, before me, of walking and carrying until my whole left side, the side she leaned upon, was numb, and my legs were leaden. After a while, though, say late Sunday night, it was as if Leah and our joining had sunk more deeply into me, so that I only did it, didn't think about it, didn't rebel against it. They say that this happens with the KGB, too.

Dana had gone to bed, leaving one lamp in the living room dimly lit. I remember looking at my watch, at the way the time looked there, eleven-fifteen, and the previous four weeks of nights, myself lying awake in fear or hope or whirring thought, suddenly seemed like a deck of shuffling cards to me, and yet each moment had been a lengthy agony. That was why the face of my watch was so familiar to me—I had looked at it repeatedly in disbelief at the tormented slowness of time. Then I remember looking down at Leah, whose face, as familiar as the face of my watch, glowed with fever and sleep. Her mouth was partly open and she breathed at me. I felt the tiny rush of it on my lips, where the nerves cluster, on my cheeks, like the first breeze after you have shaved your beard, even on my forehead. There was a fragrance to it, too, sour and pungent, the odor of sick child, but so familiar, so entwined with the lasting pleasure of holding the child's flesh to your own, that I drank it in. I lifted her higher and kissed her hot cheek, hot silk against the searching ganglia. I shifted her over to the right and she settled in. It seemed to me that I had never loved anything—object, or feeling, or person—the way I loved her right now. Love is in the body as well as the mind, a rush of blood to the surface, maybe, an infinitesimal yearning stretch of the nerve endings. I looked at her without seeing her, blinded by the loveliness of her nose, the grace of her forehead, the curl of her upper lip and the roundness of the lower. I will never see her, hard as I try to look past love. My eyes will always cast a light over her, and I will always think that this love, mine for her, is a dear thing. But it is as common as sand, as common as flesh.

After all, it was harder to cherish hers for me. Hard to appreciate the way she climbed the stairs looking for me, held my leg when I was trying to walk across the kitchen, yearned for my presence in the middle of the night, hard even to appreciate her glances into my face, her man-pleasing chatter, the stroke of her baby fingers on my forehead. And these hours of walking were unbearable, although I was bearing them. I stopped and looked down at her, thinking, Open your eyes. After a long while, she opened her eyes with a sigh, and I said, "Leah, it's time for bed."

She said, "Not go to bed."

"Yes, I'm tired. I'll walk you in the morning."

"Picky up."

"I'm going to take you to your bed now. You can have a bottle of juice. Tonight, even the dentist says you can have a bottle of juice."

"Picky up."

I carried her into the kitchen, filled a bottle with diluted juice, and began up the stairs.

"No bed."

"Time for bed. I'll lie down beside you on the floor."

"No bed."

I put her in. She was wide-awake. I lay on the rug, and she rolled over and looked down at me through the bars. Her eyes were big in the dark. She reached her hand through the bars, and I gave her mine, though it was awkward. She looked at me, and held my hand, and I fell asleep. Maybe she never fell asleep. We were up and walking by six. When Dana got up, I said, "I talked her into letting me get some sleep. I talked her into it." Dana handed me a piece of toast. I grew, once again, overconfident. The goodness of warm toast, the sweetness of cold orange juice, the attentions of my wife, the new maturity of my two-year-old. "Two years old!" I said. "I *talked* her into it." I thought I knew what I was doing.

We walked all of that day, until about six, when she got down out of my arms to interfere with Lizzie and Stephanie at their Parcheesi game. After dinner her fever went up and we walked until eleven. On Tuesday, we walked from six-fifteen in the morning until ten-thirty, when she got down for good at the sight of the Barbie bubbling spa boxed up in the front hall closet. I set it up. I found every Barbie and every water toy in the house, all the hair ornaments and four spoons. I gave her Tylenol and a bottle of juice, and then I went into the living room and collapsed on the couch. After a few minutes I could hear her start talking to herself and humming. I ached from the soles of my feet to my chin.

At noon I still hadn't moved, and Leah came in the living room to chat. She said, "Are you sleeping now?"

I said, "You're soaking wet."

She said, "Are you sleeping on the couch?"

I said, "Let's go upstairs and change out of your pajamas. Is your diaper wet?" And just then Dana walked in, her face as white as her jacket, which she hadn't bothered to take off. She closed the door behind her and, without speaking, turned and climbed the stairs. I said, "What's the main symptom?" and she said, "Aches and pains. My joints feel as if they're fracturing and knitting every second." Her voice trailed off and I sat up on the couch. Leah said, "Are you waking up now?"

Stephanie and Lizzie came in at three-ten, when I was thinking about dinner. I hadn't thought about dinner in four days, and I was ruminating over steak and baked potatoes and green beans in cheese sauce, my father's favorite meal. They threw down their backpacks and called for milk. While I was in the kitchen, someone turned on the TV. By the time I had returned, Stephanie was facedown on the couch. I was nearly jovial. I thought I knew what I was doing. I said, "Is it your turn, Steph? Have you got it?"

She rolled over. She said, "I feel bad now."

"Do you want to go upstairs? Mommy's up there. She's got it, too, but I have a feeling it will go away fast for you and Mommy." She held out her arms and I picked her up. There was Tylenol in every room in the house, and I grabbed some. She said, "Ooooh." It was a long-drawn-out and deeply resigned moan, the sound, it later turned out, of the fever rising in her veins like steam in a radiator. By the time I had carried her to her room, my shirt where she lay against me was soaked with her sweat. She said, "The yellow one."

I thought she was asking for a certain nightgown. I said, "Sweetie, you don't have a yellow one. How about the pink one?"

"Throw away the yellow one. My house."

I sat her on the bed and counted out five children's Tylenol. She collapsed, and I sat her up, opened her mouth with that practiced dental firmness, and put in the tablets, one by one. Her hair was soaked with sweat. She said, "Melon. Melon, melon, melon." I laid her out, and put my hand across her forehead. She was incandescent. I took my hand away and placed it in my lap. From downstairs came the sound of the Superfriends. From down the hall came Dana's voice, low and annoyed, saying, "Shit. Oh shit." She is not long-suffering in illness, and generally keeps up a steady stream of expletives as long as she feels bad. I sat quietly, because in myself I felt panic, a little void, needle-thin but opening. The thermometer was on the table next to Lizzie's bed. I stared at it for a long time, then at Stephanie, then at my hand reaching for it, then at my hand putting it in her mouth. The Superfriends broke for a commercial, Lizzie called, "Daddy!," Dana said, "Damn I hate this," and the thermometer, held up to the light, read 104.2.

There is the permanent threat of death. In the fifties, people used to grow trees through the roofs of their houses, sometimes, and I often think of death as an invisible tree planted in our living room. When the doors are closed and locked, the insurance paid, the windows shaded, injury and the world excluded so that we, thinking that we know what we are doing, can sit complacently at the dining room table, that invisible tree rustles, flourishes, adds a ring of girth. Any flight of stairs is treacherous, the gas furnace is a bomb waiting to go off, Renuzit may stray, unaided by the human hand, from top shelf to bottom. A child carrying a scissors might as well be holding a knife to her breast; bicycles beside the door yearn to rush into traffic. A tongue of flame can lick out of the wall socket, up a cord carelessly left plugged in, and find the folds of a curtain. From time to time, unable to sleep, I have lain in bed counting household hazards: radon in the basement, petroleum products in the carpeting, gas fumes in the stove. I don't often think of illness, but a child in the next block had meningitis last year. When Eileen, that is the mother, went to the hospital, they looked her in the face and said, "Twenty-five percent chance of death, twenty-five percent chance of severe brain damage, twenty-five percent chance of minimal brain damage, twenty-five percent chance of full recovery," and they were so matter-of-fact, Eileen says, that she just nodded and said, "Oh. Thanks," as if she were taking a rain check on a sale at K-Mart.

I wonder once in a while how my father would have reacted if one of us had died. It seems to me that he would have noticed something missing, that my absence, or my brother's, would have prickled at him through the day, and he would have upheld the forms of grief, but I don't know that he ever really looked at us, or perceived enough about us so that the removal of one of us would have been a ripping of flesh. Soon enough he would have gotten behind the stove or the clothes dryer or the dehumidifier with his electrical meter and forgotten about it entirely, as he did about us alive. Dana said that I often underestimate him, but in this case, I think he was a wise man, to have addressed himself to the world at large like that, to have stood in front of us, only half perceiving us, reassured by the shuffle of our feet and our sighings and breathings that all of us, whoever we were, were back there.

When you are in the habit of staring at your children, as almost everyone my age that I know is, of talking about them, analyzing them, touching them, bathing them, putting them to bed, when you have witnessed their births and followed, with anxious eyes, the rush of the doctor and nurses out of the delivery room to some unknown machine room where some unknown procedure will relieve some unknown condition, when you have inspected their stools and lamented their diaper rash and, mostly, held their flesh against yours, there is no turning away. Their images are imprinted too variously and plentifully on your brain, and they are with you always. When I agreed with Dana that I wanted to be "an involved father," I foresaw the commitment of time. I didn't foresee the commitment of risk, the commitment of the heart. I didn't foresee how a number on a thermometer would present me with, paralyze me with, every evil possibility. Stephanie lay there, stupefied with fever. Lizzie came into the room. She said, "Didn't you hear me? I want some more milk." She sounded annoyed.

"You can pour it yourself."

"I can't. It's too heavy."

"Don't talk to me in that tone of voice. Can't you say please?"

"Please!"

"Say it as if you mean it."

She drew it out. "Pleeeeease."

"I'll be down in a minute."

"It's always in a minute. That's what you and Mommy always say—in a minute. Then you forget."

"You aren't the only person in the house, Elizabeth."

"You always say that, too." She backed away, not sure how far she could take this discussion. She glanced at Stephanie on the bed. I said, "Stephanie has a very high fever."

"Is it dangerous?"

I turned the word over in my mind, because it is a big word in the family vocabulary, a dangerous word, in fact, that always signals to Lizzie that she ought to panic. On the other hand, I was still rather annoyed about her recent demanding tone. I contemplated sobering her up, but I needed her as my ally, didn't I? I said, "It's not good, but it's not dangerous." She nodded. I said, "Do me a favor, and go ask Mommy how she feels." She turned in the doorway and called, "Mommy! How do you feel?" Dana groaned. I surveyed Lizzie and wondered, Is this defiance on her part, ill-taught manners, stupidity? I said, "Go ask her. Be polite. I need you to help me." Now she surveyed me. I was not kidding. She went into the master bedroom, and I stuck the thermometer back in Stephanie's mouth, thinking that the Tylenol would have had time to take effect. 104.1. Lizzie returned. "She feels as if she's been run over."

"What's Leah doing?"

"Watching TV."

"Can you do everything I say for the next two days?"

"Do you mean like cleaning my room?"

"I mean like getting me stuff and watching Leah, and getting stuff for Mommy."

She shrugged.

"I think you can. It's important."

"Okay." She and I looked at each other. Her eyes are blue, too, but darker blue than Dana's, more doubtful. Simultaneously I thought that this would be a good lesson in responsibility for her and that no lessons, however good, would preserve her from her own nature. I said, "Go into the bath-

175

room and get a washcloth and wring it out in cold water. I'm going to talk to Mommy for a minute, and then we are going to try and cool Stephie off, okay?"

Dana lay on her side with her eyes closed. The lids were purple all the way to her eyebrows, as if she had eyeshadow on, but the skin of her face was opaquely pale. The blood was elsewhere, heart, brain. She was not sleeping, but I don't think she was aware of me. Her lips formed words, Fuck this, I can't take this, dammit. I leaned down and said, "Can I get you anything?"

Her eyes opened. She uttered, "Did you have these aches and pains?"

"Not really."

"I've never felt anything like it. It must be what rheumatoid arthritis is like."

"Anything else?"

"A little woozy. How's Stephanie?"

"Temperature."

"How much?"

"Lots."

She looked at me for a long moment. "How much?"

"104."

"Did you call Danny?"

"He'll just say bring her in at 105. I gave her some Tylenol and I'm going to give her a lukewarm bath."

"Oh." Her voice was very low. She closed her eyes. After a moment, tears began to run through the lashes, over the bridge of her nose, onto the pillowcase.

"She'll be all right."

She nodded, without opening her eyes.

"What's wrong?"

"I'm sad for us."

"We've had the flu before."

"I'm sad for us anyway." She snorted and wiped her face on the quilt.

"We'll be all right, too." She opened her eyes and looked at me, sober, speculative, in retreat. Not if she can help it, I thought. I said, "I love you."

"I know." But though she continued to look at me, she didn't reciprocate.

Finally I said, "Well. I'm going to work on Stephie." She nodded.

Lizzie was doing a good job. Stephanie lay on her back, with her eyes closed and her chin slightly raised. Lizzie was smoothing the washcloth over her forehead and down her cheeks. She had a look of concentration on her face, the same look she gets when she is writing something. I stood quietly in the doorway watching them and listening to Leah mount the stairs. Soon she came into view, her hand reaching up to grasp the banister, her eyes on her feet, careful. She looked up and smiled. I would like to have all these moments again.

Just then, Stephanie threw out her arm, smacking Lizzie in the face. Lizzie jumped back in surprise, already crying, and I was upon them with reassurances. "She didn't mean it, honey. Stephie? Stephie? Are you there, sweetie? Do you want to take a little bath?" She was tossing herself around the bed. She said, "Megan, don't. Don't!" I picked her up to carry her into the bathroom and she nearly jerked out of my arms. She was soaked with sweat and slippery. After the bath, she was still above 104. It was like a floor she could not break through.

I kept a record:

> 6 p.m.: 104.1
> 6:40 p.m.: 104.2
> 8 p.m. (more Tylenol): 104
> 9 p.m.: 104.2
> 10:35: 104.2

Midnight: 104.4

12:30: 104.4

3 a.m.: 104.6 (another bath)

4 a.m.: 104.4

6 a.m.: 104.2

I longed for some magic number, either 103.8 or 105, for either reassurance or the right to take her to the hospital. She writhed and spoke and sweated and grew smaller in my eyes, as if the flesh were melting off her. I kept reminding myself that the fever is not the illness but the body fighting off the illness. It is hard to watch, hands twitch for something to do. And I was beat, after those nights with Leah, but even if I dozed, I would wake after an hour, and my first feeling was raging curiosity: what would it read this time?

8 a.m.: 104.2

Lizzie walked to school alone and I took Leah to her day care. I ran home, my fingers itching for the thermometer. I was ready to believe any magic, but none had taken effect. I gave her more Tylenol, another bath, took a shower, stepped on the scale. I had lost twelve pounds since Dana's opera. The High Stress Family Diet.

9:30 a.m.: 104.4. Dan, the pediatrician, told me to keep taking her temperature.

11 a.m.: 104.4

1 p.m.: 104.4

3 p.m.: 104.4

6 p.m.: 104.4

After I read it, I shook the thermometer, just to see if the mercury was able to register any other number. I called the pediatrician again. He said that it would go down very soon. I said, "It's not impossible that it could just stay at this level, is it?"

He said, "Anything is possible." I was glad to hear him admit it.

8 p.m.: 104.6

10 p.m.: 104.6

I should say that I talked to her the whole day. "Stepha-nie," I said, "this stinks, doesn't it? We've been at this for days, it seems to me. Pure torture, an endless task. Sisyphean, you might say. I remember the myth of Sisyphus quite well, actu-ally. We read it in seventh grade. You will probably read it in seventh grade, too. I also remember the myth of Tantalus. He kept trying to bite an apple that would move out of the way when he leaned his head toward it. Sisyphus had to roll a stone up the mountain, and then watch it roll back down again. I think I remember it because that's what seventh grade seemed like to me. Anyway, sooner or later you will know all this stuff. And more. The thing is, after you know it, it will float in and out of your consciousness in a random way, so that if you ever just want to sit and talk to your own daughter like this, not having a conversation but just talking to keep her ears greased, as it were, then all of this stuff will come in handy. But I am here to tell you, Stephie dear, that every word, whatever its meaning, gets us closer to tomorrow or the next day, when you will sit up and look around, and I will breathe a long sigh of relief." The paternal patter. During the night, it eased toward 105, and I took it every forty-five minutes. At two, Dana got up to spell me, but when I got up at two-thirty, I found her passed out in the hallway and carried her back to bed.

She is light. She is only 5′ 4″, though she seems taller to the patients because she always wears those three-inch Italian heels in the office. People marvel at this, but in fact she doesn't stand on her feet all day, she sits on a stool. The shoes flatter her ankles, her hips, her waist, everything up to the back of her head, because everything is connected, of course. She is thin. She weighs 107 or 108. Once I had a good grasp on her, I could have carried her anywhere. She was wearing a white flannel nightgown scattered with tiny red hearts. She was warm and damp, her hair was askew, she would have said that she didn't look her best. A silk shirt, those heels, a linen or cotton or wool skirt, a good haircut, lipstick—that is looking her best, she would have said; a fine-grained surface, a sort of enameling. Women who are more relaxed find her a little cold, or archaic, or formal, but it seems to me that she has poured herself into a sort of dental mold, too. Dentists make a lot of money. Dental conventions are full of dandies. Two dentists in conference in the lobby of the Dallas Hyatt are more likely to be talking about tailors than about inlays. Her body is not yielding. It has a lot of tensile strength that is inherited, I think. Her brother Joe can bench-press 250 pounds, though he doesn't lift weights as a hobby. In any pickup softball game, Frances has amazing power at the plate. To lift Dana in one's arms is to feel not weight but elastic resistance.

To take Dana into one's arms, and to be taken into hers, is to feel, not yielding, but strength. When she holds your hand, she grips it hard. When you hug her, she hugs back. When you kiss her, her lips, which are firm, press against yours. Picking her up reminded me of those things, reminded me that retreat isn't always her mode, is rarely her mode, has never been her mode, is, in fact, a function of point of view, of where you are in the field of her activities. I pushed the covers back with my foot and laid her down. She groaned. I pulled her nightgown over her feet, pulled the sheet up to her chin, then the blanket.

Stephanie had been asleep since about eleven. I opened the curtains of her room partway, and shook down the thermometer by the streetlight outside. I opened her drawer and took out a fresh nightgown. The house was quiet, and I was fully awake somehow, though I hadn't had a full night's sleep in six days, or slept the sleep of the innocent in weeks. The darkness, when I closed the curtains, seemed a presence in the house, sensible, like heat. I let it envelop me where I sat on Stephanie's bed. I might have said that it pressed against my skin, got under my clothes, filtered into my hair, coal dust, blackness itself, sadness. I reached out my hand and put it on Stephanie's small hip under the covers. It submerged her, too, pressed her down against the dark pillow so that I could barely see her face. Even her blond hair, coiled against her neck, moist with sweat, gave off no light. Now the darkness felt as though it were getting into me—by osmosis through the skin, mingled with my inhalations, streaming into my eyes and up the optic nerves to seep among the coils of the brain, replacing meditation. It pooled in my ears. My pulmonary arteries carried blood into my lungs, where it was enriched with darkness, not oxygen, and then it spread through the circulatory system, to toes and fingertips and scalp. The marrow of my bones turned black, began spawning black blood cells. And so thought was driven out at last. Meditation, the weighing of one thing against another, the dim light of reflection, the labor of separating thread from thread, all gone.

I ran my hand gently up Stephanie's back and jostled her shoulder. "Time, sweetie," I said. "I need to take your temperature." I jostled her again. No response. Now I put the thermometer on the night table and lifted her in my arms. Her head flopped back against my shoulder, and I put the thermometer into her partly open mouth, then held her jaws closed. I was glad she seemed to be getting sounder sleep—she had been restless for two nights now. I counted slowly to 250, then took out the thermometer and laid it gently on the night table. Then I unbuttoned her nightgown and slid her out of it. Her skin was so damp that it was hard to get the sleeves of the clean one up her arms. I stretched her out on the mattress, smoothed the blanket over her. Then I carried the thermometer into the bathroom and turned on the light. 105.2. My hand was still on the switch. I pushed it down, and submerged myself in darkness again.

I did not have a thought, but I had a vision, or an image, a fleeting memory of the stars as they looked the night I drove out on the interstate, as many stars as worlds as eras as species as humans as children, an image of the smallness of this one gigantic child with her enormous fever. When each of them was born, Dana used to say, "There's one born every minute," but she was grinning, ecstatic with the importance of it. "Isn't it marvelous what you can do with a little RNA?" she would say, just to diminish them a little. But they couldn't be diminished. So, however many worlds and species and children there were and had been, I was scared to death. I crept to the phone and called the clinic, where, thank God, they were wide-awake. I said, "Is it possible to die of the flu?" They put a nurse on right away. Was she very sick?

"What does that mean? She has a temperature of 105.2."

"But how is she acting?"

"She's not acting any way. She's asleep."

"Is she dehydrated?"

"She urinated at around ten-thirty. We've maintained lots of fluids."

"Is she hallucinating?"

"She's asleep."

"Is she lethargic?"

"She's *asleep,* goddamn it!"

"Is it possible to wake her?" Her voice was patient and slow. Now I had another image, the image of Stephanie's head flopping back on my shoulder and the utter unconsciousness of her state. I said, "I'll try." She said, "I'll hold."

And then I went in and I sat her up and I shook her and shook her, and I said, "Stephanie! Stephanie! Wake up! Wake up! Stephanie? Listen to me. I want you to wake up!" She groaned, writhed, protested. She was hard to wake up. I reported this to the nurse and she left the phone for the obligatory hold. After a while she came back and told me to bring her in. Her tone was light enough, as if it were three in the afternoon rather than three in the morning. I began to cry. I began to cry that my wife was unconscious with the flu, too, and that I didn't dare leave the other children in her care, and pretty soon the doctor came on, and it wasn't Dan but Nick, someone whom we know slightly, in a professional way, and he said, "Dave? Is that you, Dave?" and I of course was embarrassed, and then the light went on and there was Dana, blinking but upright in the doorway, and she said, "What is going on?" and I handed her the phone, and Nick told her what I had told the nurse, and I went into Stephanie's bedroom and began to wrap her in blankets so that I could take her to the hospital, and I knew that the next morning, when Stephanie's fever would have broken, I would be extremely divorced from and a little ashamed of my reactions, and it was true that I was. They sent us home from the hospital about noon. Dana was making toast at the kitchen table, Leah was running around in her pajama top without a diaper, and Lizzie had escaped to school.

I sat Stephanie at the table, and she held out her wrist bracelet. They had spelled her name wrong, *Stefanie Herst.*

"That's the German way," said Dana. "It's pronounced 'Stefania.' Shall we call you that now?"

Stephanie laughed and said, "Can I have that one?" pointing at the toast Dana was buttering, and Dana handed it to her, and she folded it in two and shoved it into her mouth, and Dana buttered her another one. They were weak but in high spirits, the natural effect of convalescence. I went into the living room and lay down on the couch. I looked at my watch. It read 12:25. After a moment I looked again. It read 5:12. It was not wrong. Across the room on the TV, Maria and Gordon and some child were doing "long, longer, and longest." Leah was watching them, Lizzie was erasing and redoing her papers from school, and Stephanie was coloring. Dana appeared in the doorway, wiping her hands on a towel, then smiled and said, "You're awake."

"I'm resurrected. Are you sure I was breathing all this time?"

"We had a nice day."

"How do you feel?"

"Back to normal."

"How normal?"

"I'm making fried chicken."

"Mashed potatoes?"

"Cream gravy, green beans with browned almonds, romaine lettuce."

"The Joe McManus blue-plate special."

"I set a place for him at the table, just like Elijah."

The ironic middle. We were married again, and grinning. We've always made a lot of good jokes together. I heaved myself off the couch and went to the shower. Not so long ago, Lizzie came home and said, "You know when you let the bathwater out and there's a lot of little gray stuff in it?"

I said, "Yeah."

She said, "That's your skin."

I stood in the shower for about twenty minutes.

And then it was Friday, everyone in school, day care, work, all support services functioning, the routine as smooth as stainless steel. I was thirty-five, which is young these days, resilient, vital, glad to be in the office, glad to see Laura and Dave, glad to drill and fill and hold X-rays up to the light. In our week away, the spring had advanced, and the trees outside my examination room window were budded out.

As soon as the embryo can hear, what it hears is the music of the mother's body—the *lub-dup* of her heart, the riffle of blood surging in her arteries, the slosh of amniotic fluids. What sound, so close up, does the stomach make, the esophagus? Do the disks of the spine creak? Do the lungs sound like a bellows or a conch shell? Toward the end of pregnancy, when the pelvis loosens, is there a groan of protest from the bony plates? Maybe it is such sounds that I am recalling when I sit on my chair with the door to my office half closed and feel that rush of pleasure hearing the conversation in the hall, or in Dana's office. Delilah's voice swells: "And then they—" It fades. Dave: "But if you—" Dana: "Tomorrow we had better—" The simplest words, words without content, the body of the office surging and creaking. Dana's heels, click click, the hydraulic hum of her dental chair rising. In my office, I am that embryo for a second, eyes bulging, mouth open, little hand raised, little fingers spread. I have been so reduced by the danger of the last few weeks that the light shines through me. Does the embryo feel embryonic doubt and then, like me, feel himself nestling into those sounds, that giant heart, carrying him beat by confident beat into the future—waltz, fox-trot, march, jig, largo, adagio, allegro. I don't sing, as Dana does, but I listen. Jennifer Lyons, age fourteen, pushes open the door, peeps in. "Hi," I say, "have a seat." And I am myself again, and the workday continues.

And continued. And continued. She made lasagna for dinner. Saturday she got a babysitter and we went to the movies. Afterward we stopped at the restaurant next to the office and had a drink. She put her arm through mine. I watched her face. Now I could speak, but what would I say? If there was not this subject between us, I could have talked about the news, our friends, the office, our daughters, but now I could say nothing. We sat close, she put her hand on my knee. I drank the odor of her body into the core of my brain, where it imprinted.

On Sunday there was laundry and old food in the refrigerator. We mopped the floors, and Dana was seized with the compulsion to straighten drawers. I raked mulch off the flower beds and got out the lawn mower and climbed the ladder to clear leaves out of the eaves troughs. Lizzie and Stephanie spent the weekend obsessively exploring the neighborhood, like dogs reestablishing their territory. Leah took this opportunity to play, by herself, with every one of their toys that she had been forbidden over the winter. I liked her touch. She didn't want to damage, she only wanted to appraise. I thought of my temptation to speak on Saturday night with horror. Each of these normal weekend hours seemed like a disaster averted.

Monday at noon Dana and Delilah were late, did not appear. Dave was surprised at my surprise. Man to man. He didn't look at me. He said, looking at the floor, "Didn't you know that she canceled everything?" Man to man. I didn't look at him. I said, "Maybe she told me and I wasn't listening. It was a busy morning." Man to man. We glanced at each other briefly, embarrassed.

She was not at home at three, when I got there to wait for the big girls.

She was not at home at five-fifteen, when I got back from the day-care center with Leah, or at five-thirty, when I put in the baking potatoes and turned on the oven.

She was not at home at seven, when we sat down to eat our meat and potatoes. Lizzie said, "Where's Mommy?"

I said, "I don't know," and they all looked at me, even Leah. I repeated, "I don't know," and they looked at their dinners, and one by one they made up their minds to eat anyway, and I did, too, without thinking, without prying into the mystery, without taking any position at all.

She was not at home when Leah went to bed at eight, or when Lizzie and Stephanie went to bed at nine.

She was not at home when I went to bed at eleven, or when I woke up at one and realized that she was gone. At first I considered practicalities—how we would divide up the house and the business and the odd number of children. These were dauntingly perplexing, so I considered Dana herself, the object, the force, the person that is the force within the object. In the confusion of dental school, of fighting with my father, of knowing that my draft lottery number was just on the verge of being not high enough, of taking out a lot of student loans and living on $25 a week, I remember feeling a desire for Dana when she first appeared, when she paused in the doorway that second day of class and cast her eyes about the room, that was hard and pure, that contained me and could not be contained, and I remember making that bargain that people always make —anything for this thing. No doubt it was the same bargain that Dana was making right then, at one in the morning, somewhere else in town.

She was not at home at three, when I finally got up and went downstairs for a glass of milk, or at four, when I went back to bed and fell asleep, or at seven, when Leah started calling out, or seven-thirty, when Lizzie discovered that all the clothes she had to wear were unacceptable, or at eight-forty-five, when I checked the house one last time before checking the office. Dave caught my eye involuntarily as I opened the door, and shrugged. At eleven the phone rang, and then Dave came into my examination room between patients and said, "She canceled again." I nodded and straightened the instruments on my tray. At two my last patient failed to show, and I went home to clean up for the girls.

She was sitting at the dining room table. I sat down across from her, and when she looked at me, I said, "Until last night I still thought I might be misreading the signals."

She shook her head.

"Well, are you leaving or staying?"

"Staying."

"Are you sure?"

She nodded.

I said, "Let's not talk about it for a while, okay?"

She nodded. And we looked at each other. It was two-thirty.

The big girls would be home in forty minutes.

Shall I say that I welcomed my wife back with great sad-

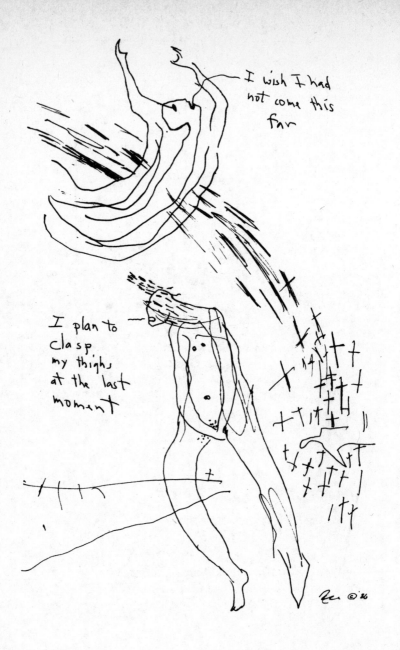

The James Poems

ZERELDA

I

She, like all the best people,
came from Kentucky; she is on
her third husband and has never been
happy since the first one died in
California, preaching the Word
of God or maybe he was
panning gold himself, who knows? A Mr. Robert
    James,
sick and biblical, passed away on
    the 22nd inst. of this year 1850
      with his penultimate breath said
      I am far from Zerelda and my boys, God keep
      them
et cetera and then shuffled off this mortal coil
(which appears to be a sort of clay snake)
having never in his life
entered a bar or tavern,
sworn out loud, read salacious literature, or
fired a shot in anger.

II

Here are her sons, Jesse and Frank,
small consolation prizes out of the goldfields;
they are her own, at least so far.
She can neither vote nor sit on a jury
nor go around without the ironclad corsets
or speak aloud of anything she knows to be true;
she is alive and yet without
a legal existence.

The law does not allow her husband to beat her
with a cane any thicker than his thumb.
So she will get another husband
who is smaller, whose thumbs
are not so big.

III

Big emotions sweep over Zerelda,
tornadoes and electrical storms; the Civil War
was made for people like Zerelda;
she does not even resist but sails off
like a barn roof.
  They are simple emotions: rage, fear,
  a desire to be noticed.
In her mouth human speech becomes a skinning
  knife:
They're going to take our niggers away,
they think they're better than we are,
  and so on.
She expands into a rage at the mill:
she thinks she's been cheated, she goes after
George William Liddle with a potato spade.
  (Can you imagine Zerelda dancing, can you
  imagine Zerelda seventeen years old and
  dancing in Kentucky?)

IV

At the end of the line of wagons at the mill there
is a black woman with two sacks of field corn and a
jar of zinnias. She is taking the zinnias to her
  mother
if she can. The woman sees the conflict coming and
  backs
the mules. "Sshh-back, sshh-back" and the zinnias
  nod

with accurate brown centers. She has to get the
    field
corn ground into kitchen meal and back home and
    now
look what's going on. The woman is owned by a
    man
named Billy Garshade who lives at Cracker Neck.
COLORED RECRUITS! $100 BOUNTY
AND PAY NOT EXCEEDING
$300 TO LOYAL OWNERS! She can easily
imagine herself
dancing. The mules back up against the singletree
and the trace chains crash with a noise like water
or hope.

V

The boys don't like to see their mother cheated,
they believe her, they have always believed her
    and now it is Civil War.
Down the road comes a troop of local Union militia
in blue uniforms;
leading them is George William Liddle.

V I

Frank has already joined the guerrillas.
Jesse is fifteen and plowing in the fields
when the militia rides in, they shut
Zerelda up like the whole neighborhood
secretly wished somebody would shut
her up, with a rifle butt.
They find Jesse at the plow and beat him half
to death with the reins.
This is called Civil War.
Enormous thoughts or desires crash and
collide with each other, theories, ideologies.

Zerelda is screaming of course, they
will finally burn her out under
General Order Number 11.
> (Can you imagine Zerelda dancing? Can you
> imagine Zerelda seventeen years old and
> dancing in Kentucky?)

VII

As the years go by Zerelda gets more dramatic.
Oh, Mother, say the huge famous bandits.
They are sick of problems with no solution.
Look up from your soap-making, Zerelda, stop
    muttering
to yourself, possessed by rages, cheated, vengeful,
thinking you are in actuality making soap.
Stop talking to yourself.
The larger questions of life are for you as well
down the ladder of summer cumulus, out of the
arctic of noon, out of the cosmic laundry of
gigantic clouds comes either death or eternal life.
Detectives throw a bomb in the window.
Archie is killed, Zerelda's hand is blown off.
Oh, Mother.
> (Can you imagine Zerelda dancing?)

VIII

Zerelda learns to make soap, wash clothes,
    clean the lamp chimneys, shovel the ashes
from the fireplace with one hand;
    the other is a steel hook.
Does she appear like a monster-woman from
    folktales or legends?
She is,

she didn't get this way by herself,
she had help.

FRANK INVITES JESSE TO JOIN HIM IN QUANTRELL'S GUERRILLAS: SEPTEMBER 1862

I am coming back for you, leave the house after
    supper,
meet me at Low Gap, I will come with two horses,
    one in each
hand, they will be striped with darkness and the
    shadow
of deep wells.

We will move like clocks through the night hours.
    We will work
for ourselves and when we like we will be
    unemployed as the
goldenrod and the grass. It is better than owning
    things, it is
better even than getting elected.

Meet me at Low Gap. I will give you a horse of
    violence and
delight, I will give you a horse of agency and black
    powder.
The world is different than we used to think,
    houses catch fire
more easily than they said, killing is simple,
    dynamite is

also fast. The world around us is made of
    matchsticks and
rye straw.
I am telling you, reality is unstable.

Sit on the rails by the salt spring tonight, I will see
    your
cigarette, wait for me at Low Gap, under the broad
    shoulder
of Rattlesnake Hill, stars spark in the dark roach of
    its
diamond back.

We will not be officially counted and no one will
    have time
to call us by our names.

Only saints and killers know firsthand
the red fragility of the human body,
the low gear-ratio of the human mind.

FOUND POEMS

There were bands of robbers moving continually
through (Cooper) county, who cared nothing for either party,
who robbed and killed without discrimination or regard to
party. During the year 1864 many good citizens belonging to
either side were shot down, first by one side and then by the
other, and many citizens abandoned their homes, seeking
places of more security. The details of these murders and
robberies are too disgraceful and sickening to enumerate in
this brief history.
    The History of Cooper County,
    Steam Book Job Printers, St. Louis, 1879

GUERRILLA WARFARE: MISSOURI
1856–1865

I

It is a war we have invented to our own liking.
It is homemade, off-the-wall,
we have invented many new ideas in our war
with our neighbors;
the new ideas are:
bushwhacking
leading Quakers into ambushes
killing all the men over the age of twelve in any
particular town
(Lawrence, Osceola, Danville, Poplar Bluff)
and throwing people down wells.
Anyway, they are new to us.

Altogether we make something bigger than one
      alone,
more explosive, a group of men reaching
critical mass.
We are the atoms of an unstable substance, moving
      toward
fission,
we suddenly fuse and go off.

I I

The unarmed federals leaping out of the cattle cars
in Centralia yell stop or something.
Our rifle barrels are hot as pokers
we can't stop ourselves
we are being run by something
that lives in us as if we were an abandoned house.
It is watching and watching out of our eyeholes.

I don't know what it is or what it wants, but I can tell you this:
we don't come natural to it.

III

Frank's house is not abandoned,
after all the killing and escapes he
lays up in a corncrib west of Rocheport
reading the constitutional theories of Robert
    Ingersoll,
fingerprints of grease and black powder marking
    the
hot-lead print.
Bloody Bill and Charlie and Taylor Fletcher are
    suspicious
they eat their sidemeat and fried mush watching
    him,
they know the only thing
looking out of Frank's eyeholes is Frank.
Leave him alone, says Jesse. *You just have to leave him*
    read.

COLUMBIA MISSOURI STATESMAN:
SEPTEMBER 27, 1864

Included here is a list of the members of Company A,
39th Regiment of Missouri Volunteers, lost near Centralia by
Anderson's Bushwhackers.

This is a correct list of all lost and missing. There may be
such a thing that one or two may come in, but nearly every man
was found and recognized on the field and scattered in the
neighborhood within a few miles, some as far off as six miles
from Centralia.

PENNY DREADFUL

Read here how the Missouri Guerrillas rode
    through storms of shot (how does
it go?) and anyway, the killing, you'll love it.
    Bloody Bill Anderson is not very efficient as
    guerrillas go but
he alone is worth the price of admission.
    Read how he rides in to the attack weeping and
    foaming at the mouth
after the federals killed his sisters in a Kansas City
    prison (they didn't
mean to, it was mainly that the building collapsed
    but to hear B.B. tell
it), tears rush down his face as he screams and fires,
    his mother
    throws her apron over her head and sobs,
    When will it all end?
    What do you mean, end? We just got started.
    Fletcher Taylor does heroics, Charlie Pitts starts
    fires, and
Frank, reserved as usual, takes time out for a good
    cigar.
    Jesse is hard to see
    he survives
    he is sixteen, he knows already to stay very
    quiet and
    aim for the middle
    he operates like an empty space, he shifts.
    Around him are atmospheres while in the
    foreground
    more heroics; a cover story.

THE END OF THE WAR: RETURNING
FROM AN ATTEMPTED SURRENDER:
JUNE 1865

This is the story of how it all started. Of how none
    of this was our
fault. We are trying to get home, telling ourselves
    this story.

We are taking the long way around, Jesse's chest
    wound leaks down his
shirt, it makes his belt sticky, at night we have to
    pour hot water

into his boots before we can get them off, he is
    soaked in fluids,
blood, and plasma, we only had one frying pan and
    Charlie Pitts

lost that. Jesse was riding into Burns' Schoolhouse
    with his hands
in the air, calling out he was coming in to
    surrender. We may be

guerrillas but we knew the etiquette, you're
    supposed to hand in
your sword or something and say, Thank you for
    the lovely war,

we'll do the same for you next time, and they fired.
    The first shot
took off half his middle finger, left hand, the
    second shot got

him in the chest and he went flying backwards out
    of the saddle
and took the bedroll with him. It was him and
    Fletcher Taylor.

Fletcher went back to get him. We laid up for a
    week in a triangular
hogpen somebody had knocked together in the
    corner of a rail fence.

Jesse said he's had it up to here with surrendering,
    if he keeps it
up it'll be the death of him. Then it was a matter of
    getting him

back across the Missouri River, riding on the
    strange sliding action
of the flooding water which was like a long material
    being drawn and

drawn underneath the ferry, the far shore coming
    at us in the night
with a slow, expanding movement. We walked past
    the detachment

of federals on the other side like visiting angels on
    our way to
some other annunciation. Jesse said it made him
    feel shameful

and incontinent to be breathing in two places at
    once and in front
of strangers. Charlie wakes us up too early in the
    mornings, he

has either nightmares or visions, he said he saw this
    giant
guinea hen in the oaks two mornings ago, skulking
    there with

its head bowed, quoting text from Leviticus. "It was
mournful," he said, "and fearsome." The worst
    thing about Pitts

is that somebody taught him to play the juice harp.
    Jesse rides
upright now, the wound is shutting itself like a
    bank vault

over his safe and valuable heart, nobody notices the
    rare skeletons
of birds or the sudden hair of milkweed, our pods
    are not broken,

the soul does not float on the octaves of the wind,
    all the wars
and reasons for wars are lost, but we will make up
    our own

reasons. We will make up our own story. At
    Appomattox the federal
government learned its fatal lesson; that anything
    can be solved

by the application of superior force. This is what
    happens to
winners. They begin to believe in winning.

And now the federal government believes in guns.
So do we.
We believe in guns.

JESSE MEETS HIS FUTURE WIFE, ZEE MIMMS

Here she is coming in with medicines, with
    bandages for
his infected life.
She can see everything in this big hole in his
    thoughts.
She can see the faulty reason beating and beating,
the lost causes,
the parts that are missing, the blood and the lungs.

There are things that live inside of wounds;
a certain memory fixed in his body forever,
a hole in the heart of Dixie, just south of his
    breastbone.
It was the last time he ever exposed his heart.
It was the last time he ever put his hands
above his head
except for her.

Every man is owed a wife; wives live in a different
    country,
a country of women without civil wars, or trains, or
    motivations.
They arrive with bandages; he imagines they never
    surrender
except to him.

She will make a design of his life, a quilt pattern
rusty with blood, made up of the rags
of women's dresses.
Log Cabin, Courthouse Steps, The Road to
    California.

He says: Marry me.
He says: I want to be able to stop,
just stop and watch you,
a hawk pouring out of the long prairie air
carrying between your wings a commission from the
    fertile sun
and your soul, which will have to serve for us both
and move through us both
like a wind through the bottom fields
an invisible comb, I will be moved and marked
and finally harvested.
Why don't you marry me, he says. Tend to all these
wars, and the broken thoughts, and the open
    wounds.

THE KILLING OF JOHN W. SHEETS: GALLATIN, MISSOURI, 1865

This is a stick-up:
your money or your life.
We are beginning to understand they will always
    choose the money
but a force has been filling Jesse for days, he is
    under
pressure or water,
he turns at the door of the bank and you could see
his whole soul and the entire static charge pour out
not once but five times.
The Gallatin Farmer's Bank crashed with the noise—
flashes, bangs, hot blue surprises.
Life flies out of the man with his hands up
like the air from a balloon.

Jesse's blaze-faced sorrel horse bolts and drags him
down the main street of Gallatin
banging his head off the town pump.
I pulled him up behind, my horse sank and lunged
carrying two grown men and a sack of dollars,
two heavy men and a sack full of money.
He said he thought he was going to get blown away
but it was kind of an exciting feeling.

TESTIMONY
Frank's trial
by General Jamin Matchett

I lived three miles from Winston at the time of the
robbery. Believe I saw Frank James at my residence on July 14,
1881. A Mr. Scott was with him. One of the party rode a bay,
the other a sorrel with two white hind legs. I came downstairs
to the front door. They wanted to know if they could get
dinner. I said I would see my wife, who objected somewhat, as
she was washing, to which they remarked they were in no
hurry, and I then told them they could be accommodated.
When they rode up I noticed they were wearing heavy goods
for that time of year and had gum coats or blankets strapped
to the saddles. The defendant said his name was Willard
. . . and came from the Shenandoah Valley. I inquired of
Willard where he had been between the Shenandoah Valley
and this section, and never answered me, but said, "What do
you think of Bob Ingersoll?" We discussed Bob for some time,
till we differed, so that I went to my library for a volume of his
lectures, and he read some till he fell asleep. [After dinner]:
Willard wanted to pay for the dinner, and I declined at first,
but finally took fifty cents. In conversation with Scott he ob-
served he would take me for a minister of the Christian
Church, and I answered that I was. He said he thought if he

ever united with the church he would join the Christian Church and referred to his wife as a Presbyterian. Willard acquiesced in that, but said there was no man ever lived like Shakespeare, and declaimed a piece and remarked, "That's grand!" which observation I endorsed. Finally Scott said something about going and I invited them, if they ever came that way, to call again, which they said they would be pleased to do, that they were going to Gallatin, where Willard said he had not been for ten years.

Cross-examined: I am this confident the defendant is the man who stopped at my house that if he hadn't paid for the dinner I would say, "Mr. Willard, I would be pleased to have the amount of that board bill." [*Laughter*]

ROBBING BANKS: 1865–1876

After a while they get good at it,
it becomes easy and practiced;
like anybody who does the same trick over and over
    they
get bored.

Charlie is still setting fires, playing
the juice harp, Fletcher went to Oklahoma
a long time ago, the Youngers argue with
each other about land or general principles,
Frank wants to go somewhere and farm.

Jesse keeps them at it, the only solution
for the boredom is to make mistakes once
in a while, or get married, or rob
something more complicated.
So he does all three.
One of these solutions is fatal.

It was back when the art was still primitive:
    they used cap-and-ball
    getaway horses
    everything was slow motion and
four-four time,
    a ballad in fact, with end-stopped lines
predictable
    nothing could move faster than a running horse
except trains, the telegraph, or
    the human mind.

Maybe the human mind is not as fast
as we thought.

REWARD

Western Union Telegraph Company, Jefferson City,
    Missouri, December 24,
1869. Rec'd at Independence, Missouri, Attention
    Sheriff of Clay County.

You will at once organize, arm and equip as militia
    thirty or more men and
aid Tomlinson Deputy Sheriff of Clay County if
    called on in capturing
or killing Frank James and Jesse James or hold such
    force in readiness
to aid you in such capture or killing if they be
    found in your county.
The state will pay expense of force for actual
    service and five hundred
(500) dollars for capture and killing of each. I write
    by mail. J.W. McClurg

PAULETTE JILES

WANTED POSTER

Jesse Woodson James: five feet eleven inches tall, brown hair, regulation killer-blue eyes. In photographs appears to be considering shooting the photographer. Does not test out well. Approaches casual strangers in an intimate way and interferes massively in their private lives. Is trapped in the dead hole and neither moves nor changes. Steals horses. Inhabits a discolored landscape through which only one, treacherous path is known to pass. Has the appearance of many ballistics with a flat trajectory. This man is occupied by an army of scars, tip of middle finger left hand missing, and one large scar on chest which oft has spoken with bloody lips. Is always breaking out afresh. Cultivates a desperado aura and can most often be seen in the penny dreadfuls, spotted regularly in novels, poems, ballads, and folktales. Men claiming to be James can be differentiated from him in that they pose willingly in front of cameras, they make political speeches. These people are not the genuine article and are confused. Jesse James was never confused about anything in his life, which will last exactly thirty-seven years, five months, three days, fourteen hours, and ten minutes.

ESCAPES

The front end of the horse is the suspension,
the back end is the drive,
in sudden plunges down shaly slopes your
heels are jammed down, the Achilles tendon
taut as a bowstring, providing forward impetus and if
you come to a sudden halt caused by things such as
bullets or fence rails you
will be shot from the saddle like a bolt from a
crossbow, you
will decorate trees, that whiteoak there for
instance, they call them hanging trees.

The detectives who are not far behind in
geospace or relative time on this
train of thought will crowd up on
their present tense, they will
fire at will, they will
look into each other's eyes, it will
be a kind of true love,
    they will all shoot each other.

Or maybe they will try to turn him like spies or
informers are turned we need a man like you Jesse
and have been looking for somebody of your caliber
to give out our press releases
    a kind of cosmic postman
America's Candygram, a Western Union
of all our underground intentions
our hard copy whose statement is this:
bang.

Sitting up all night in Dick Liddle's
dirty whorehouse near Richmond by lantern
light he's filing down some metal piece and
    clearing his throat, he's waiting
for them,
    he is either crazy or so self-contained that
there is no room for anything else but himself and that's no heroics, it's just the simple
single-mindedness of rattlesnakes.
    A bullet stops the detective's horse
the detective emerges from a hard run into a
    treetop
    there's something I've been meaning to tell you
    and
that is, I don't like it when you come up
    behind me like that.

BANDITS' WIVES

What Zee is doing all these years is a mystery, or
  maybe not so
much mysterious as ignored
    no different from any other housewife in the
    nineteenth century,
in Missouri
    she has to balance everything carefully, how to
    make Jesse the
center of her life but yet not become too
    dependent, after all, her
husband's work takes him away from home all the
    time, she has to make
some decisions by herself
    but then on the other hand she can't get too
    independent, Jesse
likes to be the head of the household, you know
    how it is, the money
she spends is not her own, it's not Jesse's either but
    let that go
for now
    can you imagine being engaged to a bank
    robber for seven years and
he's your first cousin besides, the marriage was
    fairly quiet
    Oh well it's all in the family and those Missouri
    rural clans are
tight
    Zee never wanted to end up like Belle Starr or
    Cattle Kate or
Poke Alice, those violent whores are attractive to
    historians but

they are usually diseased or dead after a while, the
    whores I mean,
and besides it's no fun having people spit on your
    skirt
        Zee is a good Missouri girl from the right
        background
        her life and that of Frank's wife Annie is the
        kind of life you
have to imagine or invent, such as the time
        the chimney fire nearly burnt the house down
        and Zerelda said
you have to pour salt down the chimney! and sent
    Annie up on the roof
with a washpan full of salt and Annie's petticoat
    lace caught on a
nail and it all tore off in a strip and nobody noticed
    it till later,
Frank saw this strip of lace hanging from the roof
    gutter like a celebration,
        yes, everybody laughed about it for years, and
        the time
        Frank taught Annie to play poker and so Annie
        went over to Zee's
house with a pack of cards and taught her, and
    then Zerelda caught them
playing at gambling and said what the hell are the
    people at the New
Hope Baptist Church going to think about this? so
    Zee hid the cards
in one of Jesse's socks and Jesse never did figure
    out where they came
from and the time
        Zerelda borrowed Annie's little portable sewing
        machine and never

gave it back no matter how many times Annie asked
    her for it, and one
night Frank came in and said, *We've got to go to
    Tennessee, right now,*
get the kids ready, they'd done another bank robbery
    or something,
so Annie and Zee went over in the middle of the
    night and got the
sewing machine and hid it in the wagon so they
    were halfway to Jefferson
City before Zerelda even knew it was gone. When
    they were going along
in the wagon Annie said, "Well, I guess now I'm as
    big a robber as you
are, Frank, ha ha ha," and Frank didn't know what
    the hell to make of
that and the time
    Jesse and two of the gang were at home doing
    as little as possible
and Zee said she was feeling like homemade sin
    with this cold, "Jesse,
give me a hand with the house, would you?" and
    he did; you talk about
a desperate outlaw doing the dishes, wearing that
    Navy Colt five-shot
revolver, standing at the sink, soap bubbles caught
    in the blonde hair
of his forearms, singing "I'm A Good Old Rebel"
    and he said, "Honey, I'll
get the sitting room," and he lifted both hands
    above his head to straighten
a picture of Dan Patch whereupon Robert Ford
    shot him in the back twice
at close range.

JESSE IS THROWN OUT OF THE NEW HOPE BAPTIST CHURCH
(Founding preacher, Reverend Robert James)

Minutes of the New Hope Baptist Church,
Kearney, Missouri
August 12, 1876

The covenant of the New Hope Baptist Church
was called for and read.
A motion that the church get seven spittoons
for the use of the
congregation.
Carried.
It was requested Sister Dixie Thompson be
excluded from the church,
she being found guilty of dancing. Moved that the
hand of fellowship
be withdrawn.
Carried.
Brother Elias Halloway confessed to having
made a false impression
and requested forgiveness. He having made suitable
amends, the question
was considered.
Forgiveness voted.
The case of Brother Jesse Woodson James
being considered, charges
of revelry, robbery, murder, intemperance, and
other un-Christian acts
being preferred, and he manifesting an impenitent
spirit, motion that
the hand of fellowship be withdrawn and he be
excluded from the church.

Carried.
On motion of Brother Hancock, Sister
Georgina Williams to be excluded
from the fellowship of the church upon charges of
    walking disorderly
and having run off to join the Campbellites.
    Carried.
    After sermon by pastor, the doors of the church
    were opened to
membership. None responded.

    Clerk: Jon Burnett

FOLK TALE

One day Frank and Jesse and Bob and Cole were
    riding down the road
to home with saddlebags full of gold. And they
    came on a farm where a
woman was out doing dishes in the yard. They were
    all hungry so they
stopped and said,
    Say, ma'am, would you cook us some dinner,
    we are real hungry
    (They didn't have any restaurants in those days,
    my mother explains).
    And the woman said,
    Hell no, can't you tell a person's doing a
    laundry when you see it?
    But, ma'am, we are real hungry, and we will
    pay you for it.
    No, I ain't going to do it, she said.
    But look here, you could cook us a chicken, I
    see you got a lot of
chickens there and I'll even kill one for you.

And he whipt out his pistol and shot the head
off a chicken.
Well now, since you done kilt that chicken you
can just gut it and
pluck it, she said. She was so mad she was hopping
around the yard, lookt
like somebody killing snakes with a switch.
And all the boys razzed Jesse and laught at him
and shoved him off
his horse and he had to sit down and gut and pluck
that chicken. And she
went and fried it for them and charged them a high
enough price for it,
I can tell you. And the boys never let him live it
down, when they would
be riding hard away from the law and they saw
some chickens somebody would
yell
Oh, Jesse, I want my dinner, go shoot me that
chicken. Oh, Jesse, we're
hungry, blow the head off that rooster, will you?
There are good days and bad days in the life of
a bank robber. My
mother swears this story is true. The farmer's wife
was trying to teach
them that you have to eat what you kill.
Think of yourself as a chicken.

FOUND POEMS

*Trial of Frank James: Testimony: Clarence Hite's
Confession*

Jesse killed Ed Miller. He killed him in Jackson or
Lafayette counties last spring was a year ago. They were in a

fuss about stopping to get some tobacco, and after riding some distance, Ed shot at Jesse and shot a hole through his hat and then Jesse turned and shot him off his horse. The watch I got out of the Blue Cut robbery is at home. Just before I was arrested I hid it between the bed ticks. Frank gave the jewelry to his wife he got out of the Blue Cut robbery. Jesse said last summer if he only knew on what train Governor Crittenden was he would take him off and hold him for a ransom—thought he could get about $25,000.

CONFESSIONS OF GANG MEMBER CHARLIE PITTS, KILLED AT NORTHFIELD, SEPTEMBER 7, 1876

I rode into Northfield, Minnesota, with voices in my
    head telling me forget it,
it's not worth it, but I stopped listening to them
    ever since these voices
I mentioned told me to eat axle grease for my sins
    when I was ten and I
ate it and was damn sorry. Nothing east of
    Hundred and Two Mile River
except big dead chickens and rusty pig snouters
    nowadays. Upside my head
is a strawberry mark big as a dollar. This means I
    have good luck and
foresight and get flashes of things that come up out
    of the back of my head.
Listen to the happy pistols clicking and saying their
    piece. Nothing makes
Jesse so content as shooting people. We got other
    people living inside us,
just under the skin, these inside people are not
    male nor are they female,

they are kind of purple-black like the skins of
    garden onions, and they
have the same pearly shine. Last night mine begun
    to slide out of me
through the hole in the top of my head through
    which so much else has
escaped too, when I was looking after my horse
    Sweet Pea, she had a great
big locust thorn stuck in her gums. This onion
    creature began to get
fed on the lantern light and slide out of my person.
    I would have been
struck blind and dumb, I would have went and eat
    axle grease again. This
is the thing makes everybody kill people.

Here we go up to Northfield now, this is us getting
    close to Northfield.
We're going to die here and get shot up until we
    look like sieves. They're
gonna run us into a swamp and yell, Surrender,
    and one of the Youngers is
gonna yell back, We don't surrender much, and it
    will get writ in a book.
I'll never get to tell anybody or any one person
    what it is makes us kill
people. Whatever we get in life is provisional. It
    will eat you in
sections and you will die all at once. This thing has
    been talking out
of my mouth all my life and now I will be hit in
    that selfsame mouth.
People who have messages are struck dumb and
    folks who don't have a damn
thing to talk about never shut up. Oh, God, how I
    loved shooting people.

Me and my onion woulda blown up whole cities if
    I'da had the gunpowder.
I will finally win the argument with the purple-black
    party inside, which
was flying out toward the simple lantern in the barn
    and Sweet Pea and
the world. Leaving me to voices and rye straw. This
    is Northfield, my
Minnesota onion war.

POCKETS

In the pockets of the corpse of Bill Chadwell, killed
    at Northfield,
there was found a map of the Western states, a
    pocket compass, a box
of salve, a Howards gold watch, an article on the
    Yale lock torn from the
local paper, gold sleeve buttons with enameled
    leaves, and a gold ring.

In the pockets of Clell Miller, killed at Northfield,
    there was found
a gold Waltham watch, ten cents, an advertisement
    for a Halt's safe with
an engraving depicting a robber giving up on trying
    to enter it, and a
business card from a St. Peters, Minnesota, livery
    stable.

In the pockets of Charlie Pitts, alias Samuel Wells,
    there was found
five cents, a label from a whiskey bottle, and a
    Spanish onion.

FRANK GETS NERVOUS ABOUT
JESSE'S KILLER INSTINCTS

You grow blue in the steamy days of July, the
    depths of heat in your
shrunken house in St. Jo, blind shadows.

I hear cries, shouts, the final appeals of men
    working out some
predictable destiny in a swamp, out of ammunition,
    crude as ore.
These sounds appear to come from my dreams.

Sometimes you are there, soaked in oak shadows,
    the hard shells of
mental ammunition, green shade moving like
    suspicious neighbors where
next door is always full of armed men, the very
    guinea hens call your
name as if it were the announcement of a fabulous
    act, the very yard
dogs appear quiet and stiff with intent as
    undertakers, nobody pities
your hard, red karma.

This is what was made of you, stuffed into a
    five-button cutaway suit,
the fingers into gloves, arms into the linen shells of
    drover's dusters;
we see you coming a mile off, riding right through
    Clay County and into
folklore, clashing with real federal silver dollars,
    realer than we
have seen in a long, long time.

Through the blackberry and sumac east of
    Otterville, at Rocky Cut,
you get the drop on everybody. Talk about trains.
    It was so daring
and so daylight.

It was too bad about Northfield. If only you had
    asked the right people.
But all along the turnpike behind, here comes our
    long company: Captain
John W. Sheets, D. W. Griffith, Joseph Lee
    Haywood, Frank Wymore, Frank
McMillan, the unarmed federals we were shooting
    three at a time at
Centralia.

What I will answer for is not the federals or the
    bank clerks but that I
came back for you at Low Gap, full of persuasion
    and leading horses.
I cocked you like a pistol, you were efficient and
    fifteen. "And I
said: Oh, that I had wings like a dove! For I would
    fly away and be at
rest. Lo, I would flee far away and live in the
    wilderness." Psalm 55.

The young men who are joining us now are
    treacherous and don't remember
the war. Something moves and grows in me like an
    apology, a hope, a
mass demonstration. At night when I sleep my
    hands fall each to one side
empty as clothes without people in them. I think
    this is how husbands
are, in their own beds, in their own time.

RAISING HOGS

September of 1876 Frank rides quietly away from
    Northfield
toward Tennessee like the whole thing was just
    embarrassing;
it was hardly human, he won't let Jesse drag him
    into
these things again.
Frank's going to Tennessee and raise hogs
he crosses the river at Cape Girardeau
it's a very hot river town, the Mississippi is actually
    hot
it's steaming, nobody asks who you are.
He is seduced by all the simple normal people at
    the
ferry landing, he will send for Annie and the kids,
he is crossing the river into Little Egypt
he's going into agriculture as if it were a religion
the Holy Fire Church of Prophesy and Pigs.
There will be peace in Waverly County
they have relatives down there they can count on
never go anyplace you don't have relatives.
It's all in how a man comports himself
walking upright amongst the swine.

JESSE: HIDING OUT IN TENNESSEE

He is having an adventure. It is very seductive and
thrilling. He has changed names many times now. He is hiding
out in Tennessee, a hot night, an old farmhouse, listening to
the clock's neurotic metronome, nobody knows where he is.
He finds this very moving. He moves through the Tennessee
night and nobody knows where he is. He changes names.

He investigates things with complete freedom. He looks into drawers. He is carrying a gun in case somebody interrupts him. He is the secret agent of a great and important cause, the last of the underground Confederate Army, the Dixie Mafia, the End of the World Gang. Everybody down here thinks he is a Mr. Howard, and the people in Kentucky thought he was a Mr. Woodson, and the people somewhere else will think he is a Mr. Hite. Behind all these names is a sentence of death, which he has escaped now three times: once from fright, once from spite, and once from a desire to show off.

All day long people have been looking at him and choosing what to think about him, there have been whispers behind his back, he has nodded amiably at certain statements. But now in the private night his image and impression is not being appropriated by all the daylight people who walk the daylight earth down here in Tennessee. Now nobody knows where he is and so they cannot think about him. Only he can think about them. He can think about them and watch them from under his hat and choose not to appear to them. He cannot now be robbed of his face or taken to jail or taken aback or think straight. He is not really thinking straight.

It was really just a process of getting rid of his name, and after that his image, and after that his body, and after that his presence. Now what burns in him is match struck at the very center of his brain or mind. A coal-oil lamp is sucking the thick night air into itself in the middle of the table. It's going to be hot all night long. The coal-oil lamp is hot too but he has to have light to disappear by. He realizes he is going through somebody's desk drawers and he has a revolver in his left hand. He's going through Frank's desk drawers. It's a scene. He's having an adventure. You can't have an adventure unless you have a gun. His wife and children sleep as if they were suspended in spring water and the whippoorwill is releasing note after note in a rain of musical fluid. This is what the adventure is all about, it's about Frank. Frank knows his real name. The moon rises from behind a hill, it focuses on Tennessee and out of the mind of the moon walks a blaze-faced sorrel horse. The devil's trumpet flower opens its red mouth and says, *Yes.* Jesse listens as the horse speaks in the language of human beings. Don't talk back. Don't say anything. Because you have abandoned your daylight self with such urgency and such joy, because nobody knows your name, there is the danger of being absorbed by the language of animals.

He realizes he lives among *vegetables.* The oak forest cover, the tulip trees, the standing field corn all night long hacking and sharpening its coarse leaves, down in the bottom fields under the moon. The Cherokee Bukka-man hacks and sharpens his coarse leaves, down in the bottom fields, all night long. Human slavery never seemed to bother him much. It changes names.

Without an identity he begins to grow huge and to evaporate. He can't sit quietly and watch it happen by the light of a coal-oil lamp. It would be a kind of surrender, here in Tennessee, without a name. Without a name anything can take you over, anything can fill you with its language. In his brother's desk he discovers an envelope; it has a name on it, Dick Liddle, and the return address says Richmond, Missouri; evoking the grubby and restless pleasures of Cracker Neck. Gratified, he puts it back. It is a sign. It is a portent. All this night he has been adventuring around without a name, going to and fro in the earth, walking up and down in it. In Missouri something is waiting, but at least he will have a name for it to happen by. "And not even the angels shall know the hour of his coming." Back to Clay County, where at least they will have the right

name to put on the headstone. All the visions cloud over and
then shatter; he blows out the lamp.

TESTIMONY
Dick Liddle, who turned state's evidence at Frank's trial

The baggageman was standing in the side door and
Frank seized him by the leg and jerked him out of the car and
left him on the ground. The engineer pretended he could not
move the train as the brakes were down. We then struck him
with a piece of coal and told him we would kill him if he did
not start the train. He then threw open the throttle and started
it under a full head of steam. Frank jumped up in the cab and
stopped it. I went back after Jesse, who was still in the express
car. Jesse jumped first and then I followed. We got $700 or
$800 that night in packages. It was all good money. Jesse killed
McMillan. Frank was in a rage about it. Jesse said, "I thought
the boys were pulling out from me. I wanted to make them a
common band of murderers to hold them to me."

ASSASSINATION

I

Jesse is not being helped by all his good reasons,
his Black Flags, his secret underground army.
Behind him is a trail littered with corpses.
To other people Kansas City and St. Jo look
     normal
but to Jesse they look like something out of a
penny dreadful, maybe
*Frank Reade, the Inventor, Chases the James Boys
with His Steam Man.*

You never know who has been taken over by these
mechanical devices, the offers of rewards,
Zee or anybody might be one of Them.

The creak of the floorboards and also
turning a page of the *St. Louis Post-Dispatch*
makes a sound so loud
it thunders like distant artillery.
Concentrate on the print, read the
river news:
The river is at 24 feet, 10 inches.
The *Henry Frank* has come in from Memphis
carrying 9,226 bales of cotton, steamboats
are crossing the water, the two sides of
his heart are crashing together with mounting
violence.

By now he only has these two alternatives:
he wonders what it would be like to be killed
        instead
to be the innocent victim,
he thinks all victims are innocent,
it is familiar and inevitable as a Bible story.
He turns to straighten the picture of a
racehorse, his back
to history, the final solution.

11

Bring on the angels of rain, of newspapers and
celebrating sheriffs, Jesse has reached
his evening.
Now everybody in St. Jo remembers
they sold him coal or shook his hand
or petted his dog.

James W. Graham takes the death picture
with 8 × 10 dry plates;
they had to rope him to a board to get
him upright, there is something strange
about the picture, his fingers appear to
be missing. It was Graham's first day
at work.

III

Jesse's gift was the skill of sundering, parting,
to divide the soul from the body, the flower from
    the
stem, the banks from their money, the being from
the life it held lit and sheltered
in an irreducible heart;
patron saint of the dismembered, the exploded,
the spilled and the broken

and his last gift was to make a secret of everything.
Zee weeps and sells his guns for groceries;
    —6 dozen eggs at 8 cents a pound
    —1 pound of sugar at 7 cents a pound
    —1 1/4 yards domestic at 15 cents a yard
    —4 1/2 pounds of butter

Everybody splits and
Frank surrenders.

FOUND POEMS
The St. Joseph Western News, May 19, 1882

Robert Ford, the slayer of Jesse James, is the biggest
man in Kansas City. He is appearing on the stage three nights
a week, for which he is paid $100 a night. The morbid curiosity
of the people of Kansas City is beyond human comprehension.

CONFESSIONS OF A SORT: JESSE

If I could have my body back again
    for a little while, my good old body, the one
that fits the handmade gloves and the riding boots,
everything the way I liked it, what bargain
    can a person make
    nothing to replace it but
    small shines in the shadow of wild underbridges
    a broken china woman in the long pools of the
    Meremec
    the Gasconade,

    think how little I wanted.

I only wanted your money,
the lives of a few individuals nobody
would have heard of otherwise,
    the joy of some derailed trains
    my name in *The St. Louis Post-Dispatch*
    the secret life in the backwoods
    people to shoot
    cornbread, good horses, Sundays at home
    the happy splinters of express-car doors
    starbursting into the celebratory air
the good old boys and the private war cries, our
conspiracy of cruelty and bad manners, the iron
wives we invented at leisure.

What would you give to have my world of limited
    distance
with a safe horizon and no overhead missiles, where

everybody had a biography, a pistol, the old happy
    aggression
we thought would last, like the soil and the rivers,
forever?

    You invent murder so big you can't even think
    that big.
    The planet is so small you can't even think that
    small.
    I am your last warhead. Behind me is the
    evening.

If I could have my body back again
    I would release the thing that inhabited me
    that went out at night, with a gun, looking for
    more
    it would fly out of me in some lamplight.

Then we could ride toward Green Ridge
where there is a tavern with
    neon advertisements for Pabst and Michelob
pickled eggs swimming in a jar
a jukebox and a pool table
we could lean over the cosmic
geosynclines of the baize, like
divine forces, we could smash the balls
like tiny planets.

FRANK SURRENDERS: OCTOBER 5, 1882

"I have known no home, I have slept in all sorts of
    places . . . I am tired
of this life of taut nerves . . . I want to see if there
    is not some way out
of this."

Since I was seventeen I have carried
on my person
twenty pounds of iron.

I want to see if there is not
some way out of this.

I am expecting now the approach
of the psalmist, like a sherriff
he will disarm me and speak
his arresting word: Appomattox.

Or I will be a piñata
and the psalmist, with childlike erratic blows
will break this heavy clay
and let all my common and inexpensive gifts
rain down on this world, this
private war, this
terrible birthday party.

And now I have made up my mind,
who do I surrender to?
Who will accept these obsolete and heavy
sidearms, who is going to break
my hardshell case with a magic stick?

THE TRIAL OF FRANK JAMES, 1882

As he lays his pistols down on the governor's
    polished desk
we can see him pausing for the photographer
among the globe lamps, facing the man with the
    black hood
on his head, who is using
an 8 × 11 dry plate with a double plate holder.

We, too, are looking for the right authority
to whom we may hand in pistols we do not have
and confess to robberies we have not committed
and apologize to corpses we have not murdered.
We, too, hope for a trial packed with old
    confederates.
We expect, like you, to get off scot-free, revealing
little of our lives or personal disasters before
an admiring crowd
stripped of nothing but our sidearms. You can
    always
buy more sidearms.

If we, too, could find the right one to whom to
    surrender—
but we are choosy—
before whom we could unbuckle everything and lay
    down
our old defenses, drop them
on a mahogany desk, and the Authority, looking on
with mild and kindly eyes, would not know or
    would have
forgotten what we have done
    unspeakable things
which now seem like nightmares or war footage or
    blue movies.
And the Authority says, That's okay, Frank or
    whatever
your name is, it was a typographical error, you were

assigned the wrong parents, the wrong war, an extra
Y chromosome by mistake.

No one ever says I am your prisoner without
believing somehow in clemency, in mercy
    or in short memories, it is

not something said
by battered wives or people
    held in unnumbered rooms or
children with cigarette burns. It is not said
by those who can no longer talk.

FRANK RETIRES

I'll shake hands with anybody that
walks up the road.
At the age of forty-nine almost anybody who
    matters
to me is dead,
in the clean fields
in the simple and uneventful woods,
most by violence.

When I handed in my guns, everything stopped.
It stopped, and there was no more screaming,
the sound of running horses and black powder,
it was all gone.

How slowly people move
and with what patience the horses search
for horseweed in the fields.
I am amazed, I am amazed with what fixed intent
we move from the porch into supper.
I sit down carefully, I am astonished now at
    everything—
the plates with flowers, my big old mother praying
over the food and my shiny hands.
I am free as the unemployed goldenrod and the
    clouds
move in from Kansas, dry and clean.

THE LAST POEM IN THE SERIES

The scholar who studies the life of Jesse and Frank
    needs solitude.
This person approaches a cabin through fields and
    some woods, slowly,
seriously, as if they were going there to take vows.
    Everything else
has flown away.

There are no other people.

The flame shapes of cedar and scrub oak are
    drawing something huge and
nourishing out of the clay subsoil, a substance we
    can only guess at.
Johnson grass burns in its low fires, the color of
    prairies. The
sky at this hour and season is a gemmed glass, blue
    and refreshing,
it has raised our broken sight many times before
    this. In the cabin
are the voices of the original angers. They wait. It
    is up to the
person who wants solitude to abandon them. If you
    release them they
will fly off like birds or trains. Your skull is very
    small under
the awning of the universe. All the time you walk
    toward the cabin
huge electrons are raining down on you out of the
    heart of the sun.

What do you think of that? Before you can step in
    the door, surrender
and disarm. It is a kind of bank, and can be robbed
    only by the
anti-bandit.

This is the end of the story of Jesse and Frank.
The grass pours by in the white wind like a river
    out of the hill
country, flooding and breaking, and you are
    smoothed by its lengthy
currents.

And so you walk in the door of the bank, your
    hands are empty.

Whoever We May Finally Be, Said Rilke

It is horrible to look on the dead at Belsen,
the sinews, hollows, straining arms of the Jews.
But how much worse to see them piled on the
    ground
and think of those thin nudes of El Greco's
aspiring to heaven in Christian ecstasy.
To remember the strange Venetian luxury
of his bodies while watching two women
in German uniforms dragging more of the dead
and throwing them loosely down into the pits.
Seeing the bodies at Belsen is not simple.
Bodies the shape of their bones, mouths,
and the fresh holes in the earth.
The illusion of tenderness in the arms and hands.
The people who were in charge standing in warm
    coats
on the dirt ridge above watching the excavations fill
with corpses. Other soldiers carrying other dead.
Two pulling a body with its lax hand dragging
on the dirt. Worst of all is seeing
how beautiful these bodies are in their ruin.

Transcending

The small marble head I've found
is worn away by eight thousand seasons.
No eyes, nose, or mouth. Only shape
and the stylish way she fixed her hair.

Inside the Same As Out

There is a violent sound of too many chickens
in one place. A child sobbing and the mother's
    voice
and the sobbing stops. Someone drags a metal
    wagon
over cobbles in the street outside. But the sea
    carries
its one silence no matter what the weather makes it
    do.
Peace remains always where it is. Where those in
    love
walk for a long time and then see the other
    standing
by a wall. He makes a formal speech, as one plants
a tree in an empty world. Not to talk.
For what is inside is known without words.
There may be sex, but not much touching
    beforehand.
It is not what you call romance. An orange is seen,
then eaten. Makes a ringing everyone can hear.

Since History Is a Marriage
of Geography and Race

All week I've been thinking
About the house on Interboro
Avenue with its wood floors
And throw rugs and old upright
Piano, about the amazing flight
Laundry took down the stories
Of its chute. I've remembered
That bottle of holy water
For the first time in years,
And sitting next to my aunt
At table after they'd buried
My Uncle Arch. I've been thinking
About the landing at the top
Of the stairs in the old house
On Sixteenth Street, how standing there
Made me feel as if I were hovering
Up against a corner of the room.
I've even been dreaming about
The waters on the front porch
In Emsworth, about one cousin's
Braces and another's breasts,
The round dark of the car barn
In which trolleys were housed
Overnight. All week long
I've found myself surrounded
By closets, basement shelves,
The green fire of the elm tree
Whose branches shook my sleep.
I've been struck by the ways
Of knowing such places bring

To life, by a friend's father
Who listed the same old address
No matter where he happened
To be living. Unlike me
He knew he'd move back in time
To become part of the light
Angling across the floorboards,
The flowers which turned to amber
In the honey of his walls.

Road Kills

Lately, wherever I walk I find them,
Halfway to heaven on the roads.

They are becoming new again.
The insides of their bodies glisten,

Their bones jut into the sky
Like girders or fresh-cut planks.

All over again they keel into time,
Tufts of them fraying loose

In the gravelly storms of traffic.
Watching the bowels turn black

As fallen apples, the skulls
Break down into the asphalt,

I think about the two-hour life
As matter your baby sank through,

Lungs like small wet leaves,
And the world flooding his eyes

Like headlights. If I told you
That death begins in such sweetness

As any of us would drown in,
Would it help? If I said

Death is the place we start from
Out of each hard loss and delivery?

Those brief pounds weigh me down—
To have nothing to give you

But what passes for resurrection
And then simply passes from the roads.

Fire Poem

This was before the dark
Behind our house was torn down
And sectioned into suburbs,
Before the trolleys stopped
Humming like parlors of light.

I had yet to unfasten the pale
Fronts of blouses, or labor
All night in the deafening mills.
Slag heaps were still sunsets
On the far shores of Clairton

And railroads simply carried
Their ignitions past our home.
It would be years until ECT's
Began burning my father's brain,
And years more than that until

He was flashed all to ashes.
I had never even heard the word
Incineration before I helped
Unload the car. Before I stood
Swaying as the man slid back

The immense slab of concrete
And I saw beneath our streets
That all I had thought of as solid
Was empty instead, and enormous,
And a place of continuous flame.

The Anniversary of Weather

Once again, this year,
  I am not making mincemeat,
    Encrusting the great fist of suet,

Hanging it below me
  To burn in the cellar dark.
    November's come around again.

A year's worth of weather
  Has fallen through the corn.
    Again this year I am not going home

To the woods behind my house,
  Or to the house my parents sold,
    Or the streets I cannot find

Even in my dreams—
  Everything changing but the way
    Rivers keep siphoning the land

And my aunt bends to her oven,
  Every year of my youth,
    To carry back into the room

The jeweled flesh of mincemeat.
  Walking out among the fields
    Again this November

I think of her descending
   The cold steps to her cellar
      Where the suet hangs like a moon.

Daily now I imagine her
   Counting the weather down
      The season's familiar notches

And crawl space of the bones.
   My hands take up weeds,
      Feathers, sylphs of peppergrass,

As if by holding such frailty
   I was keeping faith
      With whatever riffles the surface

Of the pond or flutters
   In the bark of the hickories.
      I watch as she takes all of it—

Wing, blood, and moonlight—
   And puts it in the pie,
      Then turns in the dark toward home.

The Knife

It is always in December,
No matter when, this whiteness
Cindering into gray,
The flakes as light as ashes.

I stand on my porch watching
Snow swirl down onto blacktop
Until it starts to haze.
Soon it will be covered.
At some point everything we are
Or have meant to be
Will be as endless and white.

Yet even here there are distances
I stare across to where
It's always summer, and all along
Alberta Street the maples
Float upwards in lamplight.

Whenever it is, Morgan and I
Are halfway through our teens
And dying for the sudden
Bird-shaped breasts of creatures
Who used to be girls.
Our aches are simpler then.
Our dreams are driving Chevies,
Moons on all their wheels,
Up and down the streets of heaven
In Homestead, Pennsylvania.

We have not yet stumbled
Against the furnaces of steel
Mill and marriage.
                    Tonight
It is his father who careens
Into the room, smiling and drunk,
And holding to his mouth
A blood-soaked towel
And the knife he's been using
To cut loose a tooth.

Through that smear of grin
He talks to us about the ways
To get at pain, about buckrubs
And legs gnawed off in traps.
His towel flowers the length
Of his song, the maples lift
Into night again this evening,
Light falling slantwise along
The branches.
                    Everywhere I look
It's cold, December,
The year sliding farther away.

And yet it is the knife,
Forged and honed, and the way
He holds it, that cuts, even now,
So the sharp air tastes of metal.

On the Blackness of Sidney

The first day he came to us, he was outside,
on the ledge, staring through the picture window,
burrs clinging to his haunches, patches of fur
    missing,
mad with hunger and dermatitis, fugitive from the
    woods,

accusing us, pressing his soundless cry against
    glass.
He ran off. Next day, we saw him beneath the blue
    spruce,
his body absorbed into the darkness of the ground,
eyes like lights risen from a depth. We knelt, and
    called,

saved him from a diet of crickets, removed swollen
    ticks,
black blood bursting over thumbnails, spoke to his
survivor's nervousness, arguing a world safe, where
    love
growls in every tree, mercy squeals, the heart fails.

We saved him again as we returned from the beach,
the smell of sand and sea clinging to towels
and folding chairs. He came limping toward us,
    wincing
at our touch, panting like an old miner with black
    lung.

His bladder blocked. Those little stones
accreted from his ashy fears, anger's alkali
    unfulfilled,
he would soon bloat like a child dying of hunger,
acting out the news of crop failures, helpless,

empathic. The vet removed his penis.
A urethra now wide, to pass the sediments of
    maleness,
made him no more female than Ethiopian marble
or the altered bulls of Miura. That didn't matter.

What astonished was his reaction to the anesthetic:
his balding stomach; a grayish pink showing
    between
his incipient nipples. It was knowing he wasn't
    ebony
to his bones. It was the soft feel of his baby skin,

the gradual, darkening fuzz of his body's
    assumptions,
the way he pulled at his fur, combing it with his
    teeth,
the tips of white hairs like slivers of moon-fire
flickering in the space between his golden eyes.

The Family

Annie Green,
mother of Roosevelt,
twenty-eight, of Georgia,
convicted of the kidnap,
rape, and murder
of a girl, eighteen,
watched his execution
by electric chair.
The papers said she
kept her calm.
A little tight about the lips,
but calm,
the boy a little tight
about the thighs
when they strapped him in,
but calm.
God was with him
in his innocence, he said.
He hoped He was with others,
he had been reborn.
His father,
though he wished to be there,
had to wait outside.
They were afraid
he would not keep calm.
When it was over
the doctor,
a little pale but calm,
emerged to tell him
mother and son were doing fine.

Music

The English horn,
however close it calls,
is always in the distance.

How clever of music
not to let the foxes know
how near the hunters.

The Moth

Skimming the pantry shelf
his motors were still running,
his wings slowing toward peace
when I brushed the moth away.
He became, all of him,
at that moment, ash.
All his body entered it,
devoted what solidity it had
to that thin performance
of mere stain.
It was as if,
scooping a finger to test for dust,
I had created it,
made of casual inquiry
small death.

My thumb's erasing
only spread it there
like a constable to shadows.
And I could feel its wealth,
this payment passed in darkness,
this loam more lasting than a life.

One Day

One day it will be like this.
The low sun will tilt above the sea
gleaming like a monocle,
as though a head bends to approve,
a slight smile at the horizon.

Suddenly it will seem to grow, perhaps to rise.
The man rocking on his balcony will blink,
not believing, but it will be true.

He will stand, as though wired to attention,
his lips will separate
dumb as a blinded infant for a spoon,
and he will all but know.

He will turn to his furniture and rooms
and run, as though the added distance,
the closed glass doors to the event avail,
and words will fall from him
like fruit from a tumbled basket.

He will scale steps to the street,
two, three, four at a time,
as though it were a matter of time,
as of course it is, and over his shoulder
the sun will be white now,
having bled its color to the sea,
the grass, the rail he cannot grasp.

And it will be no eye or disk,
no wafer for an easy morning tongue,
but the featureless mask above the birth
when the lights snap on, the last
bandstand shell of light the patient sees
before the darkness rises to his street.

He will not know
whether to keep his clothing for a canopy
or tear it from the bonfire
taking hold just now in the dry
wood of his bones, and a sudden
storm of bodies like his own
will blow with his question.

And the sun is an outrage now.
He holds his ears against it,
but like terrible news it is in his throat.
He is all breath and particular as angels,

one by one,
as the sky sets at the heel of the sun,
they sift back to where they were
and where they would be found.

Lovers

When I hear men boast about how passionate
they are, I think of two cleaning women
at a second-story window watching a man
coming back from a party where they had
lots of free beer. He's running in and out
of buildings looking for a toilet. "My Lord,"
the first woman says, "that fellow down
there surely does love architecture."

Maybe She Is Here

She might be here secretly.
On her hands and knees
with her head down a little, tilted
to peer around the doorjamb
in the morning, watching me before
I wake up. Only her face showing
and her shoulders. In a white slip,
her skin honey against the simple
white of the thin straps
and the worked edge of the bodice.
And her right hand a little visible.

Falling in Love Again

Two years after Michiko went away
he still wondered what the marriage
was like for her. He knew there must be
some things she didn't like. So he went
to her best friend and asked what
she complained about. It's all right,
he kept saying, I don't ask because
I'm afraid. It's because I want all
of her. Until the friend gave in.
"She said sometimes you made a noise
drinking your tea if it was very hot."

Stealing from Donald

Sometimes in the evening when the day cools
I cross the empty valley to see my friend.
Two months ago he told me a strange story
and I said there was a real poem in that.
He's been trying to write it ever since.
I did my version weeks ago, but it's still
his story. So I can't tell you what happens
over there outside his one-room, dirt-floored
hut most nights in the moonlight one by one.

A Ball of Something

Watching the ant walk under water along
the bottom of my saucepan is painful,
although he seems in no distress.
Walks at leisure, almost strolling, except
when he encounters a ball of something
and seems almost scared as he struggles free.
Afterwards, he continues on. Lifts his head
twice and pitches forward curled tight.
It's not clear whether that's the end.
Perhaps he's waiting for someone to pass
whose ankle he can grab and ask for help,
hoping for pity. But maybe not. Maybe
he just lies there hugging himself, smiling,
liberated at last. Dreaming of coming back
as Byron, or maybe the favorite dog.

The Difficult Beauty

The air full of pictures no matter where
you reach in. Great caverns in the earth bright
with electricity and covered with language.
Because you are on the fifth floor, on Sundays
you can look in the synagogue where people sing
in Spanish secretly together. You up there
trying to get the galleys marked which are so late
because of love that Yale threatens not to
publish the book at all. The noise finally
so loud you have to look outside and see everybody
gathered on Fourth Street to eat ice creams
and watch the guys carrying the naked woman
        down
the fire escape with difficulty who had been
promising all morning to jump. But best of all
are the gardens. Hidden places where they have
burned buildings and kept the soil poor
so the plants won't grow with vulgar abundance.
Like Japanese gardens made only of rocks and sand
so the beauty would not be obscured by
        appearance.
Like the maharajah who set aside the best
        courtyards
of the palace for the dandelions he imported
from England to be kept alive with difficulty
by the finest gardeners against nature.

Heart to Heart Talk

She recoils at being told
You've a heart as large as all
outdoors. Why for god's sake
outdoors? How large is that?
She sees her heart spanning
the Continental Divide,
a kind of pulsing red barrier,
a bloody barbed-wire fence.
Or resting on a rock ledge
half way down the side of
Whiteface Mountain, staining
the snow with its outrageous
ooze. What about a heart
fit for interiors,
one the very size of
lamplight on an open page
or a lump of amber to be
fondled and stroked like
Grecian worry beads?
She wants her heart handsize
and manageable, no sprawling
extravagance. A domestic ticker.

His heart was grandsize.
It contained a leaky valve
requiring surgery. He thought
he could outfox the experts
once again, catching the largest
salmon in the contest, telling
outlandish stories like a pro.

259

He thought his strength was as
the strength of ten because
his heart was as large
as all of Oregon: coastline,
forests, streams and cities
spilling their place names
all over the map.
Damned if he didn't
almost do it, trick death
out of this bighearted boy.

But death grew impatient,
waiting at the top of the dunes,
grinning in the sea salt spray
that whipped his face.
And down he went, a crash
of branches, limbs tearing
at the heart of the hill,
ripping the air on the expanse
of sand and scrub and rock.
He might as well be chopped
for kindling, loaded on a truck
and hauled home. What is this
great outdoors, anyway?
A mystery stop in her train of thought,
the station deserted, kiosk closed.

Coyly, to His Mistress

I beg to be excused.
My live-in lover has a
headache, sore throat,
cracked knucklebone,
faulty haircut, parking
ticket, scorched saucepan,
sudden run in her pantyhose.
She is unable to phone for
the rescue squad, osteopath,
cockroach control, paper
hanger, her personalized
shopper. Her throat is
too hoarse. She's lost her
voice, her nerve, her
alligator purse, her mind.
I know we had a date to
make love, make up, make
matzo-ball soup, tell
each other every little thing.
And you, poor thing, all the way
in from Albuquerque, Altoona,
Alabama, Great Neck. Great God,
you must try to
get yourself a bite to eat.
We must try to
get together real soon.
I'll be sure to
be in touch real soon.
I sure would like to
touch you.

The Lover

Lately I've taken to driving around
as in the homeless teenage 1950s,
gliding through stop signs,
careening past old ladies and not caring
from one end of town to another, wanting
to be not anyplace specific.

Close to thirty years since the Chevy
and nothing's changed.
Still railing at the moon,
yearning on a star,
more comfortable with longing than with anything
that ever took me in its arms.

Still looking for the cure
and still thinking of you
because, baby, the way I feel about you I wouldn't
    care
if you were male or female.

Kiss me.

Cynthia

When I take off your red sweatpants,
sliding them over the ass I love,
the fat thighs, and now my hands
are trembling, my tongue is muzzy,
a fire runs under my skin.

Cynthia's red-gold muff caught
the morning light as she strode from my bed,
upright and proud. Her body was
a vehicle for pleasure. It had carried us
into sleep as if we were children,
protected forever from the void and dark.

She slept with him
if at dinner he pleased
her. If he did not, she
did not. She was free
to choose, without
the drags of love.

Every day I wonder about you—
why it is your eyes look so wild,
sometimes. Other times, so naked,
so pure-blue naked. Your shields, you say,
speaking of your diaphragm, your contact lenses.
Nevertheless, you think of yourself as being at
    home
in this world in a way I am not.
I understand it is my myth-making intelligence
gets me in trouble, makes me want to fix you

as earth nourisher, source of comfort,
when it is what is lost and erratic in you
brings you to my bed, beatings against fate
or circumstance, stabbings toward transcendence
that leave us both bruised and happy in ourselves.

To be with her
was to be in a cloud
of sexual joy—hair, eyes,
speech. The merest
flick of her tongue
on a word set off
resonances.

I fell in love with
one of the poisonous tomatoes of America.

Mind-fucking at 3 A.M.
because where are you
and that's where you are.

At the instant of her coming, she makes a throaty
        sound.
It is back beyond words, low in the throat,
away from the tongue. I never try to translate it,
anymore than I would translate sunlight or deep
        shade.

Before sleep, C in my arms, her back towards me,
puts my right hand on her left breast. If I
could make an amulet of that.

She is beautiful to me
as she wakes from sleep,
sits straight up—
force, energy, and purpose
in her straight spine.

I wonder where her cunt is tonight
and her proud head. She did
make me happy, more than once.
One Sunday morning, light everywhere
in the living room, she on the couch
facing me, garbed in my blue bathrobe,
one breast shapely through the opening
of the robe while I drink my coffee, happy.

The last time
I went down on Cynthia
was the last time
though her petals
in the rose red light

She said she had taken on seven students the previous
night on her visit upstate, and that all had watched,
masturbating as each colleague performed. One had her
in the missionary position, one took her from behind,
one made her ride on top, one came in her mouth, one
had her lean over a table, one did her on his lap, one fucked
her up the ass. The last to have her, she said, because
he had come six times, had trouble achieving an erection.

After she had told all this to her lover, fiction or fact,
he became the eighth man.

    There'll always be room for you
    in my capacious vagina, she said.
    At the elevator door. Some parting.
    ("Capacious quiff" would have been catchier.)

    All the questions she asked him
    he answered from another life.

    He was trying to understand
    the nature of the pain.
    Maybe when a woman
    aborts a child
    it is like this: killing
    something in oneself.
    Someone else has already done
    the killing, yet there
    is more left to kill.

    She was hidden in his thought
    like a tick in a dog's fur.
    He could feel the rise with his finger
    where her mouth sucked blood.

In Paris en route Cairo with group of six harebrained New Orleanians being led by broken-down, emotionally upset Egyptologist from Boston.

New Orleanians have not stopped drinking champagne since the flight from New York. All they talk about is cocktails, nightcaps, and champagne. I am only sober member of party.

When I grow fearful—of impending trip to Egypt—Africa, the Third World—they say, "Oh, Nancy, it'll be fun—we'll have cocktails!"

"There's such a thing as too much fun, you know," I say.

After three weeks in Egypt I also learned there's such a thing as too many mummies. There's such a thing as seeing too many mummies, and I saw too many for my own good.

New Orleanians discuss similarities between Egypt and New Orleans—Nile Delta/Mississippi River Delta, semitropic climate, tourism.

New Orleanians (aka the King Tut Social Club) have brought tuxedos for the boat trip on the Nile, and records of Oriental fox-trot music—type of crazy 1920s violin jazz—for one member of my party, George, is bandleader of local orchestra playing same.

Aside from George, my party is composed of John (who lies Wallowing in Depression in hotel in Paris because concierge has just refused to ice champagne); a genteel, somewhat stunned, sixty-five-year-old lady from Shreveport; daughter of famous local bon vivant and restaurateur; and one other elderly society lady.

Just thinking of madcap activities, alcoholic intake, and relentless socializing of New Orleanians en route to Paris and Cairo made me tired. Am exhausted. Nor have we even yet reached Egypt.

Third night Paris.

George just fell apart. Who wouldn't who had drunk that much champagne and had that many nightcaps?

Ladies closeted in their rooms drinking vodka, a ritual which they practice religiously every evening beginning at five.

I am rapidly losing confidence in the Egyptologist, who has a nervous condition.

"Do they have cocktails?" George asks wanly, with rising hope, on the way to the airport.

And so, under these conditions, we arrived in Cairo.

Cairo is a Third World capital of twelve million people. There is no sewerage system and no mass transit except for decrepit buses. Traffic at catastrophe level. Garbage is not collected. A group of people known as the Untouchables, who live in tombs, sometimes collect the garbage.

Much of the architecture is modern, housing projects and skyscraper hotels. The housing projects are built unfinished—that is, the top story remains unfinished so that it may be built on later. The result is that, among the new construction, you can't tell whether the buildings are being torn down or put up, adding to what is already effect of Total Chaos.

Decaying nineteenth-century Beaux Arts villas and administrative buildings. An odd sight in the East—Western classicism and grandiosity amid the dust of Africa. They seem almost madcap here, for they do not intrinsically belong, and there is a pathos in it.

Philosophical Crisis at Muhammad Ali mosque in old Cairo. Fell apart. Coptic churches and Islamic mosques, smoldering medieval bazaar. Smoldering Babylonian prison.

The boulevard leading to the pyramids once was a stately one, lined with eucalyptus and acacia. Now is frenzy of new construction and traffic problems. Camels, Arabs, Egyptian families on picnics, a raving Arab who had a fit next to pyramid, French sports cars with loud Egyptian disco music blaring.

The guide said that life was but a short dream to the builders of the pyramids, and that is why the pyramids and tombs exist intact and not the palaces. It would not matter to them if they lived in a mud hut, the guide said, because this was not the life that mattered. This life we live is not and never was what mattered in the East. Sinai, Israel, the Arab world, and war across the desert. It is all religion here. It always was and still is all religion here.

I was filled with fear. Camels, tombs, mummies, dead people, religion, Egypt, Africa, the Third World. But camel riding turned out to be my favorite thing. It was the thing I was most scared of, and then it became my favorite thing. The weather is clear and dry, though prone to extremes of temperature, hot and cold, throughout the day and night. The weather, the light, the desert, in my Arabian headdress galloping on the camel in the desert off toward Mecca, among the inscrutable Bedouins.

The myriad of palms, the verdant green adjacent to the desert. There is a ribbon of cultivation along the Nile, but beyond it, the desert. At Memphis is a monumental statue of Ramses II—Shelley's Ozymandias.

New Orleanians always dressed to the nines—suspenders, suits, and ties. Headdress of Arab sheiks, however, with their suits and ties.

I practically expect to see them with tuxedos, steamer trunks and gramophones, in a caravan with swami music winding through the desert. Old Africa, safari hats, and drumbeats on the Nile.

Leaving Cairo, we drove into the country, along the verdant Nile. The Nile with its date-palm groves and the desert beyond. Sugar cane, egrets, Coptic monasteries, drumbeats in an African rhythm not unlike that which we hear at carnival in New Orleans.

George entertained the party with his Oriental fox-trot songs ("Egyptian Ella," "Nymphs of the Nile," "Belles of Baghdad," etc.) and had the old ladies in stitches. Later he deteriorated and took photos of our party in the rearview mirror. I, too, began to fall apart. Egyptologist driving me crazy. Fellow travelers driving me crazy. Contemplated my loathing. Ladies discuss carnival balls and convents and nuns in genteel Coptic whispers in back seat—many of the party being devout Catholics. Discussion of world religions. Religious Crisis. John discusses his cousins and their debut parties and the time one of his cousins' mother-in-law's horse won Kentucky Derby.

Temples to Hermes and Thoth. Tomb of the Baboons. Mummy of Isadora. Tomb of sacred bulls. Mummified crocodiles at Kom Ombo. They mummified everything in sight. You name it, they mummified it. Mummies driving me crazy.

New Orleanians discuss plots of *The Egyptian,* with Victor Mature, and *The Mummy,* with Boris Karloff.

Pass banana plantations along the Nile, prompting sudden discussion of Robert E. Lee's horse, Traveler, among New Orleanians.

The genteel accents in the back seat—"That was the night of the Nereus ball" or "Anne honey, the lecture is beginning" or, "It's lovely, sweetheart"—honey this and sweetheart that, much discussion of cousins.

Arrived at El Minya, sweltering town on the Nile in Africa whose like I never saw before or expect to see again. Besotted nineteenth-century colonial palaces, decrepit horse-drawn carriages, Arabic music, Muslim chants. Comparison of El Minya to Biloxi, Mississippi. George suggests Arab version of *Streetcar Named Desire*. This sweltering, besotted town with its ruined Beaux Arts mansions, grandiose architecture of West in remote outpost of Third World, lost in old Egypt on the Nile in Africa. Streets of dirt lined by eucalyptus trees toward main square, a circle of date palms and sweet olive bounded by wrought-iron rail, Coptic spires and Islamic minarets in distance. Green shutters, Corinthian columns, and balustrades on balconies of besotted villas. Galleries, tile floors, bentwood chairs. Majestic Hotel. Everything besotted with worst squalor I have ever seen.

Luxor, Egypt. I have now panicked. The *Middle East Times* —religion and war—Christians, Muslims, Arabs, Jews—weird articles like "Dining Out in War-Torn Beirut"—I wish I were returning with the guide to Cairo instead of going farther. Famine to the south, trouble on all fronts, how could one be carefree on the Nile? This land is filled with sorrow. Egypt, how I wish I were far from thee.

New Orleanians have cocktails.

Winter Palace Hotel, a sprawling rose-limestone building with long, empty halls, seedy grandeur. Elaborate garden with monumental palms and ocher-colored dirt, cane chairs. The seven-thirty prayer to Allah going up. Full moon.

Luxor and Karnak temples, connected by the famous avenue of sphinxes. George sang Grand March from *Aida* on the sacred lake.

We board the boat to Aswan.

On the Nile, my cares stole away. They folded their tents like the Arabs and, as silently, stole away. One could sit transfixed for many hours straight on the boat on the Nile. Mostly palms, many palms, also sugar cane, banana plants, and tamarisk. There is no industry, no traffic on the Nile. An occasional other pleasure boat. The green palms, the blue Nile, the waning afternoons. Schubert played on deck. An unknown pathos. Befitting, for it was a sudden ecstasy, the beauty of the Nile.

Dignified Egyptian travelers from Cairo. At night Strauss waltzes played. Italian pleasure-seekers. New Orleanians wore Arab djellabas over their tuxedos, and George wore a monocle and a fez and carried a dagger that he got in the bazaar. Sang ("Now old King Tut was just a nut," etc.). Italians did bawdy pantomimes. George sang "I'm cooking breakfast for the one I love."

Left boat in sort of frenzy—last morning on deck—George fell apart—relations strained—Egyptian violins. Arrive at Elephantine Island on the Nile in Aswan. Barbaric luxury. Tropic paradise. The bougainvillea. Royal palms from Brazil in botanical gardens. Nubians. Proximity to Sudan.

George like traveling Busby Berkeley production number. Sang ("If you Sheik on your mama, your mama's gonna Sheba on you"). Nubians on dock start snapping their fingers, etc.

George ate seventeen pigeons at lunch. Famine worsening in Ethiopia. Relations strained.

Return to Cairo. Texacized at Ramses Hilton. Relations deteriorating. Each time we arrive at new hotel, John comes in my room and repeats his litany: "Your room is bigger than ours." Ladies went to St. Catherine's monastery in Sinai. Then had facials. John fallen apart. Lies in bed in hotel room on drugs. Competition arising as to who can do the most exotic thing. Ladies returned from Sinai ask John what he did. Said he ran into friends and had lovely buffet lunch at British Embassy in Nile-green ballroom, even though he lay in bed all day. Then said went to oldest church in world.

Smoldering medieval bazaar. Chickens being slaughtered by woman who would bite their heads off and pull their feet off before they were even dead, next to man being shaved by his barber in middle of spice emporium. Plate of olives fell into our taxicab in traffic jam among vendors, Vespas, cars, donkeys, and horse-drawn carriages. George bitten by rabid cat in restaurant surrounded by ostriches. Ladies had their nails done.

And so the New Orleanians return in time for carnival, though missing Babylon parade, George comments wistfully. I went to Cairo Tower with one of my many Arab admirers (our guide) and looked at last upon the dust of Africa, and so we bid adieu to Cairo, never to see it again.

Whirling dervish in lobby. Q

"If they can send a man to the moon, why can't they send them all?" Somebody says this to this friend of mine, Jenny, and for a while that is how Jenny thinks it should maybe be—all the men on the moon, all the women on earth. Maybe there would be mixers, but otherwise no communication. And in ten years' time, which of the genders would be happier? Jenny would like to think the women would. Jenny would like to think the women would make earth fertile again. Jenny would like to think that the men would right away take to the lightless and ruinous lunar landscape. But, really, Jenny knows that you would not solve this thing, this whole man/woman thing, by simply making all the men on earth move out.

I think I'm qualified to say what Jenny thinks; I know her pretty well. I know Dave well, too. If you know a person well, that person lives a life inside your mind sometimes far more epic than that person's own life. Inside my mind, there is a Jenny and a Dave, and inside my mind, they think.

Jenny is thinking about this, the man/woman thing, about a week ago. Even though it is the beginning of summer, Dave still has his place and Jenny could keep on living with him if she wants. Jenny lives with Dave, although she would not call him her boyfriend. Jenny knows the rules: to call Dave her boyfriend or to even think it in her head, even to imagine, say, that she and Dave are at a malt shop sharing a soda through two straws, or that maybe he brought her a corsage when they went to the high school prom together—although in real life, Jenny did not know Dave in high school, and she did not even go to the prom—even to think one thing like that or imply it with a word like *boyfriend,* would make Dave feel tied down, and when Dave feels tied down, he has a fit. Besides, Jenny is too cool to think that what she and Dave are doing has anything to do with romance, or even emotion. What they are doing is screwing.

But it is not because of this semantic problem of not knowing what to call Dave—*boyfriend* is out of the question and *the guy I'm living with* also dangerous—that Jenny decides to move out of Dave's. Jenny moves out because of Dave's fits. Really, Dave has fits whether Jenny makes him feel tied down or not. Really, Dave has fits according to some inner schedule of his own that has nothing to do with Jenny.

Dave has a pink, purple, and green bowling ball he bought at a garage sale. Everyone calls this bowling ball his planet, because Dave sometimes tries to stand on it and twirl around. Jenny can't even lift the thing, but when Dave is having a fit, he throws it around, sometimes at her head.

The other thing Dave does when he is having a fit is come up with theories. He will take something you say, even something about the weather, and he will argue against you for hours, using theories that are intricately insane. He will use insults if necessary. He will look things up in books, quote scientific formulas. There is no way to make peace with him when he is like that.

It is after a particularly bad fit of Dave's that Jenny finally moves out. Dave and Jenny are watching the news and the news people are saying how America has declared war on this or that Third World country and Jenny says, "I can't believe this. Those assholes!"

"You dumb shit," says Dave, "can't you see we've got to bomb them into the ground?" Dave starts on his bomb-them-into-the-ground theory. Jenny knows that this is not really what Dave thinks, but once the theory has taken him over, it does not matter what Dave really thinks. When Dave has a theory, it comes out of him whether he agrees with it or not. It is an uncontrollable physical reaction, like vomiting.

So Jenny goes to stay on Beth's farm. A month before, Beth had dumped her man, moved to Maine, taken a lesbian lover, and begun to till the sweet earth with her shirt off. Jenny thinks Beth's farm could be like the manless planet earth—not a solution, but something worth trying for a while.

Jenny is there only a few days before Dave calls. Dave does not exactly say he is sorry, not in so many words, but by way of saying he is sorry, he tells her a story.

When he was little, falling stars were really UFOs landing. It was in one of these UFOs that he came to earth. The UFO dropped him off at his parents' house. His parents raised him as they would a human child.

Jenny is not surprised. Jenny has always suspected that something of the kind is the case with Dave.

Jenny says, "You're not human, then?"

Dave says, "Sometimes I lose control and the other thing comes out." Dave changes the subject. Dave does not like to talk about what is inside him. Dave says he's been thinking of coming up to Beth's farm to hang out for a few days.

"Okay," says Jenny, even though, officially, she has broken up with him.

After she hangs up the phone from talking to Dave, Jenny asks Beth if it's okay for Dave to stay on the farm. Beth says that the whole point of a feminist farm is not to have any men on it; it's like when boys build a fort and put a sign on it that says No Girls Allowed. When you make a place where only one gender is allowed, you can be yourself there. Beth says all this, but then she says that if Jenny really wants Dave to stay, the rules can be bent.

Then Jenny calls me up to get my advice on this whole thing. I tell her if she lets Dave come up, she will just get back together with him again. I run through a quick list of Dave's faults, but even as I'm talking, I can tell Jenny cannot be convinced that Dave shouldn't come up.

I guess you can send a man to the moon, but you can't make him stay there. **Q**

Jonathan Yardley, writing in *The Washington Post*, castigates "the little world of literary publicity" for being concerned with what I write, since, he asserts, ". . . Harold Brodkey, who in 1958 brought out a volume of stories called *First Love and Other Sorrows* . . . has not, to all intents and purposes, been heard from since." In the 1960s, in *The New Yorker*, I published sixty-five or sixty-six thousand words, enough for a good-sized book of three hundred pages pleasantly printed, if anyone would have printed it. In the 1970s, I printed in *The New Yorker* alone sixty thousand words and perhaps half again more in *Esquire* and *New American Review* and *Partisan Review*. Mr. Yardley refers to "snippets" I have published: the word means in this context "short extracts from books." One story I printed in the seventies was more than a hundred pages. In the 1980s I have so far already printed more than sixty thousand words. What I do is considerably rewritten as story and only two things so far published are possibly extracts from the book as such, but they are not snippets, one being fifty pages long and the other longer yet. The Jewish Publication Society recently printed a small book in an edition limited to three thousand copies of *Women and Angels*. Perhaps Mr. Yardley intends an insult to *The New Yorker* and to small publishers, or to small Jewish publishing houses and to *Esquire*, or perhaps he is not thinking. Surely he is saying that *The New Yorker* does not exist, a statement febrile, menacing, and absurd. If he minds it that he was not called on to review those long pieces, he might take that up with the editors of the best-story anthologies who passed them by. Or perhaps he considers them to have been reviewed in that fashion. Individual expression of interest in what I publish outside the adventure of publishing a book hardly seems a fit thing to attack in the manner he adopted (a manner I would characterize as scurrilous, discourteous, suicidally and carelessly murderous at the start: he calms down later a little).

In the past, Mr. Yardley, so far as I can recall, praised two long stories of mine that were in those best-story anthologies in the 1970s. He singled them out and called them "perhaps great."

Since 1958 I have published the equivalent of one middle-sized novel each decade. I'm not hiding from anyone. A number of people including Jonathan Yardley keep a gingerly distance from me.

He writes: "As best can be determined, the novel's principal subject is Harold Brodkey. He said as much recently in a long interview. . . ." No. Mr. Yardley perhaps intends by *subject* the meaning of a *thinking and feeling entity,* but even then, no. Other people have said that the narrator of the stories so far published is largely me, but I have never said it or implied it, preferring not to give simple and probably wrong answers to what are complicated matters of representation. Harold Brodkey was the subject of the interview Mr. Yardley mentions. Surely it would have been wrong for me in the interview to pretend not to be the subject under consideration. I wasn't asked about being Wiley or about being in the novel in the simplistic manner Mr. Yardley uses here; and my answer was complicated and then was simplified by the reporter, for good reason, in his piece, but not to the point Mr. Yardley claims in his piece. The subject of the questions and answers had to do with reality and reporting it or representing it. The reporter had to represent my answer as a form of reporting on it. I said I didn't do that. I thought I was showing a strong sense of duty to the occasion and to readers in appearing in the interview as myself, rather than in some impersonation. An interview may be an art form, but it is not a form useful as masquerade for purposes of public deception, useful as an art form. Then it is something else, a form of joke perhaps. One can remark here that fiction is not autobiography; we all know that autobiography cannot be fiction. Accurate statement and fact and attestation are of one sort in autobiography. Fiction has nothing to do with those three categories of useful language. Each of the stories I have printed so far from the time I started writing has been accused of too much life or lifelikeness by some; and the recent stories have been open to much more serious imputation of lifelikeness and presence. This has to do with art—with linguistic representation and linguistic perspective as it can be set up on something very unlike canvas, on the level of consciousness that reads and interprets and responds. And it concerns observation and expression, and notions of reality and representations of memory of a more complex sort than have yet been attempted by others. What I do is more seriously revolutionary than I have been willing to admit publicly until now. It seemed corny to say, *Look, here is some revolutionary prose, you guys.* And then to supply a chart saying what had been rethought and so on seemed like a commercial describing the new additives in a food or the new engineering of an engine. The quality and extent of the escape from conventional representation and the extent and degree of the effect of truth and presence in what I do is clearly not of the sort associated with the form we call autobiography; and a little thought might show that we do not have before us an exercise of memory in any usual sense. And not in a Proustian sense either. In my recent stories, the realities of childhood were embedded in the realities of being in the care of adults, and it was the presentation of adult realities among the testimonies of childhood realities pictured in a new way that was at the center of the stories. The reasons for doing it had to do with art and creation. I seriously doubt that it is me who is Wiley. The formal means by which we name ourselves and name events make it impossible for us to be sure to any even small degree of those selves and those events seen with means other than those formal ones. This does not mean the element of confession is untrue—it means the confession would not hold up in court even if I insisted Wiley was me. And I would, if I thought that was truer than the reverse, or that saying Wiley is a little like me and mostly not, or some variation of that. The adult and child realities I write about are set in a universe I take as moral but obscure, and in a world I think we ought to take as immoral and perhaps more obscure than we do. These realities cannot be projected by a child. They cannot be part of childhood memory in the usual sense; and they are not part of any automatic act of consciousness in an adult. This is, I think, generally recognized by my readers. I don't mean to be mysterious or unduly self-protective about any of this: I would like to be careful, however.

Let me proceed by taking up a point Mr. Yardley attempts to make, which, if we unravel it, might make some of this a little clearer. Mr. Yardley quotes some remarks by an unknown woman, who might very well be Mr. Yardley himself. I will refer to this unnamed woman as he. His remarks are praised by Yardley as *nicely and tartly stated.* Here is one sentence: "For if he [Harold Brodkey] is devoted to pounding the moments of his life for each note up and down the scale of memory, he has found undoubtedly how time changes the music of our souls by taking on a drumroll here, a string progression there, the angry blat of an offkey horn until childhood's simple melody swells into a symphony that can finish only with death!"

I do not know what meanings of *nicely* and *tartly* Mr. Yardley had in mind. *Pounding the moments of his life for each note up and down the scale of memory* presents problems of redundancies, first in *each note* and *scale* and then in the phrase *of memory,* since *the moments of his life* cannot be conceived of as being present in unison outside of memory.

What is present in the above sentence is, on one level, a

description of Proust's novel in small part, which uses a number of his key images for his book, including the idea of its being a symphony; but which does not credit him with these notions and does not make it clear which part of this is what I do and which part of this the writer of this note is claiming as his own and as general literate knowledge. Mr. Yardley's commentator does not present a logical or an original notion or one likely to be applicable to what I write. Furthermore, his description is full of miraculous frames for theatricalized encounters with the past as a known quantity in all its aspects—this is a notion of a certain kind of Southern fiction, very dear, but perhaps not entirely serious except as a sentimental—and commercial—enterprise. But it cannot itself be a term of explanation for something it is used to explain or illumine if that something is not itself: it has no built-in mechanism for widening out into life or into an example of something real. *The moments of his life* are lumped as a single thing, a piano; memory is seen as a formal organization of the *sounds* that can arise from the initial term when it is pounded. So far, it is dangerously unclear—dangerous for truth or study—and it is still more dangerously without any foundation in logic or emotion or prettiness or comedy: it has no given logic at all. It does not suggest the aleatory result you might get if you pounded on a scrapbook, or got drunk and tried to remember, or if you studied old documents and unmounted pictures and souvenir programs. The writer conceives of a fixed process by which a writer has a life and pounds on what must be a memory of parts of it and gets stories or chapters to order, in a scale, in a naturally limited system. I don't know why the writer is willing to live and write in this way. I presume the writer takes pleasure in some association on his part with books and stories already written and not with the thing itself newly and more accurately looked at. The possibility of melody is implied to be

forgone for scales simply played (pounded) in automatic entirety. This suggests that my recent pieces are those of someone playing the scale(s) up and down, that the stories
represent predictable permutations. This in turn might mean
that the stories give an effect of truth and that this truth once
it is recognized feels basic to him, the maker of these images,
and unarguable, or not happily arguable just yet. The work,
the ideas in it, the pleasures and suggestions of logic in it are
not recognized as discovered or created or found or given out.
The accusation is an inversion of saying that work of the sort
in the stories with memory (and life) is like Bach inventing
keyboard music, the rules of it. I use a grand image to show
the perversity of the attack. The attack consistently refers to
something unsupportably grand. The underlying thrust of the
image is to attach blamingly the history of music from Bach
through Mahler, the person's fundamental image for sincere
art, I would guess, to questions raised by what I do in my work.
The assailant takes for his own field of knowledge the subject
of the changes time makes, but he does this in a set of phrases
empty of allegorical meaning, and he does it in grab-bag images, supposedly tart but hardly *nice* unless *nice* means thinner
than farce or bludgeoning: "a drumroll here, a string progression there, the angry blat of an offkey horn. . . ." Little thought
has gone into this claimed knowledge, which we then might
assume is actually haphazard critical comment by which we
might judge the seriousness of intention of the writer. *Time,*
Yardley, or Yardley's alter ego or Yardley's friend, says, *changes
the music of our souls by taking on* various bits of orchestration.
Now, on the face of it, time does not take on the bits of
orchestration; it confers them. But if I might be permitted to
attempt to lessen the confusion in the image, I think we might
get something like this: here are the moments of Wiley's life
in their reality and entirety; here are the scales of memory

being sounded; now the parts of an orchestra come into existence, slowly, around this other thing. The music becomes complicated, symphonic. This is a process, we are told, that can end only with death. Now we do not know who is doing what, and we do not know what really is happening, but the scale of the description can be seen. And where is the orchestra? In Wiley? In memory? In the prose structures—i.e., as in Proust? Is it in the soul? If so, shouldn't the headline of Mr. Yardley's piece have been: THE SOUL ENTERS AMERICAN LETTERS? *The music of the soul,* this person writes. The passion of the writer is neither nice nor tart to me.

Childhood reality recalled in whatever passes for wisdom and longing and humor latish in life becomes symphonic. Why is this person saying that as if it is his idea and not Proust's and that it is somehow somewhat to my discredit? Why is he saying it accusingly? Consider the nouns in that sentence: *moments, life, note, scale, memory, time, music, souls, drumroll, progression, blat, horn, childhood('s), melody, symphony, death.* The supposed writer of the letter complains earlier of "all the writers and would-be writers who will [now] spend long hours lying on couches and producing horrendously dull and obscure contemplations of their own lives. . . ."

This writer's notion of memory as fixed in patterns but capable of infinite numbers of senselessly varied orchestrations as time changes the rememberer is particularly unpleasant spiritually and psychologically. And it is on the grounds of the above argument that it is important to Mr. Yardley to say it is Harold Brodkey that is the subject of the novel. He uses as "evidence" an interview and not the stories that have so far appeared. Mr. Yardley does not attack my writing. He says it does not exist. He says also that it consists of snippets. And that it can be nicely and tartly said to consist of pure automatism of recall. I don't know what can be done in answer to an argument along the lines of *We will not recognize what he has done, and no one else ought to recognize that it exists either,* except to suggest that such an argument does us all too much discredit and is a considerable folly for literate people to engage in—unless being ostriches compulsively amuses them.

Now let us consider the unkindness of my reply. Put self-defense and service to truth to one side, along with love of literature and the hope of clearer-headed and truer writing about books and people, magazines and American writing—I mean put them aside as possible motives of mine. Let us consider that the man who wrote this is the same man who wrote the stories—the ones that do not exist. The same man means he has the same name and he lives at the same address. Mr. Yardley says it is not possible to separate the artist from his art and that it would be foolish to try, and that is certainly true; but is the artist the same artist in his poems as in his letters, in Keats's case, or in his music as in his letters, in Mozart's case? Actually he is not. In fact, the artist is only unreliably present as the same artist in different works: consider the arguments over the attribution of paintings and unsigned manuscripts, and even signed ones. Then consider whether the artist is an artist all the time. Mr. Yardley may be the same man away from the typewriter that he is when he is at it, but I am not. Nor am I the same man, quite, or the same artist, writing this kind of thing as writing other things. And the variations are not minor. If we are clear-headed for a moment we can see that there is no way for us to "know" the artist except in his art: everything else is guesswork about him, and it's not all that clear who he is in the art either. The autonomy and control through *his* autonomy of a piece of work that an artist does, does not exist in life for the man or woman the artist is away from his or her work. And even at his own work, a man is not necessarily the artist who seems to have been there when the work later appears to be good. That is because the artist comes and goes, edits and pauses, and perhaps rarely, very rarely, fully exists. He exists in flights and spurts and by accumulation. Right now it is popular knowledge that Mozart the man and Mozart the artist were not the same being and could not be. An artist cannot give an interview as an artist of the same kind as he is, perhaps is, when he writes. A character named Wiley Silenowicz first appears as a narrator in my stories in the early 1970s. (Anyone who likes can look up the third-person narrations I wrote during the 1960s.) The issue whether I am really he or he is really me interests me, of course, but not very much: I cannot be him except at certain very few moments of composition and not for very long and not very well. Whatever *sensible*—old-fashioned—answer I give depends on the distance I take from the work. If I say to myself that the work does not exist, that it is not very good, if I am distant in that way, it seems to me Wiley is, in a very bedraggled way, someone who resembles me from a distance too great to be of any meaning to me as therapy or pride or shame or whatever. The slightest sense I have of virtue in the work I do, and the loss of distance then, the more that seems, contrarily, to make the distance between me and Wiley enormous. I am an interesting and complex man, but I am not transferable to paper in structures of narrative; and actually, I am not very interesting or very complex except as the originator of Wiley Silenowicz. Mr. Yardley is being very wicked in what he says.

He says, he writes: "Harold Brodkey may or may not be in the process of producing a modern masterpiece—and if he is, more power to him—" Mr. Yardley is very calm about a matter that one would expect him to be intense about in his interest and duty as a reviewer. He goes on: "But his unabashed self-preoccupation is paradigmatically contemporary." These twenty-four syllables in seven words seem an attempt to be bluff—in English one doesn't need to do that to be impressive. Usually, in English, we consider such pomposity as an indication of self-love and insincerity, an unabashed and self-important preoccupation with oneself.

His evidence for my preoccupation with myself is less direct: my not publishing and what can be inferred from something attributed to me in an interview.

Mr. Yardley, then, ruthlessly murderous toward his own standing, attempts to establish as an axiom of fair literary attack that anything he says about Philip Roth—and Elizabeth Hardwick and Renata Adler—then applies to Harold Brodkey. He attempts to establish a critical principle by writing that "no matter how you slice it" Philip Roth is "writing solely about himself." It is not possible. Mr. Yardley is far closer to it than Roth is, but it is not possible for Mr. Yardley. Roth has subject matter, themes, characters, a world. Roth's worlds are refracted through sensibilities more directly present than is the case for the sensibility portrayed in Paul Theroux or Eudora Welty. Let me be direct: Is Mr. Yardley proposing the argument that literary works that openly or covertly report on specifically Christian and peripheral communities are ipso facto superior to works concerned with urban individuals, particularly if the individuals are Jews or urbane Irishmen or even more urbane Frenchmen?

Mr. Yardley knows that part of all public writing in every culture is what one can think of as country-club stuff. And fine stuff it is, too. But it is also dismissible cant admirable only when it knows its place—which is not the case with people.

I would like to see Miss Welty get a Nobel Prize, and I admire the others on Mr. Yardley's list of admirations. And I agree that some people ought to be discouraged from reading my work. We are trying to set up a board of licensing to which readers can apply. Mr. Yardley can be goaltender on our ad hoc hockey team and he can pass on applications for demotion back to the country-club level by disappointed readers of my stuff if he will just be a bit clearer as a heroic defender of merit and a seeker after truth by telling us what is "The Cult of the Self" that he talks about? One uses one's life to judge the merit of ideas and to check against statements one has read, isn't that so? And one mulls over one's life in relation to fate and nonsense all the time. One is always judging one's life and one is always being returned to contemplation of it. At what stage does this minimal practice of citizenship and individual responsibility for what one thinks and says become the hurtful stuff of "The Cult of the Self"?

By the way, Mr. Yardley, I am willing to be judged finally on what I have published so far. It would have been far too difficult to grow to the age I am without publishing sufficient work for that willingness to be the case when I haven't published *the book* and when the work involved in publishing it is so onerous. **Q**

TWO PIPES IN BOP TIME

Characters in the Masque:
Big Old Cracked-up Pipe
Little Shiny New Pipe
Tiresias Theban, a fading queen
Little Miss Dreary, a chimney sweep
Medea, a bad apple
Fishbait Capaneus, a Leather Lane monger
Professor Fasttalk
An Unknown Poet
Chorus of Language Poets
Chorus of Structuralists
Ballet of nude Ping-Pong players

Setting:
The Stanton Street Palladium.
Flashing lights. Wax figures of demented dancers by
Jill. Music begins sweetly with *Zwei Herzen im Dreiviertel
Takt,* but quickly modulates to aboriginal rock.

BIG PIPE: Wot yer smokin' terday, little shiner?
LITTLE PIPE: Just the useral.
BIG PIPE: That doan smell ter me like Dunhill Number
13.
LITTLE PIPE: 'Tis too.
BIG PIPE: Are you hidin' something from me, duckums?
Like a bad habit?
LITTLE PIPE: Wodzit to yer?

BIG PIPE: You promised not to be flaky.

LITTLE PIPE: Don't a girl need a few kicks now 'n' then?

BIG PIPE: You promised.

LITTLE PIPE: See ya roun'. I'm headin' for the Gargoyle Club.

(*There is the sound of a door slamming, as in* Doll's House)

TIRESIAS: This has all happened before. I've seen all this happen before. I think it was in Crete, but I can't remember.

MISS DREARY: Keep your pecker up, Mister T. I've seen a lot worse things, comin' down chimbleys the way I do.

MEDEA: Are there any kids around here today? I'm hungry. I haven't et a good kid in two weeks.

TIRESIAS (*Mumbling*): Everything has happened before.

MISS DREARY: You should watch TV, Mister T. Lotsa new things on the tube these days.

CAPANEUS: Nothin' much new happens to me. I've always wanted to ride on a dolphin, like I read about.

MISS DREARY: Don't worry, Mister T., I'll never leave you. I'll lead you around when you go blind.

MEDEA: I'm so hungry.

CAPANEUS: I've got some real nice pompano in my stall today. Shall I get one and cook it up on the hot plate? Better than La Tulipe, you'll see.

MEDEA: Piss off, Cap. I want my useral. There must be some kids around here somewheres.

PROFESSOR FASTTALK: I can talk faster than anyone else can talk.

MISS DREARY: You sure can, Jack, but do you say anything anybody wants to hear?

PROFESSOR FASTTALK: I have seven honorary degrees from great universities. I talk good.

UNKNOWN POET: Once upon a day I sat,
                Shelling walnuts in my hat.
                The flames came up and burnt my chin
                But still I rolled those walnuts in.

MEDEA: I hate walnuts. No body to them.

UNKNOWN POET: I'm expecting a Pulitzer any day, and maybe later the Nobel.

TIRESIAS: Homer never got a Pulitzer.

CHORUS OF LANGUAGE POETS (*From offstage, Stockhausen music*):
      "pardon quickly / adroit breeze / argue
          tonic / in issue / practical
      platoons /
      returns slowly / that make
          mason isospheres / unheard relief"

TIRESIAS: I think I've heard that jazz somewhere before. Maybe it was in Alexandria.

CHORUS OF STRUCTURALISTS (*Offstage, music of Webern*):
      "One of the members of a family absents himself from home.
      An interdiction is addressed to the hero.
      The interdiction is violated.
      The villain makes an attempt at reconnaisance.
      The villain attempts to deceive his victim in order
          to take possession of her . . ."

MISS DREARY: What's that all about, Mister T.? I don't get it.

TIRESIAS: It may be about you, dear, but don't worry. Things will come out all right in the end.

INTERLUDE

The ballet of the nude Ping-Pong players. The music is Ravel's Bolero. *Their* poitrines *bounce as they dance.*

> *Rising applause in the audience as the music gets faster.*

BIG PIPE is slumped in his chair in despair. He has finished his bottle and has no money for more.

The telephone rings. BIG PIPE rushes to answer it. We hear the voice of LITTLE PIPE amplified.

LITTLE PIPE'S VOICE: I'm sorry, Big Pipe honey, I didn't mean to be flaky. Come get me at the Gargoyle Club. They have me tied to a chair. I'm scared.

(BIG PIPE *rushes out*)

TIRESIAS: "Men and things come round again, eternal as the seasons."

> (*The lights dim. Exeunt omnes, to the strains of Schubert's* Ave Maria)

Pipe figures courtesy of Dunhill of London.

The tone of the play is from Kenneth Patchen's *The Old Lean over the Tombstones*.

The Chorus of Language Poets is from Charles Bernstein's *The Difficulties*.

The Chorus of Structuralists is from Vladimir Propp, as quoted in Robert Scholes, *Structuralism in Literature*.

Tiresias's final line is from Rudyard Kipling.

About the piece of fiction I have with you in this issue —I just wanted to say that I leave a lot out when I tell the truth. The same when I write a story. I'm going to start now to tell you what I left out of "The Harvest," and maybe begin to wonder why I had to leave it out.

There was no other car. There was only the one car, the one that hit me when I was on the back of the man's motorcycle. But think of the awkward syllables when you have to say *motorcycle.*

The driver of the car was a newspaper reporter. He worked for a local paper. He was young, a recent graduate, and he was on his way to a labor meeting to cover a threatened strike. When I say I was then a journalism student, it is something you might not have accepted in "The Harvest."

In the years that followed, I watched for the reporter's byline. He broke the People's Temple story that resulted in Jim Jones's flight to Guyana. Then he covered Jonestown. In the city room of the San Francisco *Chronicle,* as the death toll climbed to nine hundred, the numbers were posted like donations on pledge night. Somewhere in the hundreds, a sign was fixed to the wall that said JUAN CORONA, EAT YOUR HEART OUT.

In the emergency room, what happened to one of my legs required not four hundred stitches but just over three hundred stitches. I exaggerated even before I began to exaggerate, because it's true—nothing *is* ever quite as bad as it could be.

My lawyer was no attorney-at-last. He was a partner in one of the city's oldest law firms. He would never have opened his shirt to reveal the site of acupuncture, which is something that he never would have had.

"Marriageability" was the original title of "The Harvest."

The damage to my leg was considered cosmetic although I am still, fifteen years later, unable to kneel. In an out-of-court settlement the night before the trial, I was awarded nearly $100,000. The reporter's car insurance went up $12.43 per month.

It had been suggested that I rub my leg with ice, to bring up the scars, before I hiked my skirt three years later for the court. But there was no ice in the judge's chambers, so I did not get a chance to pass or fail that moral test.

The man of a week, whose motorcycle it was, was not a married man. But when you thought he had a wife, wasn't I liable to do anything? And didn't I have it coming?

After the accident, the man got married. The girl he married was a fashion model ("Do you think looks are important?" I asked the man before he left. "Not at first," he said).

In addition to being a beauty, the girl was worth millions of dollars. Would you have accepted this in "The Harvest"—that the model was also an heiress?

It is true we were headed for dinner when it happened. But the place where you can see everything without having to listen to any of it was not a beach on a bay; it was the top of Mt. Tamalpais. We had the dinner with us as we headed up the twisting mountain road. This is the version that has room for perfect irony, so you won't mind when I say that for the next several months, from my hospital bed, I had a dead-on spectacular view of that very mountain.

I would have written this next part into the story if anybody would have believed it. But who would have? I was there and I didn't believe it.

On the day of my third operation, there was an attempted breakout in the Maximum Security Adjustment Center, adjacent to Death Row, at San Quentin prison. "Soledad Brother" George Jackson, a twenty-nine-year-old black man, pulled out a smuggled-in, .38-caliber pistol, yelled, "This is it!" and opened fire. Jackson was killed; so were three guards and two "tier-tenders," inmates who serve other prisoners their meals.

Three other guards were stabbed in the neck. The prison is a five-minute drive from Marin General, so that is where the injured guards were taken. The people who brought them were three kinds of police, including California Highway Patrol and Marin County sheriff's deputies, heavily armed.

Police were stationed on the roof of the hospital with rifles; they were posted in the hallways, waving patients and visitors back into their rooms.

When I was wheeled out of Recovery later that day, bandaged from waist to ankle, three officers and an armed sheriff frisked me.

On the news that night, there was footage of the riot. They showed my surgeon talking to reporters, indicating, with a finger to his throat, how he had saved one of the guards by sewing up a slice from ear to ear.

I watched this on television, and because it was my doctor, and because hospital patients are self-absorbed, and because I was drugged, I thought the surgeon was talking about me. I thought that he was saying, "Well, she's dead. I'm announcing it to her in her bed."

The psychiatrist I saw at the surgeon's referral said that the feeling was a common one. She said that victims of trauma who have not yet assimilated the trauma often believe they are dead and do not know it.

The great white sharks in the waters near my home attack one to seven people a year. Their primary victim is the abalone diver. With abalone steaks at thirty-five dollars a pound and going up, the Department of Fish and Game expects the shark attacks to show no slackening. Q

635

Apples I set up to paint went rotten and fruit lady says she won't get any more of that kind until next year. Fruit lady says try winesaps, they taste just as good. That is not the point, but it is no use explaining Art to fruit lady, so I end up buying five winesaps to be polite.

636

Drove to Virginia to see if Derby apples are still in season there. No luck. Lucy says I should paint plastic fruit.

637

Father says it is high time I thought about paying off my law-school loan, but I am not of the corporate world anymore. I am an artist. How did those painters in the seventeenth century get patrons? Should I send my work around to rich people?

638

Maybe it was the eighteenth century.

639

For first time since I began painting two years and four months ago, I have not painted or even thought about painting. I have been helping Lucy set up her studio. They say the creative process always goes on, so maybe I am getting some work done after all.

640

Mother says she believes in my art but maybe I should take job at HBO that Father wants me to take and paint on the side. She says HBO would be creative and they must have some art series I could do the legal work for. Mother says many artists do other things. David Mamet sold real estate, according to Mother, and he won the Pulitzer Prize.

641

Lucy showed me a new design for her sashes. She is getting over her phobia about showing her work to others. Hooray.

642

I have been experimenting with color. No mixing, just apply the colors in as pure a state as they are in the tube. The effect is luminous.

643

Man from HBO called to set up interview for job having to do with copyrights. Told him I could not think about jobs right now. This color thing is too big.

644

Lucy and I saw the Turner exhibit. I feel Turner's watercolors are didactic, but Lucy disagrees. How can she be so blind? I had hoped Lucy would come and live in my apartment and a kind of colony of artists could spring up in the building, but now I am not so sure. Besides, Lucy says there is not enough tub space for her flax.

(*Query:* Lucy bleaches her hair blond. She is naturally a brunette. Is it "true" to paint her as a blond?)

645

Man from HBO told Father he had pulled many strings to get me copyright opportunity at HBO and I was a very ungrateful person. I told Father I do not approve of cronyism. HBO buys a lot of office supplies from Father, so he is somewhat annoyed.

646

Exterminator who came today told me that he got rid of pigeons for Tony Randall and that Tony Randall has a painting in his kitchen that is just like my *Bad Apples* but not as good.

647

Mother told Mrs. Glover about Tony Randall and Mrs. Glover came over to look at my *Bad Apples*.

648

Things to Strive For:
  1. Reach my quota of three paintings a day.
  2. Dream in autumnal colors.
  3. Convince Father to let Mother hang my *Bad Apples* in den.

649

Lucy says I am probably the only artist who has never had a single work of art destroyed.

650

STUDIES OF LINES

651

Found a store that still sells Derby apples. Bought four pounds. Tried to paint them, but light is not right for Derby apples anymore.

652

Borrow more money from Father so that I can study light in Amsterdam.

653

Paul Gauguin was once painting the portrait of a native in Tahiti when a tidal wave swept the island. Though the native almost drowned, Gauguin managed to finish the portrait during that sitting. I admire that.

654

I may have developed a technique for painting using only water, no paints. It is a simple idea, but aren't those the best?

655

Father maintains there is no difference between pointillism and connect-the-dots.

656

Lord & Taylor is going to buy Lucy's sashes (the "Butterfly" series). I hope this will give her the courage to explore new forms in her art.

657

On Wearing Glasses while Painting:
    Is This Cheating?

658

Beauty.

659

Father says you can make no money in painting. That is not the point of art, but I send Father a clipping of how Rembrandt Peale's portrait of his brother sold for $4,070,000.

660

Mother says she will pay me to paint a portrait of Donny and me for Father's birthday, but I cannot paint without inspiration.

661

A Thought:
A still life ceases to be when it moves.

662

Rembrandt Peale is dead, says Father, and does not need $4,070,000.

663

Lucy is taking a textile course. ("One cannot break new ground in art if one walks on the clouds and never looks down at the ground that's around." Lucy Lerner, 2/12/86)

664

Went to my first Art History course tonight, but it turns out the course is really about Arthurian Legend, sixth to twelfth century. They abbreviated in the catalogue.

665

Lucy feels Rembrandt is too painterly. Isn't that the point?

666

Donny got New York Hospital account for Father. New York Hospital buys more office supplies than HBO, so Donny will get a big commission. Father says reason I do not want to make money like Donny is because I am so intent on attacking Father.

667

A confession: I would like to achieve immortality through my art, but I would like to know before I die.

668

A woman came up to me in the park and asked if my sash was a Lucy Lerner. How will Lucy's commercial success affect our relationship? Are the Artist and the Professional viable together?

669

Lucy told me she never loved me. She doesn't believe in my art. She thinks I should take the job at HBO. I told her she could still store some of her stuff here.

670

I have made a decision. I am more interested in bringing art cheaply to the public than in reaching the critic or the wealthy connoisseur. I have been grappling with this concept for a long time.

671

Sent Lucy some sketches which suggest new ways to think about cloth.

672

Lucy cannot accept criticism. Her art will never grow beyond the sash. Q

For a long time Squeaky Fromme used to write me letters and worry about my health. And for a long time I responded and sent her books and worried about her future.

I also wanted to exploit her. She had the weird celebrity of murder (at least by association) and I wanted to know a murderer. The kind that killed strangers for obscure reasons and not because they were disappointed in love or on a pass from a mental hospital. I wanted her to believe that I would help her, so that she would tell me how it was. I wanted to know if she had found a power in surrender that made the self elemental and weightless, and so able to strike more dangerously and with no apparent fuss.

In the old days before the murders, she and her friends would creepy-crawl into a dark house, rearrange the furniture, and tiptoe away. Nothing missing except a few doughnuts from the refrigerator and one's sense of balance and claim to the space in which one lived. For a long time I thought that she was on to something. That the "Family" understood how to make even the dullest features of life—furniture arrangements, for example—seem as if they could blow up in your face.

From the beginning I wanted to remember everything there was to know about them. I clipped newspaper articles until my drawers were stuffed. I memorized even the gratuitous details (like Patricia Krenwinkel's excess of body hair). From the beginning I sensed in them the chance to rid oneself of personality but still remain alive. Manson knew where the button was that made you leave your life behind as if it had never happened.

Their two-day murder spree is one of the four events from

childhood by which my friends and I remembered our place in the world: I know precisely where I was then and cannot recall another moment from 1969. The other things I know for certain are where I was when Marilyn Monroe, John Kennedy, and Jayne Mansfield died. None of these people meant a thing to me then, but they were tied to recognizing the way language worked and how memory is a function of grammar: from Monroe I learned what *suicide* was; from Kennedy *assassination;* and from Mansfield what *decapitate* meant. Nothing you could think of doing or that could happen to you was without a name. There was a word for everything. The world became at once larger than ever imagined and more claustrophobic. It was impossible to get past the words. It made the urge to do something that would send the rest of them scrambling for a sentence to define it at least understandable.

Squeaky Fromme hated writing letters because she felt the written word lacked the hypnotic power of the voice. Her letters were ten pages long and her voice as tinny and hollow as a child's. She punctuated her sentences with a smile and two eyes. And until I sent her a postcard of a slashed blue face by Picasso, the only adornment on her walls was a photograph of a fat girl eating a bowl of cereal and a painting of a farmhouse by Andrew Wyeth.

She was a member of the Quality Paperback Book Club. The book she wanted me to send her most was *Gray's Anatomy*. She wanted to perfect her understanding of the body, since she had the mind under control. I began to distrust her, believing she wanted to train herself to slide knives through muscles without nicking a single bone.

She told me I needed to be more open to life.

She wrote: "There are hundreds of Napoleons and Jesus Christs on the rim of some bowl like a cornflake that hardens when not washed. We need to wash our bowls and be open for the truth of another day. This is not to say that if you open yourself up you'll become a murderer. But that every day is a new beginning."

She said, "Manson was new to the world because he'd done so much time inside. He was never in the in-crowd, actually."

When I asked her what had gone wrong, she wrote: "We were just a little ahead of our time."

She wanted me to visit her. She wanted to embroider me a shirt. She wanted me to tell her one thing I knew for certain.

I was afraid she would get out and sleep on my couch. I began to realize that some official was reading my letters before they were given to her. She began to make connections. Her parents lived down the hill from my grandmother, but my grandmother said it wasn't true. My aunt lived near Sharon Tate and I was sleeping there the night of the murders. It meant something. I began to exist in her orbit.

She thought she could win me over by appearing kinder than she was. She wrote constantly of love and the simple truth between friends. I wanted her to tell me what people said before they were killed, what bargains they were willing to make at the last possible second. Her friends believed that if you were willing to kill your parents, it would set you free. I wanted her to ask me, so I would know for once just how far I would go.

She denied she ever said "Anybody can kill anybody," as it was said she had said.

She complained that her hand got cramped from writing.

When I asked her whom she admired, she sensed a trap and wrote: "Jesus Christ, Shakespeare, and Socrateze."

I ceased to think of her. But for a long time I used to dream that I married her and that we spray-painted two men in business suits bright pink, even the irises of their eyes. **Q**

Was when we to the graveyard went, checked out the stones. Walked high down the grass, climbed two hills, flagled wood, strendled a stream strembling through. An old Dutch Craven. Place of simple, stergend people, unhurried in their verdin lives, grackel and God-fearing, grain-fed and willow-shaded sandstone slabs.

Once a year, in the fall when the slides of the Hudson stinge to the eye from red red to the high down drift brown. It's Tarrytown. The bridge of wide plank Brom Bones strad-dles Pocantico on the river top where Ichabod Crane came barrelassing by on Old Gunpowder, long kneebone whipping that light nag to the Tappan Zee. That's fear, man. That's eyeballs to the black nothing.

There, feelbe down the sloping through soft earth hollow. Old years have gained this sleep and wish them well. Across the road, George Washington rest brown gravy on his grits, got the troops grazled and sturdy for battle, foggled down flagons of warm rum groggles and banged with his pointing finger on a woodgrain tooth thinking of a wrinkle for muscooting the canons and manueling his arms. History, man. All what we be.

So once a year, here, in the tenth month the valley and hill do produce one winter son. Coloren bright like the inner eye of a god's fashion lunch. Modeling oak and chestnut whip through the breeze. Wear wool for the infant hawk and swaddle his scarf to the neck, loan him some shades. Pumpkins try to show up. Hollow bones are in the wings. This hawk could be father to the man.

Farther up, the hill can judge the Hudson. Real lives once cut in fieldstone say: Work this land. That wife, some faithful children straight and good enough for him, for me. All fear the witch, and so I do. Quiet times are what we're owed. Men alive are trouble. Makers. **Q**

Ted and Phil and Pop Collis ran a counter for fifty years on Church Street, two blocks from the center of town. Pop died after twenty-five, blind, rich just owning half the place. His will gave that to Phil, who did the cooking, who did the books on Sunday, who was and is steady and regular like the eggs just so on my dad's plate for thirty years, every working day and Saturday, or from time to time irregularly when I drop in after writing all night or when Dad brought me here as a kid for a treat. Phil had half already, got from the old man in three bites, by saving and lending to Pop, when the place moved down the street, when they expanded into the back, and when they put their kitchen into the building next door. Ted is the friendly one, and he has always met the public, and they always think of Collis's as the Greek's, Ted's. But he got nothing from his dad but a job, and the same from Phil, because he is not steady enough to handle anything so fragile as a business. Ted takes care of the regulars and gets stock tips, which he ignores now, because he got rich in the sixties and got out in time into rental properties. Phil took care of business, and got rich. They educated all their kids. None of them is about to get up at four every day to get into the business. They are professionals. They're old now, Phil and Ted, and their pop has been dead a long time, and serious people inquire often about buying the business.

The kid, Sam, calls his dad Red and the customers call him Jock, and it was his dad Jock, a true redhead, who opened the counter on Elm Street before the big Depression. It's a long counter, and nothing else, with the mirrored wall behind you and a pie case in your face as you sit. The kid and Sam and a girl, at lunch, do a dance that makes sense from the food to the customer, passing to one another, passing by one another, seldom touching. You've got to wait a minute to sit there, at lunch, but you get service quick. It's just Jock and the girl when Sam's at school. Sam played hockey with my kid brother on Smedley, the Connecticut traveling team. He skated into a college, easy. Sam sets tricks on the girl when he is there and she isn't, like sticking a stack of cups together, and Jock takes them apart before she gets to work. Jock takes on a woman who's got a hard time, a mother alone, a substitute teacher, maybe with a drinker or some creep in her life. A girl quits when she gets it together, but they love Jock, and sometimes there's three or four tough women together there having coffee and staring at Red, who is covered with brown hair, and I stare down the counter at the side of one, and the backs of them all in the mirror, and I remember them from the front, from behind the counter, and I wonder if the kid will keep the business going through all the lunches ahead.

The other counter place I go in my town is Louis's, where the third and fourth generation abuse the customers and they fight back, ordering extravagant delicacies and getting hamburgers. You can get hamburgers to stay or to go, with or without cheese or the works. You can't get them on a roll, but you can get them without bread or with the crusts trimmed, but you have to insist, and you'll get them that way for the rest of your life, like it or not, no matter if you asked for it when your mother brought you there when the old man's dad or his grandfather Louis was running the place, and you're an old man now. The old man is the third generation and his name is Ken, and he saved the place when my city led the nation in urban renewal and destroyed all the neighborhoods, all the organized places where people knew what a good life was and fought the politicians and the reformers for it. Ken put his place on a truck and moved it out of his blighted neighborhood to a lousy location by a vacant lot. Louis's is a tiny place, once the shipping and receiving office of a tannery, and when Ken trucked it away, one wall stayed with the tannery to be demolished, so he made a brick collection from all the great old buildings the villains destroyed in town, and bricks his customers brought him from great old buildings all over the world, and walled up the open side. It's a tiny place, in a lousy location, where still you can't get a seat for his burgers at lunchtime. It's a racket, like Jock's place, which only serves seven to two. Ken opens at ten and closes at four, and stays shut all August for an inventory of spoons. I go at two or three, when it's calm, and eat two or three cheese, works, and drink lemonade made out of lemons, and ask Ken questions about the bricks while his wife and his son clean up.

By every outbuilding I know in the country there's a stick or a lumber scrap on the ground which you need to level the door so the bolt slides, or a key on a nail under an eave or flat on top of the back wall. These shacks are places where people who have use for them are meant to get in. The heart is like that, and so is a life. I got a call from Dad on my machine after my shower on Saturday morning, saying that my old swim coach, Bob Isaacs, was dead. I went for breakfast and Jock told me he just dropped dead, a heart attack. I stopped around the corner at the shoe store Mr. Isaacs managed, to tell his brother, who owns the place, that I was sorry. Then I walked through the college where I went to school to my father's law offices, a block from Collis's, where I write at night and weekends. I live strangely, but I do it in a regular way in the place where I was born, where I moved when I grew up. **Q**

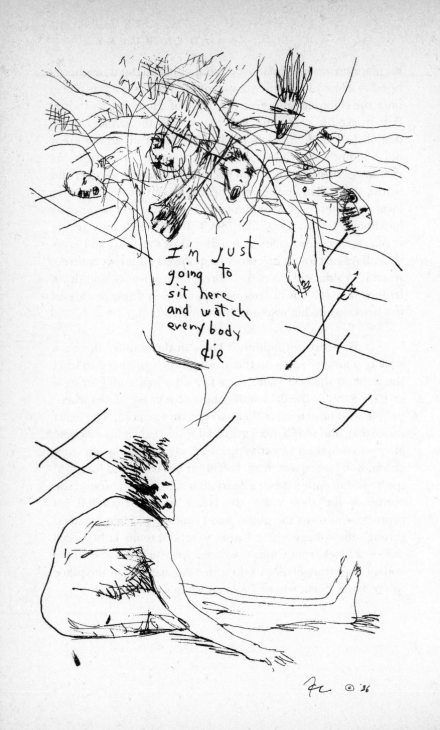